CW00494323

ANNA GIAKOUMAKI

SPINALONGA

The true story

I SBN: 9781983113277

CYPRUS 2020

Translated from the Greek by:
Maria Lazaridou

English edition revised and edited by:
Donald Morgan Nielsen

e-mail: ekdoseisopsidianos@hotmail.com
Frontcover art by:
Opsidianos Publications

Cover photograph:
Nikos Sarantos

Author photograph by:
Stella Meligounaki

The layout and technical production of this book was done by:
Opsidianos Publications atelier

Production by:
Anna Giakoumaki

Prologue

Dear Reader,

The book which you hold in your hands is the fruit of twelve years of research and nearly seven years of writing. It portrays real people and is based on actual events.

The gathering and cross-checking of information was a long and challenging process for a number of reasons, chief among them being the scarcity of living witnesses. Moreover, the prejudice surrounding leprosy and its social impact is evident to this day and makes gathering information even more difficult. Many people were reluctant to talk, but by revisiting their past they provided a rare perspective on the island and their experience with Hansen's disease. My research is based on documents of the time and on the testimony of simple people who were either confined on Spinalonga or somehow connected to those on the island. Excerpts from hand-written documents and transcribed testimony of people who lived during that period and experienced the disease are included here as confirmation of the events and situations I describe. Of special importance are the accounts of actual witnesses, since articles often fail to reveal the real story behind certain actions and events. The names of two principal protagonists, the Medical Officer and his close friend and accomplice, have been changed in this telling, to Rasidakis and Platakis respectively, so as not to cause offense or discomfort among their relatives. This book was not written in spite or to seek revenge for past wrongs. It is simply an effort to portray the events as they actually happened, to let the truth emerge and to dispel any lingering myths regarding this disease, social attitudes and the reasons behind the confinement of people on Spinalonga. It is important to note that all the information in these pages has been cross-checked with separate sources and that no "facts" were fabricated in service of the narrative. After all these years of delving, searching and interviewing, the old story and entrenched beliefs about leprosy and the case of Spinalonga falls apart, as has happened in so many other cases throughout history. Much of the "official" story of the island was intentionally fabricated to hide a dark truth. But the facts speak for themselves and lead us inexorably to a fresh conclusion, supported by documents which can be checked and by the direct testimony of those who lived through the events described. With a sense of great responsibility, I will share with you what I have read and seen and heard. This is the story of the lepers of Spinalonga. Once you have read it for yourself, you can draw your own conclusions.

Anna Giakoumaki

In loving memory of Pipina
and dedicated to all those
whose rights and dignity
were so ruthlessly denied

Sitia, 1926

Late afternoon, and the sky was turning a deep, rusty pink. The families working the fields sense the change and begin gathering their things, ending another tiring day. Eleni gathers her family's clothes and other items and loads them onto the donkey, while Pantelis picks up the heavier tools and distributes them between the two wicker baskets tied to the animal's sides.

'Kostakis[1], come my child, let's go!' Eleni calls to her son, gesturing with her hands. Kostis approaches, and Eleni grabs the boy under his arms and lifts him onto the donkey's back.

'Hold on now, ok?'

'Ok, Mama.'

Kostis' parents scan the field one last time to be sure they haven't forgotten anything; then Pantelis unties the donkey, and they head for home. On the way they run into many of their fellow-villagers, also returning from a day in the fields - a rendezvous repeated every day at this exact time, despite the scarcity of watches or clocks. The villagers' common clock, the life-giving sun, never betrays them. Sundown signals the end of outdoor work, but other work, especially for the women, never really ends.

---

[1] When added to names, the *-akis* or *-aki* suffix turns the name into a diminutive expressing affection and intimacy, in this case: *"My little Kostis"*.

The woman of that time had to cook, clean house and yard, weave and take care of the old people. The man took care of the heavier tasks that remained; building, cutting and hauling wood, making repairs and so on. But once night fell, he would visit the village *kafenion*, the traditional coffee house. With a glass of ouzo, a cigarette and good company the men banished the cares of the day.

Eleni, Pantelis and the boy arrive home. After lifting Kostis off the donkey, Eleni unties the *drouvas*, the woollen bag filled with *horta*, the wild greens she has picked during the day, and slings it over her right shoulder. Then she unties the cloth holding the bread, cheese and olives that remain from their midday meal.

'Leave it, Eleni, I'll get it. You go inside.'

Pantelis takes the rest of the things off the donkey and puts them in their places. He then leads the donkey to the shed and pours water into the drinking trough. Meanwhile, Eleni has spread the *horta* on the *sofras*, the low, round wooden table, and is busy cleaning them...

'Are you making *horta*, Mama?'

'Yes... and there are two eggs...' Eleni looks at Kostis. 'Will you fetch some wood for the fire?'

'Ok.'

Kostis runs out to the woodpile at the back of the house and picks out five or six pieces which he thinks will be good for the fire and carries them to his mother.

'That's my good boy. Leave them there,' she says, pointing to a spot by the hearth. As he is setting down the wood, there is a knock at the door.

'Who's there?' calls his mother.

'It's us, Kyria[2] Eleni,' answers the voice of a small child. She wipes her hands and moves to open the door, while Kostis peers from behind her skirt. In the doorway stand four barefoot urchins in short pants – Kostis' friends who have come to pick him up.

'Good afternoon, Kyria Eleni!'

'Look who's here,' she says, greeting them with a big smile. 'How are you?'

'We're fine. Can Kostis come with us?'

'Where are you going?'

'To play in the lower neighbourhood.'

'Go along then, but don't be late.'

'We won't, Kyria Eleni.'

Kostis looks happily at his friends.

'Kostakis, don't you want to eat something before you leave?'

'No, mother. I'll have some *horta* later,' he replies, reaching up to give her a quick kiss on the cheek.

'Where are we going?'

'To the lower village,' replies Nikos.

'Who else is coming?'

---

[2] "Kyria" for women and "Kyrios" for men, is a formal greeting and equivalent to the English terms "Mrs." and "Mr." – used to address elders or as a token of respect.

'It will be us, Kosmas the barber's son, Tasos the tinsmith's son and the girls of the lower neighbourhood,' added Stavros.

'Good...'

'Shall we race?'

'Let's go!'

The children start running.

'Last one there's a fool!' shouts Stavros, at once making the contest more interesting.

A few minutes later, the first boy reaches the finish line.

The children of the lower neighbourhood watch the others arrive at the meeting place one by one, laughing and out of breath. Artemios stumbles in last, all sweaty, and the other four immediately start chanting: 'Fool, fool, Artemios the fool!'

The children of the lower neighbourhood quickly grasp the situation and burst into laughter. After picking on Artemios for a little while longer, they settle down and start to organise their evening games.

Manolis: 'What shall we play?'

Stavros: 'Football!'

Erofili: 'Not football again...'

Nikos: 'So what do *you* want to play? Dolls?'

The boys all laugh together.

Pipina: 'How about something we can *all* play?'

Andriana: 'Let's play hide and seek!'

Artemios: 'Again?'

Kostis: 'Let's play marbles!'

Stavros: 'But we can't all play...'

Katerinio: 'How about *homata*[3]?'

Andriana: 'Yes!'

Nikos: 'I agree!'

Stavros: 'I'm in!'

Kostis: 'Me too!'

Katerinio: 'Manolis?'

Manolis: 'Yeah, I agree.'

Katerinio: 'Who'll go first?'

Stavros: 'Let's draw straws.'

Nikos: 'I'll get them. How many are we?'

Andriana: 'Ten.'

Nikos returns clutching ten straws in his fist.

Nikos: 'Well, there's a short one and a medium-sized one. Short one goes first, and medium covers the first one's eyes. Ok?'

Kostis: 'Yes.'

Nikos: 'Go on, draw!'

The children all rush to grab a straw.

'Hey, slow down! One at a time!'

In a fraction of a second, Nikos is left holding a single bent straw, and the children huddle to compare straws.

Nikos: 'Let's see...' he says, bringing the straws close together.

---

[3] Dirt, soil.

Manolis: 'Katerinio's is the shortest!'

Nikos: 'Yes!'

Pipina: 'And I've got the medium.'

Stavros: 'So, Katerinio and Pipina go first.'

Erofili runs to the edge of the square and plucks a sprig of basil from a flowerpot in front of Kyria Alonomaria's house.

Erofili: 'And here's the sign!'

Stavros: 'Good. Shall we begin?'

Katerinio: 'Yes!'

Stavros: 'Ok, Katerinio, pick up the *homata.*'

Katerinio crouches down and scrapes together as much dirt as she can hold in her two cupped palms. Erofili then sticks the sprig of basil in the dirt so it stands up like a little green flag.

Pipina: 'Are you ready?'

Katerinio: 'Come on, I'm ready!'

Standing behind her, Pipina reaches around and firmly covers the girl's eyes with her hands.

Pipina: 'Can you see, Katerinio?'

'Not a thing...'

'Good. Let's go.'

From behind, Pipina starts guiding Katerinio to a good spot for the *homata.* The rest of the children gather around the two girls and do their best to distract and disorient Katerinio. The rules of the game are simple; one child, with eyes covered, holds the *homata* and sign, while the other acts as blindfold and guide. Meanwhile, the rest of the children call out confusing directions and other loud chatter so that the blinded player carrying the dirt loses all sense of direction. The children use hand signals to communicate with the "guide" and try to lead them to some place in the village that the player won't recognise with her eyes closed. When they arrive at a suitable spot, the player is instructed to place the *homata* and sign on the ground – then they lead the (hopefully) confused child back to the starting point, usually by a different route to further complicate matters. Once they're back at the starting point, the player's eyes are uncovered, and he or she must try to figure out where they have left the little pile of dirt. The truth is, to win this game, all the senses must be alert, and a storehouse of village landmarks and memories need to be deployed: a neighbour's voice, a whiff of basil, lavender or fresh-baked bread, a barking dog or even a cobbled lane with a particular incline – any clue can lead to victory.

Pipina slowly guides Katerinio, while the other children dance around them making an excited cloud of noise to mask the sounds of the neighbourhood. This goes on for another fifteen minutes until they have circled the neighbourhood twice to thoroughly confuse Katerinio. Back and forth, up and down paths and alleys, in between and around houses until poor Katerinio is dizzy and lost.

Finally, they find an ideal spot, one they haven't used before, and they signal to Pipina to lead her there. It's a small field owned by Kyrios Andreas, about two and a half metres below the dirt road on the edge of the village. Pipina leads her to the edge of the road. Just below them lies the chosen field where the children have decided Katerinio should leave the *homata*. Pipina looks at the others, and they signal her to continue.

Pipina: 'Katerinio, put down the homata.'

Katerinio follows Pipina's command, but instead of dropping the *homata* from a standing position and possibly scattering the little mound of dirt and basil, she abruptly kneels down and slightly forward catching Pipina by surprise. Katerinio's knees, expecting to meet firm ground, find nothing firm at all – only air. Both girls pitch headlong over the edge of the road and tumble over thistles and stones into Kyrios Andreas' field, where they lie in a tangled heap and begin to cry from pain and fright. Katerinio is holding her arm and wailing, and Pipina's face is scratched and bloody from the fall. The other children stand at the edge of the road above with their mouths wide open in shock. Coming to their senses, the boys carefully pick their way down to the field to help the two girls. Stavros reaches for Katerinio's injured arm to help her up, but she swats him away with her other hand and screams, 'Leave me alone!'

'Does it hurt?'

'Yes!'

'Does anything else hurt?'

'No...'

'Just your arm?'

'I think so...'

'Try moving your fingers.'

'I can't,' she wails.

'Don't cry.'

'It hurts!'

'It will pass. We'll take you home now. You'll be fine. Pipina, are you hurt?'

Pipina is sobbing and rubbing her knees.

'No.'

'Let me see your knees.'

Pipina lifts her dress to reveal two bloodied knees, the sight of which makes her cry even harder. Moved by her tears, Kostis gently strokes her head.

Manolis: 'Come down here and help!' he yells to the other children.

As the four boys crouch around her, Katerinio, still crying, blurts out, 'What are you going to do?'

'We're taking you home now. Come on, Katerinio, can you walk?'

'I think so...'

Kostis: 'And you, Pipina?'

'Uh huh.'

Stavros: 'Good. Nikos and I will hold Katerinio. Kostis, you and Artemios hold Pipina. Kosmas, quick, open the gate for us!'

'We're going home now.'

Katerinio is sobbing inconsolably.

Manolis: 'Why are you crying? Does it still hurt?'

Katerinio: 'If anyone in the neighbourhood sees us and tells my mother, she'll beat me with a stick! Oh, what am I going to do!'

Nikos: 'Hush now, Katerinio, Kosmas will walk ahead of us and keep a look-out. Kosmas, get up on the road!'

Kosmas scrambles back onto the road.

Manolis: 'Is anyone coming?'

Kosmas: 'No, it's all clear.'

Nikos: 'Come on. Stop crying and help us,' he tells Katerinio.

Stavros: 'Ready? Here we go!'

Erofili and Andriana look fearfully at the other children.

Erofili: 'Should we come?'

Kostis: 'You two better go home.'

Manolis: 'Yes. You better leave or you'll get in trouble too.'

The two little girls get ready to leave.

Nikos: 'Andriana!'

'What?'

'Not a word to anyone.'

'Ok.'

Erofili: 'Why? What will happen if we tell someone?'

Manolis: 'Are you stupid? They'll never let us play together again!'

Kosmas: 'Go on now! Off you go!'

The two little girls quickly vanish among the village's narrow alleys.

Tasos is holding open the gate and urges them to hurry.

The boys quickly lift the two girls off the ground.

Manolis: 'Tasos, you go in front with Kosmas.'

'All right.'

Kosmas: 'Come on! There's no one around.'

Supported by the boys, Katerinio and Pipina gingerly pick their way out of the field, Katerinio still quietly sobbing because of the pain.

Nikos: 'Katerinio, stop crying, or they'll know something's wrong.'

'But it hurts...'

'Be brave till we get home.'

Manolis: 'Who are we taking first?'

Stavros: 'I think we should split up so we don't draw so much attention.'

Nikos: 'Good idea. Stavros and I'll go with Katerinio, and you take Pipina.'

Kostis: 'But we need a scout!'

Stavros: 'You take Tasos, and we'll take Kosmas.'

Kostis: 'Right!'

After settling on this plan, the boys separate into two groups to take the girls home quickly and safely. Arriving at Katerinio's house, they brush off her dress, wipe her dirty, tear-smudged cheeks with a shirt sleeve and help her stand, wobbly but straight, outside her door. Then they knock and run around the corner of the house to hide. They know that all hell will break loose once Katerinio's mother opens the door and sees her daughter's condition. Indeed, when her mother opens the door and sets eyes on the girl, she starts cursing heaven and earth. Katerinio, naturally, starts weeping again.

Pipina, on the other hand, after recovering from the initial shock of the fall, tells Kostis and Artemios that she is feeling better and no longer needs their help. The two boys agree to stop supporting her on the condition that she lets them escort her home and make sure she arrives safely. Upon arriving at her house, she thanks them, asks them to leave and then knocks on the front door. When her mother, Somarou, opens the door and sees her daughter standing there, her face all scratched and covered in dirt and dried blood, her mouth drops open in shock and fright, but no curses.

'What has happened to you, my child? Come inside.'

'I fell down, mother.'

Artemios and Tasos now leave because it's getting late, and their mothers will be getting worried. Kostis, however, decides to stay a little longer and observe.

In her anguish, Pipina's mother has forgotten to close the door so he can hear everything that passes between mother and daughter.

'Did someone hurt you, and you don't want to tell me?'

'No, mother. I fell in Kyrios Andreas' field.'

'In Kyrios Andreas' field? How? Were you pushed?'

'No. I just tripped and fell.'

'You're lying to me.'

'It's the truth!'

'And what, pray tell, were you doing in Kyrios Andreas' field?'

'Hmm... nothing...'

'You must have been doing something...'

'I tried to pick a rose from the rose bush in the corner, and I slipped,' she replies without looking up at her mother.

'Fine. I'll find out what you were up to...'

'But I'm telling you, I wasn't doing anything!'

'And were the other children there?'

'No!'

'So how did you open the fence?'

'I just opened it!'

'You're hiding something... but I'll figure it out. Go on now, wash up and come get something to eat.'

Pipina goes out into the yard to wash her face and arms. She lifts the water pitcher with one hand and pours some water in her palm. She then puts it back in place and rubs her two hands together. Just then, a small pebble hits her on the shoulder. Pipina turns to see where it came from. In the shadows across the road she can barely make out the figure of a boy. She glances back at the kitchen window to be sure that her mother isn't watching and then looks back towards the half-hidden figure.

'Who's there?' she whispers.

'It's me, Kostis.'

'Go away!'

'Are you all right?'

'Yes. Now go away!'

Kostis nods in assent and waves goodbye.

Kostis returns home, and his mother welcomes him with a simple greeting.

'You're late.'

'I lost track of time.'

'How was it?' she approaches and strokes his head.

'Fine.'

But then Eleni notices the blood on his clothes and hands.

'What's this, my child? Blood?'

'It's not mine, mother; it's Manolis'... he scraped his knee.'

'How?'

'We were playing "Buck buck", and he fell.'

'Is it serious?'

'No, just his knee, he's fine.'

'You be careful, my child. God didn't make you strong and healthy just to go hurt yourselves for no reason!'

'It was bad luck, mother.'

'Take off your clothes, and let me wash you.'

Kostis removes his clothes and hands them to his mother.

Pouring some water from the pitcher into the stone sink, the mother takes a cake of soap made from cooking oil, ashes and lye and starts to scrub her son until a clean boy emerges...

The next day

'Neighbour, good morning, neighbour!' a cheerful voice calls out.

'Who's there?' Eleni replies, peering through the curtains of the kitchen window.

'It's me, neighbour! Malamatenia!'

Eleni goes to the front door.

'Come in,' she says, opening the door and stepping aside to make way for her visitor.

'I hope I'm not disturbing you.'

'Why, of course not, neighbour! Please come in.'

'Is your husband here?'

'No.'

'Where is he?'

'He's gone to fetch feed for the livestock.'

'All the better!'

'How so?'

'I've some startling news to tell you...'

'Oh? Do tell...'

'Where's your son?'

'I sent him to the fountain to fill the water pitcher.'

'Good, now listen. I'll tell you something so you'll be prepared.'

'I don't understand.'

'Bear with me.'

'Go on...' Eleni says, offering a chair.

'Was your son, by any chance, playing in the lower neighbourhood yesterday?'

'I don't know... probably. His friends came to pick him up late in the afternoon, just after we got back from the fields.'

'And he didn't tell you anything?'

'Like what?'

'About Katerinio breaking her arm?'

'No... When did that happen?'

'Yesterday, late afternoon.'

'No, neighbour. He came home a mess, with blood on his hands and clothes, but when I asked him he said that they were playing "Buck buck" and Manolakis scraped his knee.'

'He wasn't telling you the truth!'

'What? Lying?'

'So, you didn't hear that Katerinio - you know, the midwife's daughter - broke her arm?'

'No. How?' Eleni asks concerned.

'Our "little angels" were playing *homata* when Katerinio and Pipina, Somarou's daughter, tumbled headfirst down into Kyrios Andreas' field from the road! Katerinio got the worst of it, but Pipina was scraped and bruised pretty bad too.'

'Katerinio, the midwife's daughter, and Pipina, Somarou's daughter?'

'That's right.'

'I'm sorry... you mean Pipina from the leper family?'

'Is there another?'

'And who told you?'

'Kallio, Stamatis' wife; her house looks right out onto the field, doesn't it?'

'Yes, yes...'

'Well, she saw them and told us. And since I hold your family in high regard, Eleni, that's why I'll tell you one more thing...'

'Please speak openly!'

'The blood on Kostis' clothes wasn't Manolis'...'

'So whose was it?'

'It was Pipina's. Your son and Artemios, the craftsman's son, along with Tasos, picked her up, brushed her off and took her home.'

'What?' Eleni shouts, jumping out of her chair.

'You heard me right.'

'I'm going to kill that boy!'

'But he's only a child...'

'I'm still going to kill him! He'll get the beating of his life when he gets back!'

'What good will that do? Just explain that he shouldn't befriend their kind... You don't want him catching any diseases and having new worries on your mind.'

'But he lied to me!'

'And what do you expect? The truth?'

'If his father finds out he'll beat him black and blue! Oh my, oh my - that's all we need; making friends with lepers! I'll straighten him out when he gets home!'

'Easy, Eleni. I think we should keep this quiet, don't you? Anyway, that's all I came to say, so I'll be on my way now.'

'Bless you for coming to tell me.'

'I'd like to think you'd have done the same if you were me. I'm sorry for upsetting you, but I thought you should know.'

'Of course, don't mention it!'

'Well, goodbye for now and remember... stay calm!'

'Ok, neighbour', Eleni says as she walks her to the door.

Kostis opens the door and enters carrying the pitcher.

'I'm back.'

Eleni is sitting on a stool by the hearth, staring at him in silence.

'Mama, why are you looking at me like that?'

'Come here, son,' she says in a calm, steady voice.

Kostis puts the pitcher down on the table and walks towards his mother. Eleni grabs him by his pants.

'I'm giving you one chance to tell me the truth...'

'The truth about what?'

'What happened in the lower neighbourhood yesterday?'

'Nothing...'

'Did Manolakis really scrape his knee?'

The boy suspects that the news has reached his mother and remains silent.

'Have you nothing to say?'

Kostis guiltily bows his head. Eleni, irritated by his silence, continues in a louder voice.

'Have we started befriending leper families now, Kostakis?'

'What leper families are you talking about?'

'Don't act like you don't know... What business did you have taking Pipina home yesterday?'

'She fell...'

'So what? Haven't I told you a million times not to make friends with children from leper families? Haven't I?'

'But Pipina's not sick!'

'Her father is! Her brothers are - and so is her sister!'

'Well, she's not! And her mother's not either!'

Eleni jumps to her feet in agitation and grabs the boy by his ear.

'How dare you talk back to me! You are not to be friends with her anymore! Do you hear me?'

'I *will* be her friend! She's nice.'

Eleni lifts her hand and gives Kostis a sharp slap on the cheek. Kostis looks directly into his mother's eyes but doesn't cry. Then he runs into the yard.

'You'll see what happens when your father comes home!' Eleni shouts after him as the boy disappears.

Pantelis returns home with the donkey barely visible under its burden of hay and leafy branches. He unties the load, waters and feeds the donkey and heads to the house. Kostis, seeing his father approaching, quickly hides. Fearing what his mother will say, he decides to make himself scarce until things have calmed down a little.

However, his aunt Areti, Eleni's sister, has been at the house for over an hour, visiting her sister and helping with the housework. Kostis is thinking that it would be best if there were no witnesses to his beating, and his shame would be much greater if his aunt was present. He therefore decides to hide in the shed until nightfall, when his father will leave for the *kafenion*. Kostis quickly sneaks into the tiny shed, having first made sure that no one is watching him.

'Where won't they find me?' he mutters to himself, searching right and left.

'Behind the big clay jars? No... they'd surely find me there! Under the bench? Not there either... bad idea. Where to hide... where to hide...'

Suddenly, the solution pops into his head. Little Kostis turns to the huge earthenware jar that contains the family's supply of *dakos*[4]. Using both hands, he lifts the slab of stone which his mother has placed on top to keep mice from falling in. He peers inside and figures that he can just about fit. Moreover, no one would think to look for him in the *dakos* jar, so he can sit safely inside until the storm blows over. The boy carefully places the big slab on top of the next earthenware jar – still not making any noise. He then draws back two steps and then runs toward the jar, jumping up when he reaches it. Hoisting himself up over the rim, he lowers himself slowly slowly into the jar, trying to do as little damage as possible to the rusks below. Half his body is already inside, and all that remains is for him to pull the slab over him and sit quietly on the *dakos*. If he leaves the lid off, it will draw his parents' attention, and they'll quickly discover his hiding place. Kostis carefully pulls the heavy slab over his head until it is back in its original position fully covering the mouth of the jar. Unfortunately for the boy, however, it's such a tight fit that not even air – let alone mice – can get in. Kostis tries to stay calm and breathe as slowly as

[4] Oven-dried bread rusks, a Cretan specialty.

possible, but the atmosphere inside the dark jar gets stuffier with every passing minute. The child, his lungs about to burst, lifts the slab a tiny bit, just enough to allow some cool, fresh air to enter his hiding place. Although the heavy slab requires quite an effort to move and makes a scraping noise as it shifts its position, Kostis breathes deeply with relief.

Pantelis takes his place at the head of the table while Eleni is preparing dinner.

'Fix a plate for Areti too,' Pantelis instructs his wife.

'No, thanks. I'm about to leave,' Areti replies.

'Nonsense! You're not going anywhere. Have you and Eleni finished what you were doing?'

'No, but we can continue this afternoon. It's nothing urgent.'

'You'll stay and eat with us, and when we've finished, I'll head to the *kafenion* to get out of your way so you two can carry on with your work.'

'He's right. Have a seat, dear,' Eleni adds.

Long story short, Areti decides to stay and Eleni begins to put food on the plates and set them on the table.

'What can I do to help?' Areti asks.

'Don't worry, I've got it. Sit down.'

Eleni puts down the plate she is preparing and steps out into the yard.

'Kostis! Kostis!' she calls for the boy, but to no avail. He is neither seen nor heard. Eleni walks back inside and carries on serving.

'Where's the boy?' Pantelis asks.

'He's probably playing somewhere,' Eleni replies.

'And why are you calling him? Are we to beg him to come eat? If he wants to eat, he'll come; if not, so be it...'

Eleni falls silent. If she dared tell him about Malamatenia's visit and her news, both she and the boy would be in trouble.

Eleni has set the plates on the table and is now filling the wine jug from the demijohn.

'Areti, will you fetch two *dakos* for me to soak?'

'Of course. Where do you keep them?'

'In the shed. They're in the third earthenware jar from your left as you enter.'

Areti leaves to fetch the *dakos*. The shed door is half open, and Areti pushes it all the way open to let some light into the dark and windowless room where the family stores their wine, *raki*[5], oil and certain dry foods which don't want or require sunlight.

Areti steps into the shed and looks for the *dakos* jar. From inside the jar in question Kostis senses her presence, and anxiety begins to overtake him as he grows increasingly certain she will discover his hiding

[5] Traditional Cretan alcoholic distillate.

place. With every step and movement his aunt makes, his heart pounds harder and his breathing becomes faster and more desperate. Areti mistakenly opens the jar containing figs, right next to the *dakos* jar concealing the child. Kostis' heart races. It's not just that he is afraid of being discovered but that he has nearly run out of oxygen as well! Kostis weighs the consequences and decides that he would prefer to live and be whipped with his father's belt than to suffocate in a jar of *dakos*. With these choices in mind, the boy decides to lift the slab above his head. But the combination of fear and oxygen deprivation causes him to bounce the slab noisily on the jar's mouth. His poor aunt, turning towards the bouncing slab, takes such fright that she swoons and falls heavily to the floor. Hearing the thud of his aunt's fall, Kostis cautiously removes the slab and pokes his head out of the jar to see what happened. To his astonishment, he sees his aunt Areti lying unconscious on the dirt floor of the shed.

'Now what should I do?' In a fraction of a second, Kostis decides that his best bet is to flee the scene. His hiding place has been compromised, and he needs to find a new one. He leaps out of the jar and kneels over his aunt's face. Putting an ear to her mouth, he tries to detect if she is still breathing and quickly confirms that aunt Areti is still alive.

'Whew... thank God!' he says to himself. 'And now we run!'

The boy quickly returns the jar lid to its place. Then, with three giant steps he leaps over his aunt and quits the shed in search of a new hiding place...

It has been more than five minutes and still no sign of Areti. Her sister, worried, steps to the doorway and calls:

'Areti! Areti!' No answer...

'Areti!' Nothing...

Eleni walks out to the shed to see why Areti is taking so long. As she enters the shed, she is shocked to see her sister collapsed on the ground. Eleni kneels beside her and gently slaps her face to bring her around, all the while calling her name. After a moment, Areti regains consciousness.

'What happened?' Eleni asks with concern.

'I don't know...' Areti answers, still dizzy.

'But you fainted!'

Areti's memory gradually returns as she struggles to her feet.

'Let's get out of here!'

'What's got into you all of a sudden? Areti, what's going on?'

'I'm telling you we've got to go right now! There are ghosts in here!' she cries to her sister grabbing her arm in panic.

'You've got to be joking... Areti, there are no ghosts in our house!'

'And I'm telling you there are! The lid on that jar was bouncing up and down!'

'You're tired. You must have imagined it,' Eleni replies, walking towards the jars. 'Which one was it?'

'That one!' Areti exclaims pointing at the *dakos* jar.

Eleni removes the jar lid, revealing nothing but *dakos*.

'See? There's nothing here.'

'But I saw it bounce!'

'It had to be your imagination, dear.'

Eleni takes two *dakos* from the jar and puts the lid back on.

'Come on, let's get you back inside,' she tells her sister, gently holding her hand.

Areti never learned that the paranormal event in the shed had been caused by Kostis, and she never again discussed the incident with anyone. She was afraid they would think her crazy for believing that the shed was haunted. Naturally enough, however, she never quite got over her fright and never again went to fetch anything from that shed...

Eleni made a deal with Kostis; she would never tell his father about the incident in the lower neighbourhood as long as Kostis accepted one inviolable condition: he was never to associate with

Pipina or other leper children again. Kostis didn't have much choice: he could either stop being friends with them or stay at home recovering from his father's belt.

It's the official opening of school, and dozens of happy voices fill the air. All the children of the village have been in the school yard from early morning, dressed in the best clothes their mothers can make for them. New cloth bags with lamp-wick laces are everywhere. The children, although mainly barefoot, are happily running around the schoolyard. Pipina and her friends are playing "Ring a ring o' roses" while waiting to be called to order for the blessing. Kostis is sitting alone in a corner, silently watching the other children play. The teacher comes out ringing the big hand bell, and the children immediately stop playing and gather in front of the school steps to line up, boys on the right, girls on the left. The teacher welcomes the students, offers a few words of guidance and wishes them a successful new school year. The village priest then performs the traditional blessing, and the teacher signals the commencement of lessons by ringing his bell.

The children enter the large classroom single file. Their teacher calls out their names alphabetically and points each child to his or her preassigned seat at the wooden desks, where they sit in pairs. He has placed Kostis with Nikitas at the second desk to the right, and it is now Pipina's turn to take her seat. Pipina leaves the other children behind and walks to the back of the classroom. As she passes Kostis, she stares at him but doesn't say a word. Kostis opens his mouth to speak but then blushes and stares down at his hands, and Pipina moves on to her seat two rows behind Kostis. The other children don't take long to take their places, and once they're all settled the lesson begins. During class, Kostis occasionally turns to glance at Pipina, who catches his eye several times - but then Kostis, flustered, quickly turns away. At noon, when the bell rings, the children pour from the classroom in a froth of excitement and head home for a couple of hours to eat lunch and do their homework. They then return to the school again for another two hours before leaving for the day in groups of two or three.

Pipina is waiting for her girlfriends by the schoolyard gate so they can leave together. Just then, Kostis steps out of the school building and walks down the steps to wait for his friends too. Pipina looks at him, but he pretends not to see her.

'Kostakis?' Pipina says hesitantly.

Kostis turns towards her.

'Hello, Pipina,' he answers numbly.

Pipina approaches him.

'Kostakis, why won't you talk to me?'

Kostis looks around to make sure no one is watching them.

'I *am* talking to you.'

'But... every time we meet you cross the street... Aren't we friends anymore?'

'We are.'

'So why don't you come to play?'

'I can't...'

'Why?'

'I just... I just... can't!' Kostis blurts out, not daring to look at her.

Pipina looks at him in shock and astonishment.

At that very moment, Eleni arrives at school to meet with the teacher about the school books. Seeing her son talking with Pipina, she strides over to them and grabs him by the ear.

'What are you doing with her?' she yells at Kostis.

Pipina looks at her, eyes wide with fright, but Eleni continues, still shaking his ear.

'Did we not agree that you would no longer associate with lepers? Do you want her to give you the disease?'

'But there's nothing wrong with me...' the girl whispers, looking at Eleni and nearly bursting into tears.

Eleni kneels in front of Pipina. She looks her in the eye and speaks in a deadly serious tone.

'Don't you dare go near my son again! Do you hear me!?'

'But...'

'I don't want your excuses! Go be friends with your own kind, but leave my son alone!'

Pipina's eyes begin to water. She looks back and forth from Kostis to his mother. Finally, in anguish, and not wanting to prolong her public humiliation, Pipina runs off.

Many summers and winters came and went from that dark day. A dozen more years now weighed on them both. Kostis had grown into a strapping young man of twenty with hands that could break stone, while Pipina had become a fair young woman of twenty four with velvet skin and rosy cheeks. Kostis had never forgiven himself for not standing up for her that day, and all these years had made desperate attempts to gain her forgiveness and a chance to redeem himself. But to no avail. Pipina avoided all contact and wanted nothing to do with him. The shame and sadness she had felt that day had marked her, and under no circumstances did she want to experience those emotions again. However, even though Kostis' family had treated her badly, Pipina never spoke an unkind word about them, and this increased Kostis' awareness of how unjustly he and his family had behaved. Moreover, as Pipina grew older, she attracted more than her share of attention from her fellow-villagers. If she did have the disease, as Kostis' mother claimed, she would surely bear some marks of it on her body. However, the girl's smooth, clear skin belied any such suspicions. They crossed paths many times: on the street, in the fields, at feasts and festivals... Kostis tried every way he knew to break the ice and speak with her again, but Pipina always discreetly avoided him. Until one day, everything changed...

Sitia,
1939

A sudden winter downpour has forced Kostis to gather his things from the field in a hurry and head back to the village. The sky had been overcast and threatening all morning, and the evening before when Kostis was on his way home, he had seen a frog. The minute he saw it, he knew that it was going to rain the next day, for a frog was a sure sign of rain. But he had lots of work to do in the field, pruning olive trees and burning the branches. Cloudy weather favoured this sort of work, because when he burned a pile of branches on the cool earth, he didn't have to worry so much about the fire spreading. Kostis guessed that it would probably start raining around noon, so he had set out for the field at dawn to get an early start. Once he had pruned and gathered a small pile of olive branches, he set them on fire, going in this way from tree to tree. If everything had gone as planned, he would have pruned four or five trees by noon and burned the branches as well. He would then have waited to see that his fires were out, stamped out any remained flames or embers and let the rain finish the job. Unfortunately, though, the cloudburst spoiled his plans. The fire sizzled, let out a puff of smoke and went out; the olive branches from his last tree lay scattered on the ground, and Kostis found himself at the mercy of the heavy rain and sudden cold.

His house was still a long ways off. Kostis has stowed all his gear in the woollen *drouvas* tied to the donkey's back, but unfortunately for the animal, the rain has tripled the weight of its load. Kostis walks in front pulling the donkey by its bridle rope, and they have made it halfway up the steep and muddy path, simply called "Kakodiavato[6]" by the villagers, who frequently have to navigate the narrow and dangerous route connecting the village to the fields below. It only widens enough for two loaded donkeys

---

[6] Difficult or evil passage.

to pass each other at two or three points where it meets other paths leading to gardens, fields or small vineyards tucked away on terraces on the flanks of the mountain. The footing is precarious: one treads, not on solid stone, but on small, fragile chunks of slippery shale that break apart easily and slide underfoot. The villagers are aware of its dangers but have few options; those who have fields or vineyards have no other timely way of reaching them. The donkey has begun to falter under its heavy load and unsure footing, and every now and then it stumbles and halts. The rain has almost stopped, but either way Kostis cannot return to the field to finish the job. The trees are wet and would be damaged if he prunes them in this condition. Besides, it's cold, and he is soaked to the skin. Where has he to go? He decides to finish his work the next day, weather permitting, and continues pulling the donkey cautiously up along the narrow path, knowing that such weather can prove dangerous – with whole sections disappearing under rockslides. Regardless, "Kakodiavato" saves the villagers at least one hour each way compared to the regular road, which follows a safer but much longer route, so they usually prefer to take their chances on the treacherous shortcut. Despite the usual difficulties and their fatigue, the return trip was proceeding rather well. They had encountered no rockslides or anything else out of the ordinary – until both of the donkey's rear hooves suddenly slip out from under it at the same time. The beast falls on its belly with a thud and a gasp, and its hindquarters dangle, kicking helplessly, over the edge of the cliff. Still clutching the bridle rope, Kostis is yanked backwards too, but keeps his balance, instinctively pulls back against the weight of the animal and digs his feet into the rough stones of the path. The heavy load and lack of purchase, however, prevent the donkey from scrambling forward to solid ground. Kostis pulls on the rope with all his might, but there is nothing he can do to save the poor animal on his own. And if he lets go of the rope to go for help, the donkey will slide the rest of the way off the path and tumble over the cliff onto the pile of scree and boulders nearly 100 metres below. Kostis starts desperately calling to the village above.

'Help! Help! Neighbours! Somebody help me!' he shouts at the top of his lungs.

His cries barely reach the village, where all the doors and windows are shut against the cold. Kostis continues calling for help, and by great good fortune his voice, carried by the wind, finds its way to Pipina. The young woman had been working her own family field, like Kostis, since early morning, and although she doesn't recognise his voice, as soon as she hears his desperate cries she immediately stops what she is doing and runs to help. When she reaches that section of the path, she sees Kostis struggling against the weight of the donkey and fighting with all his might to keep his footing.

'What happened?' she cries, bewildered.

'Come on, Pipina! Grab the rope!'

Pipina runs to his side, grabs the end of the rope with both hands, and they both pull together. Finally, straining and pulling, they manage to slowly drag the donkey back onto the path. Worn out from their efforts, and shaking from a mixture of exhaustion, fear and relief, they sit at the side of the path to catch their breath.

'Whew! That was close!' Kostis remarks, wiping his forehead with the back of his hand while glancing at Pipina out of the corner of his eye.

'Thank you,' he adds quietly.

'It's nothing.'

They sit in silence for a minute to regain their strength and composure. Then Kostis decides to seize the opportunity that has presented itself.

'Pipina?'

'Yes?' she replies, avoiding his gaze.

'I want to apologise.'

Pipina turns and looks at him puzzled.

'For what?'

'For that day with my mother.'

'It's all right.'

'No, it isn't. She never should have talked to you that way.'

'I said it's all right. That's how everyone is, so I'm used to it.'

'But I'm not like them. I believe you.'

'Believe what?'

'That you're not sick. I believed it then, and I believe it now. I should have stood up for you.'

'But you didn't. Anyway, there's no need to bring it up now. It's been a long time.'

'I've regretted it every day, Pipina. I can't stand you ignoring me anymore. I want us to spend time together like we used to.'

'Well, that's out of the question.'

'Why do you say that?'

'Because I know what people will say, and I can't take it. We're different...'

'I don't care! You see, Pipina, I...' Kostis loses his nerve and stops mid-sentence.

'You *what*?' Pipina urges him to continue.

'I... I... love you!' he blurts out, rising awkwardly to his feet. Shocked by his own boldness and terrified by the words he has finally dared to utter, Kostis grabs the donkey's bridle and prepares to leave. Pipina jumps to her feet as well but can think of nothing to say. Before the young man leaves, he turns to her.

'Just think about it, ok?' he says with quiet seriousness and nods goodbye. Once Kostis is gone, Pipina sits back down.

'Did I hear him right?' she mutters. Shocked and confused by his unexpected words, the young woman is lost in a tangle of conflicting thoughts. 'Did he just say that he loves me? Nah! He's young... and handsome. Can he possibly mean it? Impossible. He's toying with me. But what if he means it? What about his family? They would never accept me! He has to be lying... Can he really be so different from the others? And if he is, why hasn't he approached me in all these years? He's turned into a handsome young man, though... and a nice person too. Oh, my sweet Virgin Mary, what should I do? I'll get into trouble... and if something goes wrong I'll be ruined! I'll never hear the end of it from his mother! I'll just have to wait and see...'

A sigh escapes Pipina's lips, and a smile of hope brightens her beautiful face. Regardless of the outcome, someone has just expressed feelings for her. Pipina stands up and quickly ascends the rough path back to the village. Over the next few days, she intends to check the veracity of Kostis' words. She is a smart and resourceful young woman and will surely find a way.

Two days later

Sunday Service has just finished, and the villagers, after receiving communion and with pieces of communion bread in hand, return to their homes and daily chores, albeit at a more relaxed pace. The children will spend more time playing outdoors; the women will get more housework done, while the men, young and old, will enjoy each other's company – and a glass of something - at the village *kafenion*.

Pipina returns home and sees that her mother, Somarou, has changed back into her work clothes.

'Where are you going, Mama?'

'To the field,' Somarou replies with a sigh.

'But it's Sunday!'

'And who will go, Pipina? Your father and brothers are away... It's just you and me.'

'I'll go.'

'There's no need, dear. You should stay here.'

'But you'll be alone.'

'Don't worry, I can manage. There's not much left to do. You stay here and make dinner.'

'All right,' she replies, tying an apron around her waist.

'Go fill the pitcher too; we're almost out of water,' her mother adds.

'Ok, Mama. Will you be late?'

'No, I don't think so.'

Somarou sets off with their donkey and goat, and Pipina is left alone. She decides to fetch the water first and cook later. Besides, her mother won't be back for at least three or four hours, so there's no need to hurry. Pipina takes the large pitcher out of the kitchen cupboard. It is much heavier than the others but can hold more water, so it will save her a few trips back and forth to the fountain. Pipina folds a cloth several times to make a small cushion, which she places on her shoulder and carefully positions the large pitcher on top. The fountain she usually visits is very close to their house – just a five-minute walk. On the way she greets the neighbours along the route, just like every other day.

'Good morning, neighbour!' she cheerfully calls to a stout, dark-haired woman.

'Good morning, Pipina!' Are you going to the fountain?'

'Yes.'

'All right, take care!'

Once at the fountain, Pipina places the pitcher underneath the spout and patiently waits for it to fill up with clear, cold water. But she is miles away: it has been nearly two days since Kostis said *I love you*, and her heart is still racing. A million thoughts are running through her head, and she is puzzling to find a way to determine just how serious he is, because, to tell the truth, she rather fancies him. Kostis is a handsome young man, seems to be kind-hearted, and for as long as she has known him she has never heard an ill word spoken of him. He is respected by all the villagers, from the youngest to the oldest, and has never given rise to gossip or rumours. Moreover, he is strong and healthy; a real man, although only twenty-one years old.

Suddenly, Pipina recalls the fountain in the upper neighbourhood, conveniently close to where Kostis lives, and she contemplates going there to fill her pitcher instead. If her fellow-villagers see her going to the fountain carrying the pitcher, they won't possibly suspect that she has an ulterior motive. And she would pass directly in front of Kostis' house and could gauge his reaction – if he is home.

Her decision made, Pipina tips the pitcher to let the water run gurgling back into the marble trough. She then puts the cloth back on her shoulder, repositions the pitcher and starts up the main road to the upper neighbourhood. Even empty, the pitcher is bulky enough to make walking a chore.

As she nears Kostis' house, her heart is pounding in her ears. 'Will he be there? And if he is... should I talk to him? No, Pipina... bad idea. He's the man. *He* should speak first. As if he would! I'm sure he was lying. Even if you *do* see him you have to look the other way. That's the trick. Yes, that's what I'll do!'

Pipina has almost reached the house and sees that the front door is open. She tries to remain calm, but her stomach is in knots, and her heart is pounding worse than ever. As she passes in front of Kostis' open door, she tries not to look but finally can't help herself. Pipina gives in and turns her head ever so slightly in the direction of the house. To her immense surprise, Kostis is sitting right there in full view on a chair just inside the doorway and immediately sees her. He looks straight into her eyes and greets her with an upward nod and arching of the eyebrows. Pipina, however, is so flustered that she simply bows her head and continues on her way, perhaps a little faster than necessary.

Now at the fountain, Pipina's heart is fluttering from *both* fear and happiness. She takes Kostis' reaction as a good sign and considers that he may actually have meant what he said. Kostis, on the other hand, is trying to understand why Pipina, who lives in the lower neighbourhood, has come to fill her pitcher at the upper fountain. Has she come on his account, or are they having problems with their fountain again? He can't figure it out.

Pipina's pitcher is full, and she sets off down the road to her house. This time, when passing Kostis' door, she keeps herself from looking. Nor does Kostis respond; he merely follows her with a perplexed look as she walks past his house without even a glance. Upon arriving home, Pipina decides to test him further, taking advantage of the fact that Kostis seems to be alone. The girl empties the pitcher at the base of a large basil plant, then puts it back on her shoulder and leaves again on the same route. As she approaches Kostis' house, she sees that his door is still open.

'Good,' she thinks. 'He's still here, let's see what happens.'

Pipina passes by the house, this time fully composed and with an air of confidence. As she walks by, she glances over just as Kostis is stepping out onto the porch. He looks at her with a question in his eyes and hesitantly nods his head, thus greeting her a second time. Pipina smiles broadly but doesn't directly return his greeting. She steps up her pace and is soon out of sight, once again leaving Kostis baffled and confused. She repeats the same routine three more times, filling her pitcher at the fountain in the upper neighbourhood simply to pass by Kostis' house. When she gets home, she quickly waters the flowers in the yard and then returns to the fountain for more. All these unprecedented appearances make Kostis increasingly suspicious, and he vows to unravel the mystery later that night at the *kafenion*.

Artemios, Kostis and Manolis have been at the *kafenion* since early evening enjoying their customary carafe of ouzo. All three prefer *raki*, but the government has banned its consumption in the *kafenions*, claiming that drinking local or homemade *raki* hinders the development of trade and deprives the State of much needed revenue. Consumption of such drinks has therefore been banned in all public places, and *raki* or wine can only be drunk at home on holidays or to celebrate the name-day of a saint. The friends also prefer holidays and name-day feasts because of the added element of festivity. On Saint George's feast day, for instance, two or three men named "Georgios" together visit the house of another Georgios, without bearing gifts. They eat, drink, sing and tell stories with the celebrant and his family but never stay for more than an hour. Then, the resident Georgios joins their company, and together they all visit yet another Georgios to wish *him* a "Happy name day" as well. Often, late at night, the group might include a dozen or more merry celebrants - all named "Georgios".

The *kafenion*, on the other hand, is their daily escape and common shelter. Ouzo is the least of their concerns; what really matters to them is to get away from the harsh routine of home and field - even if just for a while.

Time goes by pleasantly in the *kafenion* for Kostis and his friends. They talk, laugh, draw conclusions, give and receive spirited kidding. And by the time the three friends say their goodbyes, they are each flush with a deep sense of contentment. Kostis, moreover, has obtained the information he wants...

On the following Sunday, Pipina again follows the same tactic. Her behaviour has no other purpose than to provoke a response and approach from Kostis.

Pipina passes by Kostis' house again and again.

'If he *wants* to say something to me... he will,' she thinks to herself.

Every time she passes, his front door is open and he is there, as if frozen, waiting for her.

As Pipina comes and goes, she glances at him and smiles. He looks back and returns the smile, nodding his head meaningfully, as if he knows her thoughts. Their hearts flutter with every look, but as yet there is no speech.

The week that followed was full of beautiful dreams, hopes and small accidents due to absent-mindedness. Kostis has confirmed that Pipina is interested in him and nothing could possibly make him happier. Now he wants to get closer to her; to confess his feelings - but how? How can he take that first step? He could see in her eyes that she wants him too. But she doesn't say a word, and whenever the poor fellow tries to approach her, Pipina runs away. She's attracted to him; that much is certain. He simply has to use his head and come up with a plan...

It's the third Sunday in a row, and Pipina is getting ready to visit the upper neighbourhood. She senses that Kostis has understood her purpose and hopes he'll be waiting for her in his usual place. As Pipina walks up the road, however, she sees from a distance that Kostis' door is closed. Sorrow spreads across her beautiful face. Pipina passes in front of the house and pauses a moment to stare. No one is to be seen. She bows her head in disappointment and continues on her way. When she reaches the fountain, she listlessly places the pitcher under the spout. As she watches it fill with water, she muses about having come all this way for nothing, not really for water, but for Kostis, who isn't here. She might just as well carry her pitcher back empty and fill it at the fountain in the lower village. 'But why isn't he here?' she thinks to herself sadly. 'He's probably at the field with his folks...'

'Pipina?' a beloved voice courses through her like electricity.

Pipina slowly lifts her gaze to meet the bright smile of Kostis, who is leaning against the far side of the fountain. Her face instantly lights up with joy.

'I was waiting for you.'

'You were? And how did you know I was coming?'

'I just knew. Do you need a hand?'

'No, thank you.'

'So... What's wrong with your fountain? Is it broken?'

'Yes...' Pipina replies with hesitation.

'Funny. I could have sworn it was working fine when I passed it last night,' Kostis replies casually.

'Well... you see...' Pipina mumbles, at a loss for words.

But Kostis breaks in and puts an end to her embarrassment.

'You don't have to tell me. I know,' he says, drawing near and reaching for her hand.

Pipina lowers her gaze.

'I love you,' he continues, searching her face for a sign. 'I will wed you.'

Pipina remains silent.

'That is, if you will have me. Will you, Pipina?'

'But...'

'Nothing else matters,' Kostis interrupts her. 'If you want me, I'll proceed.'

'And what about your family?'

'This has nothing to do with them. If you love me... I don't care what they say! Do you love me?'

'Yes,' she replies, almost in a whisper.

'In that case, I'll tell my family today. Tell your mother that I will come to ask for your hand in marriage tomorrow.'

A bitter-sweet smile appears on Pipina's lips. On the one hand she is happy that Kostis loves her and wants to make her his wife, but on the other hand she fears his family's reaction, his mother especially. She has made it very clear that they want nothing to do with her. How is she to enter their home as a daughter-in-law? It will be difficult...

'Go on, Pipina. Go home now, and come to our field tomorrow so we can make arrangements.'

Pipina nods in assent, picks up her empty pitcher and begins to walk home – but not before casting the sweetest of smiles on her beloved.

Kostis is nervously pacing the floor waiting for his family to return from the field. Tonight is the night he will announce that he intends to ask for Pipina's hand in marriage. He wants nothing more from his parents than their blessing. But even this simple but crucial act seems monstrously difficult. He knows they don't want her and never did. For them it's not just Pipina but anyone associated with lepers. But Kostis loves her. Once he determined that she felt the same way, everything became a one-way street, and his mind was set. He was going to wed Pipina with or without their permission. Tonight, he would simply make the announcement.

Pantelis and Eleni return home, and while Pantelis is tending to the donkey and gear, Eleni enters the house with a warm greeting.

'Good afternoon, my son.'

'Welcome back, Mama.'

'How are you, my child? Have you eaten anything?'

'Yes, don't worry. Where's father?'

'He'll be here in a minute.'

Eleni notices her son's nervousness.

'What's wrong?' she asks, suddenly alarmed.

'Nothing.'

'Something's troubling you,' she says stepping up to him and looking directly into his eyes.

'I'll tell you. Just wait till father comes.'

'What is it, my boy?' she asks again, patience not being one of her virtues.

At that moment, Pantelis walks in.

'Good afternoon.'

'Hello, father.'

Pantelis senses a charged atmosphere and asks the cause. Kostis calmly and politely asks them to sit down and listen to him carefully because he has something important to share with them. His parents have a seat and wait to hear the news. But when Kostis announces his intention to marry Pipina, the great storm that has been gathering finally breaks out.

'What? Somarou's daughter? You fool, couldn't you pick a regular girl?' Eleni cries, nearly falling from her chair.

'Please, Mama...' Kostis tries to calm her.

'Don't you please me, you wretch! All the strain and hardship I endured all these years and for what? For you to waste yourself on lepers!' Eleni shrieks hysterically, pacing the room.

'That's enough! I'm tired of hearing this nonsense! Pipina is not sick!'

'And how do you know? Are you a doctor now?' his mother demands.

'Maybe I am! I love her and I'm going to wed her whether you like it or not!'

'Damn you, boy! Damn you for the shame you're bringing on our family!'

'Mama, please... Stop shouting and give me your blessing.'

'My blessing? I'll give you my curse if you wed her! Do you hear me? My curse!'

'Father, have you nothing to say?'

'What can I say, Kostis, my son,' his father replies quietly. 'This is not a matter to be taken lightly. What if she bears sick children? But then again... if you love her... what can I say...'

'What can you say? Eleni explodes, her eyes wide with anger. 'Yes, that's all we need now! For you to support him! Don't you dare say another word or you'll regret it! I am not wasting my son on some leper family! Why on God's green earth – are there no other marriageable girls?'

Pantelis falls silent and looks at his boots.

'As you wish. But you should know... I love her, and I'm going to marry her - with or without your blessing. And until you accept her I will not set foot in this house again. Goodbye!'

'To hell you go then! And don't come back!' she flings at his back.

Kostis slams the door behind him as he leaves the house. His parents' reaction has drained and angered him, but deep down he had seen it coming. Now he has to figure out what to do next. He decides to go to Artemios' house, a little further down the road, to talk it over with his friend.

Artemios' mother opens the door.

'Good afternoon, Kyria Maria.'

'Good afternoon, Kostis.'

'Is Artemios here?'

'Yes, shall I call him?'

'Yes thank you, Kyria Maria.'

'Artemios?' Kyria Maria shouts.

'Yes, Mama?'

'Come here, my boy, your friend Kostis wants to see you.' Artemios comes to the door.

'All right, mother. Thank you.'

Kyria Maria leaves them alone.

'Artemios, invite Kostis inside and offer him something,' she calls from the other room.

'Bless you, Kyria Maria, some other time,' Kostis replies.

Kostis places his hand on his friend's shoulder.

'My friend, get ready and come with me.'

'What's the matter?'

'I'm in serious trouble. Grab your jacket and come along.'

Artemios throws on his jacket and follows Kostis out of the house.

'Where are you going, my child?' his mother calls after him.

'I'll be right back, mother. We're just going to take care of something.'

Once on the street, Kostis summarises recent developments, culminating in his flight from home.

Artemios is speechless.

'So you've left home?' he finally manages to ask.

'That's what I'm saying!'

'And where will you stay now?'

'I don't know.'

'Do you want to stay with us?'

'No.'

'Why not?'

'Because you'll get into trouble too.'

'Bah! I don't care.'

'I said no.'

'Ok, but where will you go?'

'I'll figure something out. That's not what's troubling me.'

'What is?'

'That my parents will go knocking on Pipina's door.'

'Why would they?'

'You know my mother!'

'So? What will she do? Attack her?'

'Why, don't you think she's capable of it?'

'Well, now that you mention it, maybe...'

'And then all will be lost! Pipina won't want anything to do with me.'

'Do you love her?'

'Yes, completely.'

'And Pipina?'

'Yes! She loves me too!'

'Well then, elope!'

'Elope? How?' Kostis replies, taken aback.

'Like everyone does!'

'And how's that?'

'Take her somewhere for a month or two!'

'Where can we go? They'll find us.'

'Like hell they will. If you want, I can tell you how to go about it.'

'Go on...'

'You know Pervolaris, with the truck?'

'Yes.'

'Well, he's a good friend of mine. I could ask him to take you to Myrsini.'

'What about money? Won't he want to get paid?'

'Don't worry, I'll take care of that. I'll give him some wine, and we'll call it even. Do you want me to go find him?'

'Yes!' Kostis exclaims, suddenly hopeful.

'Ok, but shouldn't you inform Pipina first?'

'Oh my God, you're right!' he says, slapping his forehead. 'I'm on my way!'

'Do you think she'll agree?'

'I'd like to think so.'

'Go on then! Hurry up and then let me know!'

Kostis runs to Pipina's house. Panting, he knocks on the door, and a moment later Pipina opens.

'Kostis, what are you doing here?'

'I've come to get you. Have you told your mother?'

'But... I thought you said you were coming tomorrow.'

'There's been a change of plans...'

'What happened?'

'We don't have time now; I'll explain later. Get ready to leave. Is your mother inside?'

'Yes,' she replies, still confused.

'Go get ready,' he says as he gently pushes her aside and steps into the house.

Somarou looks in wonder at the young man who has just stormed into her house.

'Mother,' he says and falls at Somarou's feet.

Kostis takes her hand in his, and continues, near tears.

'I've come for your blessing...'

'Have you come alone?'

'Alone,' Kostis echoes sadly.

'And your parents?'

'You will be my mother from now on.'

Somarou understands, and her heart sinks.

'Do you love her?'

'More than anything in the world.'

'And what have you to offer her?'

'I will give my life for her if needed.'

Tears of joy fill Somarou's eyes.

'Then you have my blessing, my child, my children. God be with you.'

Pipina, who was eavesdropping on their conversation, comes out from behind the door to the next room glowing with happiness and embraces her mother and her beloved Kostis.

'Mother, we are going to elope. But don't you worry, I'll take good care of her,' Kostis tells Somarou.

'Pipina, do you love him?'

'Dearly, mother.'

'Then I wish you all the best, and may God watch over you!'

Pipina quickly throws her few belongings into a suitcase, while Kostis goes to meet Artemios and make the final arrangements for their transportation. In half an hour, they will embark on their new life...

The first lepers on Spinalonga.
The financial situation on the island and wider region until 1936

Hansen's disease has plagued Crete throughout history. The need to establish a leprosarium in order to eradicate leprosy on the island was first raised as an issue in 1884. Following a proposal by Drs. Sfakianakis, Tsouderos and Vom, the Cretan Assembly approved funding amounting to 300,000 Turkish piastres for the establishment of the leprosarium – a sum that was collected but never used. The report recommended the cost-effective solution of establishing a leprosarium on some remote islet, a proposal which was implemented a few years later. The Report of the Committee of Doctors, which was published in the newspaper "*Kriti*", highlighted, among other things:

"Housing expenditures would be somewhat mitigated if lepers were quarantined on one or two of the nearby islets, for example Koufonisi or Dionysades, because they are government property and do not need to be purchased." (Report of the Committee of Doctors, Newspaper "*Kriti*", 25 October 1884).

After the Turks withdrew from Crete in 1898, the islanders began to reorganise. Assets which had been utilised by functionaries of the Ottoman Empire returned to Cretan possession, and they gradually devised a plan for utilising them. The island's developing economy was mainly based on agriculture and livestock. Every family tried to sustain itself and cover its basic needs by producing its own supply of: olive oil, milk, cheese, meat, fruit and vegetables, while foraging for wild herbs and greens. In this way, every household maintained a degree of independence and self-sufficiency.

The Gulf of Mirabello, however, was in a disadvantageous position. The land was arid and infertile, making any attempt at cultivation futile. According to testimonies, the residents of the broader area of Elounda used to wander the area in rags begging for a cup of oil, a couple of eggs or whatever people had to spare. The islet of Spinalonga had yet to be exploited, and the Turkish squires who remained on the islet did not want to give up the houses and properties they had been using for generations.

In 1900, the Cretan State unintentionally laid the foundations for a plan which would solve two major problems: leprosy and how to drive the remaining Turks off Spinalonga. At that time, the High Commissioner of the island, Prince George, summoned two European doctors to Crete: Dr. Ehlers from Copenhagen and Dr. Kanheim from Dresden, who, assisted by a Greek physician - Dr. Mylogiannakis - stayed in Crete from 26 March to 6 May 1900 and drew up an extensive report which recommended the isolation of lepers on an island, without, however, proposing a particular island.

After lengthy discussions, the Cretan Parliament unanimously voted for the exile of lepers to a specific location. The first law regarding the matter (No. 375) was titled "Law on the Isolation of Lepers" and was published on 12 July 1901 in the Official Government Gazette of the Cretan State (O.G.G.C.S., vol. B', issue 44, 12 July 1901). Up to that point, lepers used to reside on the outskirts of cities, outside the city walls. They were forced to live in shoddy lodgements called "Meskinies" or "Biskinies", which came to be used as terms to describe a person suffering from Hansen's disease. Both words are thought to be of Turkish origin and mean "dirty" or "filthy". One can still visit the caves in which the lepers used to live at the partly-preserved settlement of *Meskinia* - the predecessor of modern-day Chrysopigi in Heraklion, Crete. In accordance with the "Law on the Isolation of Lepers", it was obligatory to report individuals suffering from leprosy to doctors and mayors, while the supervising doctor, who was appointed by the Cretan State and was responsible for the diagnosis and eradication of leprosy (Article 2), would examine them and anyone else who had been identified as a possible leper. If the doctor's findings were positive, the patient would be exiled to the leper colony, the location of which had not yet been determined. Moreover, individuals who neglected to report someone with the disease were punished by a fine of between ten and one-hundred drachmas (Article 1). Negotiations regarding the place of exile continued. Law 463, which identified Spinalonga as the place where the lepers of Crete were to settle, was voted on 30 May 1903 ("Law on the Settlement of the Lepers of Crete", O.G.G.C.S., vol. C', issue 25, 7 June 1903), while Regulatory Decree 166, which was voted on 18 November 1903 ("Decree on the Operation of the Leper Colony of Spinalonga", O.G.G.C.S., vol. D', issue 25, 18 November 1903), established its organisational framework. Another Decree followed, titled "Decree on the internal operation of the Leper Colony" (O.G.G.C.S., Year E', 1903, p. 419), which complemented the previous decrees.

* *(Law 375, O.G.G.C.S., vol. B'. issue 44, 12 July 1901, "Law on the Isolation of Lepers")*

Article 1. Reporting individuals with leprosy to doctors and mayors is obligatory. Violators will be punished by a fine of between ten and one-hundred drachmas.

Article 2. A doctor shall be appointed as medical inspector for the lepers, and his duties shall include anything concerning the eradication of leprosy. The inspector shall not be compensated, but will receive six-hundred drachmas per year for travel expenses, and will not be considered a public officer.

Article 3. The medical inspector shall examine all individuals who have been identified as possible lepers, and will then decide whether they have been infected or not. To this end, the inspector is obliged to travel across the prefectures biannually and examine those suspected of suffering from leprosy. Once a year, he shall visit any known leper residences as well as the leper colony.

Article 4. Those affected by leprosy shall be separated from the healthy and sent to the leper colony.

Article 5. Lepers will not be able to leave the site without special permission from the inspector confirming that their disease has gone into remission and that there is no risk of them passing it on to those with whom they come into contact.

Article 6. Escapees from the leper colony will be liable to one month of detention in a special building on the island, while, in the event of a recurrence, to six months' imprisonment.

Article 7. All matters concerning the leper colony come under the jurisdiction of the Ministry of Interior, while a Hegemonic Decree shall regulate all matters concerning the internal operation of the leper colony, such as medical care, security, public order, etc.

* *(O.G.G.C.S., Year E', 1903, pp. 419 - 420, "Decree on the internal operation of the Leper Colony")*

DECREE

On the internal operation of the leper colony

I, PRINCE GEORGE OF GREECE

High Commissioner of Crete

Having regard to Article 7 of Law 375 and Law 463, and acting on a proposal from the Minister of Interior,

Decide and order:

Article 1. The lepers on Spinalonga may communicate with people on the Island or abroad solely in the way defined in article 5 of Law 375. The staff of the leper colony may communicate with people on the Island. Relatives of the lepers may visit them in the leper colony, provided that the Medical Director has granted them prior permission, but they are strictly prohibited from spending the night.

Article 2. The purchase of food or other products destined for the lepers, whether from inside the leper colony or from the Island, shall be made by the custodian. Sending unclean leper garments to be washed off the Islet is forbidden.

Article 3. Apart from the leper colony's service boat, which shall be operated by one of the street cleaners, no other boat is permitted to approach the colony for any reason, unless the authorities have provided it to transfer goods to the Islet.

Article 4. All leper correspondence to the Island or abroad shall be sent by the leper colony's doctor, provided he has previously disinfected it.

Article 5. All types of fishing are prohibited within a radius of 200 metres around the island.

Article 6. The burial of the dead shall take place on the Islet, at a location defined by the Medical Director. In the event of the death of a Muslim leper, the Director shall call upon the nearest imam to carry out the burial. Burial expenses shall be borne by the government.

Article 7. A yellow flag must be raised at the highest point of the Islet on a daily basis.

Article 8. The following staff, who are obliged to permanently reside on the Islet, shall be employed in the leper colony's general management, security and sanitation departments, will provide medical treatment to the lepers and tend to their needs:

a) A Director, who must be a doctor of medicine, with a monthly salary of 100 drachmas.

The Director shall receive 50 drachmas per month for the procurement of medicine, equipment and stationery, as well as to cover lighting and heating needs.

b) A custodian with a monthly salary of 60 drachmas.

c) Three street cleaners, who shall also be in charge of disinfecting and cleaning the lepers' rooms, with a monthly salary of 40 drachmas.

For the performance of sacraments and services on Sundays and holidays, the Honourable Metropolitan of Crete shall appoint a priest-monk who shall be paid by the government a monthly salary of 60 drachmas.

Article 9. The Director of the leper colony is appointed by Hegemonic Decree, while the remaining staff by Order of the Minister of Interior.

Article 10. The Director shall exercise full supervision over the leper colony, provide medical care and medicine to the lepers free of charge - always following scientifically indicated protocol - ensure law enforcement on the Islet, requesting, if need arises, the assistance of the Gendarmerie, and exercise disciplinary authority over the leper colony. He shall be in charge of maintaining records with the names, gender and age of the lepers in the leper colony; births and deaths; the year each patient was struck by the disease; the form, cause and course of it and submit precise statistical data on the leper colony's activity at the end of every year, as well as a report on his scientific findings. He shall perform microscopic examinations and microbiological cultures on every patient using all means available. He shall inquire of mayors, headmen, priests or the lepers' fellow-villagers to determine whether they have a genetic predisposition to leprosy. If the Medical Director conducts a clinical trial on the lepers, he shall receive ten drachmas per month for every patient undergoing the trial in order to improve their diet. These patients, however, cannot number more than two at a time. The doctor is obliged to communicate the results of treatment to the Senior Management every month. He shall ensure the quality of food and bread on a daily basis, and make sure that the latter is of the required weight.

Article 11. Up to two grocery stores may operate on the Islet to supply lepers with necessary foodstuffs. Every four months, the Prefect shall establish price ceilings for both foodstuffs and fuel sold on the Islet, and the prices shall be displayed on the walls of the Islet's grocery stores.

Article 12. The State shall provide the following to every leper, regardless of age, on a daily basis:

a) 200 drams[7] of bread

b) an allowance of 20 cents for the purchase of foodstuffs

c) 8 cents for clothing, footwear and bedding

The latter amount shall be withheld by the State, which is obliged to annually provide the lepers with the necessary clothing, footwear and bedding through a public tender and according to the provisions of Law 356.

---

[7] Approximately 355 grams.

Article 13. The Ministry of Interior shall carry out an annual public tender for the provision of bread to the lepers, as laid down in the tender document.

Article 14. The Medical Director and priest shall produce a bimonthly statement reporting the number of lepers in the colony, and submit it to the Prefect for approval. Based on this statement, the Prefect shall then issue a payment order in the name of the Medical Director.

Article 15. The doctor and custodian of the leper colony are in charge of ensuring full compliance with the provisions governing the leper colony. In the event of violating or failing to execute these provisions due to negligence, they shall be punished according to the relevant statutes of the Criminal Law.

The publication and execution of this Decree is assigned to the Minister of Interior.

Halepa, 18 November 1903
GEORGIOS
I. TSOUDEROS

Apart from the excuse that it was for the protection of public health - which was surely an issue, but not the *primary* issue - the exile of lepers to Spinalonga was mainly considered necessary for three reasons; the first reason, as reported in various documents, was that there were already buildings on the island, which meant that the cost of constructing a leper colony would be greatly mitigated. The second was that the Islet was both close to the mainland *and* surrounded by the sea. Therefore, any attempt to escape would be extremely difficult and immediately detected. The main advantage of the proximity of Spinalonga to the Cretan mainland was that the transportation of commodities, medical equipment and colony staff would be relatively easy. The third and most important reason was to drive the remaining Turks off the island in a peaceful manner. By transporting lepers to Spinalonga, the Cretan State was pursuing a specific agenda: to make the Turks fear that they would contract the dreaded disease - thus "motivating" them to depart voluntarily and without reservations. And so it happened.

In 1904, the first 251 lepers settled on the islet of Spinalonga. The 272 remaining Muslims were indirectly forced off the island with the promise of compensation.

There is also speculation that the Cretan State encouraged the lepers to choose their own houses and destroy the rest. Since they were enjoying a time of official peace between the two peoples, the evicted Ottomans should have received compensation for the properties they left to the Cretans. But since the lepers destroyed many of those structures, the amount of compensation payable was immediately reduced. The State couldn't drive them out by force because the Ottomans were protected by the French, who were enforcing order on the island, but they could use other means instead.

* An article in the newspaper "*Skrip*" (1893-1963), Issue: 28 October 1898, page 2, mentions:

"..... The French Consul, Mr. Blanche, who made such vigorous efforts to find a favourable solution to the Cretan Question, and for that the land will forever owe him a debt of gratitude, addressed Mr. Venizelos yesterday, saying 'it is sad that withdrawal was ordered by such a distinguished Greek diplomat, when the matter is so important for ensuring peace on the island.' Good gracious!

To the best of my knowledge regarding the matter of guards, the only withdrawal of Powers possible is limited to the removal of one hundred men at some point from the Island, for example on Gramvousa or Spinalonga. The country will stand firm against any withdrawal, to the extent reasonably possible".

* In the newspaper "*Empros*" (1896-1969), Issue: 27 August 1897, page 2, we read:

INTERNATIONAL MILITARY FORCES IN CRETE

A detailed account.

- The Turkish army in numbers.

The London *Times* provide the next account of the international military forces in Crete.

"A military contingent numbering 2,223 foreign troops is stationed in Chania and its suburbs. Most of them are French and Italian.

The Idjedin Fortress is occupied by 150 Austrians; 1,100 Russian troops are stationed in Rethymnon, while 1,800 British and 300 Italian troops are stationed in Heraklion. 320 Italians have occupied Ierapetra and, finally, the French occupy Sitia with a force of 400 men and Spinalonga with a force of 100 men..."

The first patients who were introduced to the island of Spinalonga did as instructed by the Cretan State: They removed the building materials they needed from other structures and destroyed anything they did not need. The incongruities of ill-fitting window and door frames and other materials used to equip their new homes are visible to this day. The Cretan State appraised the buildings the Muslims left behind at 130,000 gold francs. This amount was transferred to the Italian Consul General to be distributed to the beneficiaries, but they considered it a paltry sum and refused to receive it. On 24 September 1925, the Muslims came back into the picture, claiming the compensation promised by the Cretan State. According to the newspaper "*Empros*", Issue 24 September 1925, page 4:

"THE EXPROPRIATION OF SPINALONGA

According to reliable information, the issue of Spinalonga, the islet off the coast of Crete, has recently been the subject of debate. The value of the expropriated properties of the Turks totalled 130 thousand gold francs, a sum which the Hellenic Government deposited in the - then existent - consuls' fund. The Turks involved are already claiming this sum, which the consuls have deposited in the Bank of Italy. The Joint Committee will take the necessary actions so that the Italian Government transfers the full amount to the beneficiaries."

According to testimonies, the first lepers who arrived on Spinalonga were accompanied by convicts from death row incarcerated at the Idjedin prison in Chania. The Cretan State already considered the convicts a lost cause and held the same opinion regarding the lepers. They considered it wise to send the convicts to the islet as the lepers' guards, regardless of their unsuitability for the job. Moreover, the State did not really care if they contracted the disease. They were the dregs of society - as were the lepers - and no one really cared about them. But they were still human, with fears, passions and a strong survival instinct.

They say that the situation on the island in the early days was beyond anything imaginable, with constant mistreatment of patients and daily scenes of terror and violence.

In 1905, a supplementary Decree was passed to try to bring some order to the prevailing chaos.

* (O.G.G.C.S., Year G', 1905, No. 56, DECREE ON THE INTERNAL OPERATION OF THE LEPER COLONY)

I, PRINCE GEORGE OF GREECE
High Commissioner of Crete

Having regard to Article 7 of Law 375 and Law 463, and acting on a proposal from the Minister of Interior

Decide and order:

That the provisions of Decrees 166 of 1903, 195 and 255 of 1904, and 26, 30 and 116 of 1905 be replaced as follows:

Article 1. The lepers on Spinalonga may communicate with people on the Island or abroad solely in the way defined in article 5 of Law 375. The staff of the leper colony may communicate with people on the Island. Relatives of the lepers may visit them in the leper colony, provided that the Medical

Director has granted them prior permission, but they are strictly prohibited from spending the night.

Article 2. The purchase of food or other products destined for the lepers, whether from inside the leper colony or from the Island, shall be made by the custodian or another staff member appointed by the Director. Sending unclean leper garments to be washed off the Islet is forbidden. However, with the permission of the Prefect of Lasithi, two to four washerwomen are allowed to settle and reside in the leper colony to wash and clean the lepers' garments.

Article 3. Apart from the two service boats of the leper colony, no other boat is permitted to approach the colony for any reason, except if authorities have requisitioned it to transfer goods to the Islet or if another authority, outsider or doctor wishing to carry out scientific studies visits the Island in their own boat.

Article 4. All leper correspondence to the Island or abroad shall be put in the post-box, from where it will be collected and delivered to the Director, who, after disinfecting it, will pass it on to the postman.

Article 5. All types of fishing are prohibited within a radius of 200 metres around the island.

Article 6. The burial of the dead shall take place on the islet at a location defined by the Medical Director. In the event of the death of a Muslim leper, the Director shall call upon the nearest imam to carry out the burial. Burial expenses shall be borne by the government.

Article 7. A yellow flag must be raised at the highest point of the Islet on a daily basis.

Article 8. The following staff shall be employed in the leper colony's general management, security and sanitation departments, shall provide medical treatment to the lepers and tend to their needs. All of them are obliged to reside permanently on the Islet or at another location approved by the Minister of Interior, except for the Medical Director, who is allowed to reside in Plaka.

a) A Director. If he is a certified doctor, he shall receive a monthly salary of 200 drachmas; if he is not a doctor of medicine, he shall receive 160 drachmas. In the second case, a doctor is allowed to visit the leper colony once or twice a week to examine the lepers and shall receive fifteen drachmas per day. This doctor shall be appointed by the Prefect of Lasithi each time.

b) The Secretary shall receive 20 drachmas per month upon rendering of account for the procurement of stationery as well as to cover the lighting and heating of the offices.

c) A custodian, who will supervise all four street cleaners, the two boatmen and his assistant, shall have a monthly salary of 80 drachmas.

d) An assistant custodian with a monthly salary of 70 drachmas.

e) Four street cleaners, who shall also be in charge of disinfecting and cleaning the lepers' rooms, each with a monthly salary of 60 drachmas.

f) One annual payment of 300 drachmas shall be provided for the procurement of medicine and equipment. Likewise, the sum of 500 drachmas shall be provided on a one-off basis for the purchase and repair of the boat and its parts, as well as for the purchase of furniture, containers and clay jars for the office and pharmacy.

g) For the performance of sacraments and services on Sundays and holidays, the Honourable Metropolitan of Crete shall appoint a priest-monk who shall be paid by the government a monthly salary of between 60 and 80 drachmas.

h) A secretary with a monthly salary of 100 drachmas.

i) Two boatmen, each with a monthly salary of 60 drachmas.

Article 9. The Director of the leper colony is appointed by Hegemonic Decree, while the remaining staff by order of the Minister of Interior.

Article 10. The Director shall exercise full supervision of the leper colony; provide medical care and medicine to the lepers free of charge (always following scientifically indicated protocol); ensure the enforcement of law and order on the Islet, requesting, if need arises, the assistance of the Gendarmerie; and shall exercise disciplinary authority over the leper colony's staff, imposing, if needed, a disciplinary fine of between 5 and 20 drachmas, according to the existing provisions of the administrative bodies. An appeal against this decision can be lodged before the Minister of Interior within 5 days from notification. The Director shall be in charge of maintaining records with the names, gender and age of the lepers in the leper colony; births and deaths; the year each patient was struck by the disease; the form, cause and course of it and submit precise statistical data on the leper colony's activity at the end of every year, as well as a report on his scientific findings. He shall perform microscopic examinations and microbiological cultures on every patient using all means available. He shall inquire of mayors, headmen, priests or the lepers' fellow-villagers to determine whether they have a genetic predisposition to leprosy. If the Medical Director conducts a clinical trial on the lepers, he will receive ten drachmas per month for every patient undergoing the trial in order to improve their diet. These patients, however, cannot number more than two at a time. The doctor is obliged to communicate the results of treatment to the Senior Management every month. He shall ensure the quality of food and bread on a daily basis, and make sure that the latter is of the required weight. He may also discard food if he finds that it is spoiled, contaminated, etc.

Article 11. Up to four grocery stores may be established on the Islet to supply lepers with necessary foodstuffs, operated by lepers or not, with the permission of the leper colony's Director and the approval of the Prefect of Lasithi. Every four months, the Prefect shall establish price ceilings for both foodstuffs and fuel sold on the Islet, and the prices shall be displayed on the walls of the Islet's aforementioned grocery stores.

Article 12. The State shall provide the sum of 55 cents per day to every leper, regardless of age, for bread, clothing, footwear, bedding, etc.

Article 13. The Medical Director and priest shall produce a bimonthly statement reporting the number of lepers in the colony, and shall submit it to the Prefect for approval. Based on this statement, the Prefect shall then issue a payment order in the name of the Medical Director, who, in turn, shall distribute the amount to each beneficiary privately, making sure that the payment order has been co-signed by the Secretary.

Article 14. The doctor, secretary and custodian of the leper colony are in charge of ensuring full compliance with the provisions governing the leper colony. In the event of a violation or failure to execute these provisions due to negligence, they will be punished according to the relevant statutes of the Criminal Law or disciplined by the Minister of Interior.

Article 15. The Secretary shall stand in for the Director when he is absent or prevented from attending.

The publication and execution of this Decree is assigned to the Minister of Interior.

Halepa, 23 September 1905
GEORGIOS
L. KRIARIS

The first years of confinement were hard for the patients, with miserable living conditions which affected both their health and spirits. Their lives became increasingly unbearable due to a lack of medical equipment and supplies, infrequent communication with the outside world due to strict isolation measures, an allowance too small to even cover basic necessities, and, finally, being treated like criminals rather than medical patients. Their main sources of support during these times were the monasteries of the surrounding area, the Metropolis of Petra and fundraisers that were held by various philanthropic organisations.

The patients' despair and frustration often led to uprisings, which, however, had virtually no effect. Their limited education prevented them from properly framing their requests or having their complaints acknowledged by the authorities. According to numerous sources, the Islet's sole pharmacist was also illiterate. In 1913, Crete was united with Greece, and lepers from all over the country were transferred to the islet. There are, however, reports of non-Cretan lepers being sent to the Islet long before that. One example is provided by an article in "*Skrip*" (page 4, 8 July 1905): "The police have received a complaint about a Cretan leper wandering the streets around the 4th police station. There is a risk of him passing the disease on to others, because the leprosy-ridden beggar frequents a number of homes. The police have ordered the officers of the 4th police station to arrest the leper, who will be sent to Crete."

The Hellenic state included the leper colony of Spinalonga in its national healthcare plan and adopted new regulations for its operation. In a memorandum to the Ministry of Health in 1926, Prefect Mr. Anagnostakis notes: "Two hundred and fifty human beings of every age, gender and social class, outcasts of fortune, have been isolated – or, more accurately, *dumped* - on the dry rock of Spinalonga in deep despair. I inspected nearly all of the houses - or should I say, *hovels* - of the lepers, and I can honestly say that their wretched condition should inspire outrage in the conscience of any civilised person..."

The government of Eleftherios Venizelos made efforts to improve the patients' living conditions and the medical treatment they received. After several years of inhumane confinement and neglect on that infertile, arid and inhospitable island, a hospital was built. As archaeologist Georgia Moschovi mentions in her book, Eleftherios Venizelos sent a doctor to India and the Philippines at his own expense in order to learn about the newest treatment methods that were being used in organised leper colonies there. He also established a committee of scientists to recommend measures that might alleviate the patients' suffering. Shortly after this, Venizelos appointed the first doctor-director of Spinalonga's leper colony, Prefectural Medical Officer E.G., whose jurisdiction included not only Spinalonga but the entire Prefecture of Lasithi.

The first three decades of the colony's operation were characterised by neglect and inertia, although the number of people transported to the island was significant. According to reports, approximately 1,000 patients were confined on the islet of Spinalonga during the first three decades of the century.

The miserable living conditions on Spinalonga were also reported in the press, such as in this letter to the editor of "*Nea Efimeris*" on 17 October 1925:

"PROTEST OF THE LEPERS OF SPINALONGA

Mr. Editor of "Nea Efimeris"

From the first days of our confinement on Spinalonga, we have never ceased to shout out and protest about our reprehensible isolation on this β barren rock, which both foreign and local visitors call hell on earth.

But especially after the donations of Mr. Mihailinos, Mr. Venizelos and others, we hereby appeal to the Honourable Government, Political persons and - through the press - to the entire Nation, requesting the transfer of the Leprosarium to a suitable government-owned location with running water and arable land, as are the Leprosariums of Chios and Cyprus, in order to ease and comfort our troubled souls. We are not requesting great things at the Government's expense: the regular payment of our allowance, women for washing and tending to our needs, a specialised doctor and 3 or 4 employees to ensure the facility's proper functioning. However, to our great sorrow and despair, we were informed just today that the leper colony's Committee was ordered by the competent Ministry to strictly apply the provision of the new Bill regarding the operation of leper colonies, according to which Bill food will be strictly rationed, as if the 190 of us who are confined here are the dregs of humanity."

On 24 November 1928, another article on page 6 of "*Empros*" titled "Specialised Hospital for Combating Leprosy", mentions:

"Yesterday, the Prime Minister received the Governor-General of Crete in his office.

Mr. Katehakis announced to the Head of the Government that they will use the sum of 3,000 [Turkish] liras which Mr. Venizelos has set aside from the 10,000 liras which Mr. Mihailinos has donated for the execution of construction works in Crete to establish a specialised hospital on the leper island of Spinalonga to house the unfortunate outcasts who are no longer able to perform physical work or care for themselves."

Documents from 1929 prove that, following a public tender, reconstruction work then commenced on the island's buildings.

From the handwritten receipt of the main contractor for those works, Konstantinos Tsihlis or Spithas, we read:

"Receipt of 15,000 drachmas

I, the undersigned contractor Konst. Tsihlis or Spithas, have received the amount of fifteen-thousand drachmas from Mr. Angelidakis Angelos, Prefect of Lasithi, as an advance towards the procurement of materials, lime, sand and timber for the reconstruction of some houses in the leper colony of Spinalonga, following the relevant public tender.

Agios Nikolaos, 26 October 1929

Received by..."

* Newspaper "*Empros*" (1896-1969), Issue: 8 August 1928, page 6

"- The Leper Colony of Spinalonga

The director of the Leper Colony of Spinalonga has requested credit of 40,000 drachmas from the Governorate-General for the procurement of shale soil to repair the alleys between the lepers' homes. The special accounting office of the Governorate-General was ordered to make the necessary arrangements."

* Newspaper "*Empros*" (1896-1969), Issue: 31 July 1929, page 1

Article by Angelos Sgouros:

"WITH THE SCAPEGOATS OF SPINALONGA

..... THE LEPERS MUST BE TRANSFERRED FROM SPINALONGA

Yesterday, I wrote about the torturous lives of this unfortunate society of scapegoats; about the injustice that mercilessly lashes these troubled souls; about the appalling effect that the detestable environment of Spinalonga has on man's body and spirit. But still, among the silent and dilapidated quays of the old fortress, the waterless rocks, under the relentless sun and exposed to the mania of the winds off the Sea of Crete live imprisoned people. They have not committed murders or other crimes; they are not bloodthirsty bandits who have been sentenced to life in prison; nor are they murderers, crooks or forgers paying the price of their sins according to social justice; they are hapless beings who, by a simply twist of fate, have disfigured faces without eyes or noses and deformed hands and legs unable to support their own weight. The State and society at large should be doing their best to alleviate the suffering of these unfortunate beings by making their lives, if not pleasant, at least worthy of dignity and not like some dog on the island of Bosporus. The lepers need to be transported from Spinalonga; a leprosarium in the real scientific sense of the word must be found - instead of calling Spinalonga a leper colony when in fact it is a place offering only a lifetime in hellish exile. A hospital and infirmary must be established where serious scientists can dedicate their lives to research so that something good and useful may result from all this suffering. In this way, despair will leave their souls, and hope for a cure may take its place. Hope has a far more salutary effect on a despairing soul than even medical treatment can offer. An effective treatment for leprosy is still in an experimental stage. Injections of *Chaulmoogra* oil are being administered, as well as similar preparations of *Antileprol* and *Reganol*; while the well-known *413(?)* has also been used occasionally, and patients with tuberculosis are treated with gold injections. It has been reported that a systematic treatment of 700-

800 injections halts the progress of the leprosy microbe or Hansen's bacillus. On Spinalonga today, treatment is practically non-existent, and the monitoring of patients is inadequate. It is no one's fault. The lepers no longer believe in anything; they surrender to the despair of their misfortune and the additional torture imposed on them by the State's insensitivity and neglect. Some of them have had 15-30 injections, and each injection has created a terrible purulent abscess!..."

More work was done on the island. The Hellenic State finally began to allocate significant funds for the improvement of the facilities, and the Greek President, Eleftherios Venizelos, indirectly monitored the progress of work.

In 1933, after Eleftherios Venizelos was informed that the works had been delayed due to a lack of staff and funds, he sent a letter to the Directorate of Public Works of Crete mentioning the following about contractor Kon. Tsihlis or Spithas and referring to the latter's complaints:

"Athens, 3 February 1933

Mr. Director,

The contractor in charge of the works on Spinalonga has informed me that the delay in their execution is due to the fact that the staff of the Engineering Department of the Prefecture of Lasithi is busy with other projects. He cannot find an engineer for his public works and thus cannot expedite the process of submitting invoices for the work carried out. Because of this delay, he lacks the funds needed to continue the project. Because, as you know, the works were commenced 4 years ago and must be completed as soon as possible in order to improve the fate of the poor lepers of Spinalonga, I would be obliged if you would kindly provide the appropriate instructions to the Engineering Department of the Prefecture of Lasithi, whose jurisdiction includes the district where the work is being executed, and assist us in our charitable work by submitting any invoices to us as soon as possible so we can settle them immediately. I also kindly request that you convey to the said Department that I have asked Mr. Katapotis, doctor and Senator of Lasithi, to submit a reconstruction plan for a leprosy Sanatorium with approximately thirty (30) wards not costing more than one-million drachmas.

Since Mr. Katapotis will need an engineer for the selection of the plot of land and the drafting of relevant plans, I kindly request that you make the engineer of the Prefecture of Lasithi available to him, keeping in mind that the said engineer will be paid by me for his additional work.

Eleftherios Venizelos"

The works continued, despite numerous obstacles.

The renovation of the buildings, in combination with an increase in the patients' allowance, significantly improved their living conditions and spirits and allowed them to live in comparative dignity.

On the islet of Spinalonga, in contrast with other similar Greek institutions, patients now had three basic advantages; the first one was that all patients had the right to choose their own food and clothing. With the allowance granted by the State they could buy whatever *they* considered necessary. Although, at first, the monthly allowance set by the State amounted to only 20 cents per patient per day, over time it was increased. The patients' constant struggle for survival and the gradual improvement of their living conditions is well documented: hunger strikes and refusal of treatment, black flags and banners with slogans such as "BLACK ROCK" and articles sent to the press. Their protests and constant demonstrations echoed across the Gulf until they were either vindicated or their requests at least partially granted. The patients' second advantage on Spinalonga was their ability to live in proper houses instead of hospital wards (as long as they were physically able to care for themselves). The third and final advantage was that lepers on Spinalonga could get married, and married couples could legally live together.

For the time being, let us focus on their right to manage their own allowance.

Lepers were clearly in a better position than the rest of the starving inhabitants of the Gulf of Mirabello in Crete: they had money and a certain limited freedom, but they lacked commodities and other necessities. At the same time, the inhabitants of the Gulf and the wider region had commodities and other products to sell but no access to markets and, hence, no money. In short: lepers had the money, and the inhabitants of the Gulf had the commodities.

The patients had to obtain food and other basics from somewhere in order to survive. But where? The absence of a road network and the limited means of transport made it difficult for would-be merchants to access the island from remote locations. By contrast, the inhabitants of Elounda, in addition to being close to Spinalonga, also had an abundance of fishing boats. The development of commercial ties between the residents of Spinalonga and the Cretans along the Gulf was inevitable.

Countless boats carrying all manner of goods would embark from the Gulf of Mirabello and row across the narrow strait to Spinalonga.

Wood, milk, fruit, wild greens and herbs, which up to that time had little or no value to the coastal residents, could now be sold to the lepers at a profit. With the money they made from this trade, they could, in turn, put some food on their table and furnish their homes with other items.

Every day, a makeshift market would set up at the small port of Spinalonga, where merchants would display their merchandise and patiently wait until it was sold. Dozens of patients would wend their way down the settlement's narrow alleys to the market on the quay, and although this transaction was essential for both sides, fear of contagion still hung in the air. Therefore, after the usual bargaining and selection of goods, a patient would pay the clerk of the disinfecting unit, who, after disinfecting the money, would pass it on to the merchant.

As commerce grew and developed, so too did Spinalonga. According to testimonies, the island now housed two grocery stores, three *kafenions* and a number of other shops which would not have existed had the necessary supplies not been able to reach the island.

The boom in trade also affected the appearance of the shore fronting the small harbour of Plaka on the Cretan mainland: many shops were erected during that period in order to meet the needs of patients, visitors or escorts, as well as the leper colony's staff. Most of the locals quit their jobs in order to participate in commerce in one way or another. One of the oldest taverns in Plaka, which opened in 1932 and remains unaltered to this day, is "The old tavern of Maria". Sweet Kyria Maria B. opened this small tavern with her husband in order to serve the patients and their escorts. According to Kyria Maria, the tavern also operated as a guest house from time to time, accommodating dozens of patients' relatives, who would arrive in the area to visit and support their loved ones who were confined on Spinalonga.

Commerce, as we say in Crete, "provides bread" or, in other words, puts food on the table of many families.

These responses from an old man in Tsifliki are noteworthy:

'*Pappou*[8], were you a merchant too when the lepers where on Spinalonga?'

'Why, yes I was indeed! Golden times, my child!' he replied disarmingly.

'And what did you trade in, *Pappou*?' I continued with curiosity.

'Watermelons, bread... whatever they needed.' he replied.

'But, *Pappou*, you don't grow watermelons in Elounda! How did you come to sell them?'

'And who said that we grew them in Elounda, my child? I would ride the donkey to Malia, load the poor animal until its belly almost touched the ground and slowly return to Plaka on foot. From Plaka, I would put the watermelons in the boat and row them

[8] *"Grandpa"* or simply an affectionate way of addressing an old man.

across. You should have seen the poor souls' reaction when they heard the sound of my boat! Piles of patients would descend to the port to see what I had brought for them! If only you could have seen their surprised faces when they saw my goods! No sooner had I arrived than everything was sold, just like that! Poor people... what could they do? They longed for some fruit, and we needed the money, so we became merchants. I remember one time when I was taking them bread I was caught in a terrible squall just outside the port. The weather was really bad and I couldn't approach the dock to tie the boat.'

'And what did you do, *Pappou*?' I asked full of curiosity.

'Well, I threw the bread ashore and whoever wanted some would scramble to catch a loaf.'

'And what about money? Were you not paid? Was the bread a gift?' I asked naively.

'A gift? They paid me the next time!'

'But, *Pappou*, how did you know who took what?'

'*They* knew, and that was enough! They may have been sick, but they were honest!' replied the old man, using the simplest words to bring his world into focus.

Through trade, that neglected island had become an enormous source of income for the inhabitants of the wider region.

The president of the Fraternity of Patients of Spinalonga

Although living conditions on the island had clearly improved, the patients never ceased to fight for further changes. Their protests, however, rarely had any effect. Their limited language skills and humble origins earned merely scorn from those in power.

Their hopes were now pinned on some well-educated patient being sent to Spinalonga.

That day was not long in coming. On 11 March 1936, Manolis Kasapakis, a third-year law student, was admitted to the island's leper colony after being diagnosed with the disease. The patients saw in this unfortunate fellow their saviour. His education and its concomitant social status and his fluent speech caused people to pay attention to what he was saying. A practical person by nature, Manolis did not take long to adapt to his new environment, and it was soon apparent that this cultured young man would change their lives forever.

The image he faced when he first set foot on the island was disheartening: the arid and waterless rock was completely devoid of vegetation. The cobbled lanes were worn smooth and slippery, making it difficult and often dangerous for patients to move about. Squalor and stench filled the air, not only from the neglected wounds of the sick, but also from the piles of rubbish scattered across the island. The houses were dilapidated; their walls black with soot and mould, their roofs collapsing and their doors and shutters falling off their hinges. The chickens which freely wandered the yards and alleys of Spinalonga covered the cobbled roads with their droppings, while the acrid stench of the shallow, primitive outhouses further contributed to the atmosphere of neglect and despair. As bad as it was, the healthy people who lived across the bay imagined even more primitive conditions. They pictured the lepers in caves like the ones in *Meskinia*.

After he introduced himself to the older patients and was told how things were done on the island, he slowly began to express his own opinions. They, in turn, revealed their long-held hope that an educated person like himself might someday arrive on the island to help them lay claim to their rights and regain some modicum of dignity. They told him that they believed he could be that person, and that they would faithfully follow his guidance and instructions.

Kasapakis could see the respect and trust his fellow-patients had for him, and that motivated him to fight on their behalf. Being a rebel and pioneer by both age and inclination, he slowly began urging them to take their fate into their own hands and no longer simply accept their plight. There were many things that Manolis saw and did not like. The lack of meaningful occupation or entertainment led to idleness and the wrong kinds of pastimes, such as card playing, drinking, quarrelling and exploiting the weak. He urged them to wake up and take charge of their destiny, and, as a first step in distracting them from their misery, he began setting goals. Manolis summoned the twenty most senior patients to a town meeting where he proposed that they ask the institution's Director for 1,000 okes[9] of whitewash so that they could paint their houses, outbuilding and privies. Then, every able-bodied patient would help gather the island's rubbish. And so it was. In three days' time, a boat full of whitewash arrived at the island, and the patients were called by the town crier to proceed to the port and pick up their free allotment. The painting began the following day, and the whitewash changed the island's smell as well as its appearance. Kasapakis took heart at seeing the improvement in the island's image and in the spirits of his fellow-patients. Over the following days, he began expressing his opinions openly at the island's *kafenions*. Those patients who were present and could walk reported his words to the bedridden, because his opinion carried great weight, and everyone wanted to hear what he had to say. The death of the Greek President Eleftherios Venizelos on 18 March 1936 prompted Manolis to

[9] Approximately 1,280 kilograms.

prepare his next project. He understood the sorrow that was eating away at sick and healthy alike. Eleftherios Venizelos was loved by all Cretans, who admired him for his leadership and were also proud of his island origin. The residents of Spinalonga held him in especially high regard for the interest he had repeatedly shown in their situation. All Cretans mourned this grand figure. The only healthy people, however, who were allowed on Spinalonga were the staff of the leper colony. It was, therefore, a great opportunity to connect these two worlds. Kasapakis recommended that they hold a memorial service in the little church of Spinalonga in honour of the late leader. His fellow-patients and the leper colony's management were united in providing him the financial and moral support he needed. Manolis printed death notices and had them placed in all the nearby churches, and he gathered everything necessary for the memorial service on the island, including the *koliva*[10] offered to the mourners.

On the day of the memorial service, the turnout was tremendous; three boats ferried people to Spinalonga to honour the memory of Venizelos. The residents of the Gulf were impressed by how well organised the residents of Spinalonga were. Until that time, they had simply thought of them as social outcasts and pariahs. More initiatives followed - all

---

[10] Boiled wheat traditionally offered at funerals.

equally successful – and in the minds of the other patients, Manolis was now established as their leader and spokesman, while he, in turn, was now convinced that he could be of real use to them. Due to his training in legal matters, he knew that, for their struggle for better living conditions to bear fruit, they had to create an official legal entity – a union – which would be recognised by the Court of First Instance and which could officially represent the patients' claims and defend their rights. In short order, the patients received permission to create their union, which was called "The Fraternity of Patients of Spinalonga - Agios Panteleimon". Out of the 330 patients on the island, 160 of them registered as charter members at a cost of 10 drachmas each, while monthly fees were set at 5 drachmas.

Elections were held to appoint a governing council. The ability to vote and stand for election boosted the patients' morale and alleviated their sense of helpless confinement. Manolis Kasapakis was unanimously elected President of the Fraternity.

Once established and organised, the Fraternity took action by demanding certain basic improvements: better medical care, more staff to care for the helpless patients, sanitation, an increase in their allowance and the construction of new paths and lanes to accommodate the blind. But the Fraternity did not simply address these most basic needs; it also addressed the problems of free time, entertainment and education. According to testimonies, the island already housed three *kafenions.* The time had now come for them to be utilised somewhat differently. Manolis tracked down M.L., a patient who was also a lyre player, as well as G.H. and A.M., who played the mandolin and tabor respectively. At first, he gathered them in a remote house where they rehearsed for eight consecutive days, and on the following Sunday they organised the first traditional Cretan feast at one of the *kafenions.* Following the unqualified success of this first celebration, the feast was held every Sunday thereafter, each time at a different *kafenion.*

Witnesses also report other forms of entertainment on the island. They say that there was a gramophone on Spinalonga that played classical music, and that every single resident could enjoy its melodies thanks to the placement of speakers throughout the settlement. They obtained a billiard table, a backgammon board and a radio. They put together a theatrical group and even screened movies from time to time. Once in a while, the island also hosted shadow puppet shows featuring the beloved *Karagiozis*[11]. And in order to change the island's barren "bald egg" appearance, the patients formed tree-planting groups and shortly thereafter

[11] The main character in Greek shadow theatre.

planted the island's first eucalyptuses. These efforts were complemented by the planting of flowers and aromatic plants in clay containers and flower pots in the yards, doorways and windowsills. In time, boredom, idleness and despair gave way to creative occupations, involvement and hope. At dusk, the patients would gather on the northern shore of the island to spend their evening together and watch the sun go down. At that site paintings and scenes carved in the soft limestone, still visible today, depict games of draughts, boats and wounded hearts and attest to the many hours spent there by the patients - and by generations of islanders before them. As my friend Kostis Spithas says, not only can rocks talk, but they also have much to say. According to him, those lifeless rocks bear witness to the residents' deepest yearnings for love, belonging and freedom. A closer look at these limestone tableaux reveal the astonishing evolution and development of the people who have lived on Spinalonga stretching back through the mists of time. The island's residents during every era (ancient Greeks, Arabs, Venetians, Ottomans and modern-day Greeks) impressed their innermost thoughts and everyday images on those grey rocks. Boats of every size and shape feature prominently in these images – as do games. There are also, however, some isolated drawings, like the one that is said to portray the eruption of the volcano on Santorini, which inspire a feeling of quiet awe, since we know how fateful that eruption was to the people of the Aegean.

The patients who were less debilitated by the disease gradually resumed their original professions. Apart from the staff of the leper colony, the *kafenion*-keepers and the guards, the island now also had craftsmen, shoemakers, butchers, builders and others. The patients began to develop new interests which replaced their earlier fatalism, and the exploitation of the weak by the strong and clever began to yield to a kind of solidarity. But the phenomenon of exploitation was a major problem, especially in the early years.

A simple example suffices to explain what it was like on the island: A newcomer to Spinalonga, with no job or other work to do, almost always ended up passing time playing cards at one of the island's *kafenions*. There the more experienced ones made sure to relieve him of his allowance. If he couldn't pay in cash, he would have to pay in kind, often as a servant in the house of the man to whom he owed money. It was also common to loan or rent such indentured servants to third parties, and this practice led to numerous quarrels and frequent fistfights. Another common situation was for bedridden patients to be cared for by couples or other fellow-patients, who thus gained control over their allowance while their charge was alive – and their belongings after death.

But by gradually adopting the prerequisites for a healthy society, the patients began to view their lives from a different perspective.

They began to feel useful and gradually abandoned their dissolute and predatory behaviours – at least to some degree.

The initiatives and successes of the Fraternity led to the formation of another group on the island, the so-called "Union", comprising those who had not previously joined the Fraternity and which was formed expressly to combat financial exploitation of the islanders. Prior to its formation, patients would pay vastly inflated prices for the products that reached Spinalonga. A good example can be found in the letter of an elderly patient to his sister in Sitia, which consists of a *mandinada*[12]:

"I grow peppermint in the yard, to wash the dishes of the day,

for the price of sagebrush where I am, I simply cannot pay..."

They didn't have sponges back then, so they washed all their pots, pans and plates with a bit of soap and a clump of sage as a sponge or brush. While Crete is full of sagebrush, none grew on Spinalonga, so, as with everything else, they had to bring it from the mainland.

---

[12] Distinctly Cretan verse form employing rhyming couplet or couplets.

Because they had to buy everything at prices beyond their means, the creation of a union to procure goods at reasonable prices was considered a vital necessity. And so the "Union" was formed, and the two associations moved forward together.

A sewer system was created, which diverted the colony's outhouse waste into the sea, purging the settlement of its most unpleasant odours. The leper colony's managers made arrangements for craftsmen to come to the island and continue the job of reconstruction. Able-bodied patients also helped with the construction work, either as assistants or as craftsmen, since some of them had already started to pursue their old professions again. One such craftsman was Pipina's brother, Yiannis.

By 1939, the construction of a ring road was completed. A half-metre, concrete-coated wall that was built alongside the road was the crowning touch, designed to guide the blind who could now tap their way safely around the island with their canes. Ruins were demolished, and the overall air of newness and improvement changed people's image of lepers and their society.

The fair and spirited competition that existed between the two associations on the island largely benefited the patients. Their ongoing lobbying resulted in the hiring of new staff to care for the patients, as well as an increase in their allowance to 35 drachmas per month. The market of Spinalonga with its incredible variety and abundance, the entertainment they enjoyed, as well as the open-air events they organised all made history.

The living conditions continued to improve, and Manolis had the satisfaction of watching his early efforts blossom and spread. Thanks to his impetus, the people of Spinalonga had achieved great things in their small society.

The Prefectural Medical Officer of Spinalonga

The appointment of a Prefectural Medical Officer to Spinalonga was seen as a godsend by the patients. Michalis Rasidakis, a young doctor with powerful connections, was appointed Director of the leper colony in 1924 by Eleftherios Venizelos. He held the post, except for certain short intervals, until 1957 when the leper colony ceased operation. One of these intervals occurred in 1936 when Ioannis Metaxas came to power, dissolved parliament and declared a dictatorship. He soon removed the Medical Officer from his post as Director - a purely partisan political decision. But due to the Medical Officer's close connections with various high-ranking figures, he resumed his position a short while later, a pattern repeated over the years each time he was removed for political reasons.

Rasidakis was an educated, intelligent and highly articulate man. But what made the patients, and especially the residents of the Gulf and the wider region, value and support him was that he provided medical care at a time when doctors were scarce. According to testimonies, he was adept at a wide range of specialisations; and, depending on the case, he would assume the role of surgeon, dentist, pathologist or whatever kind of specialist might be needed to treat a specific patient. He was highly respected, since doctors at that time, along with priests, teachers, lawyers and police officers, were considered professionals of exceptionally high status. Dr. Rasidakis provided medical care free of charge, since money was also scarce at the time. Sometimes, however, he would accept manual labour by way of compensation. The doctor owned several almond fields, the cultivation and care of which required many hands. Patients he had treated and cured would often help him with his farm work in order to repay his kindness. His opinion also carried great weight, and no one dared question or oppose him. The power he held through his natural authority made him "a state within a state", for he called all the shots without requesting - or needing - anyone's permission, and his wish was a virtual command. The patients could do nothing without his consent, and he in turn supported them to the best of his ability, even during the difficult years of the German occupation when everyone else had forgotten about them. According to his wife, Rasidakis would write down the news he heard on the radio and would then read it to the patients, giving them a glimpse of current affairs. Since the Italians and Germans had banned all radios, he hid his device in a well close to his house in Plaka. At night, at considerable risk to his own life, he would lift it out of the well, listen to the daily news and then pass along the information to his neighbours in Plaka and the patients on the island. Even though the Medical Officer did not spend his nights on Spinalonga, the proximity of Plaka to the islet made it easy for him to go there whenever there was a medical emergency. He examined patients on a daily basis and was obliged by law to keep medical records detailing the course of their disease. Rasidakis was responsible for the smooth operation of the leper colony and supervised both patients and staff. He had the first say in anything that happened on or off the islet if it concerned either the patients or staff. He knew everything there was to know about each patient's condition and had the sole authority to declare someone infected. Based on his decision, any unfortunate resident of Lasithi could be sent permanently to Spinalonga. According to testimonies, medical examinations alone carried less weight than the Medical Officer's opinion. He merely had to say "This one here is sick and needs to be transferred to Spinalonga" for the hapless citizen to be bound hand and foot and sent to the islet. This seemingly arbitrary power terrified the residents, who made sure to keep on his good side. This all-powerful and brilliant man played one of the most important parts in the history of Spinalonga.

The Occupation and its impact on the leper society

The patients' ongoing efforts to better their condition were finally beginning to bear fruit, and the island was enjoying a period of peace, order and prosperity. But all that came to an abrupt halt with the German-Italian occupation. In anticipation of the imminent crisis, the State provided the patients with three monthly allowances in advance so that they might procure the necessary supplies and prepare themselves for the hard times ahead. The patients, however, were so wrapped up in their own problems that they delayed these purchases for too long. As a result, when they finally tried to obtain the necessary supplies, prices had skyrocketed. Ten days later, the baker stopped delivering bread because his supply of flour had run out, and all reserves in the storehouse of Agios Nikolaos had been confiscated by the occupying forces. They lived on barley bread supplied by some of the patients' relatives for another ten days. Finally, when this too ran out, despair and a well-honed survival instinct led them to petition the occupying forces, offering to join their side in exchange for food. While waiting for the occupiers' response, friends and relatives rushed to supply them with some bread and carob so they wouldn't starve to death. The lepers were of little or no value to the Italians and Germans and, naturally enough, were not inducted into their armed forces. But once the occupiers established that the islanders had no ulterior motive beyond survival, they supplied each of them with half a loaf of white bread per day for the following month. At the end of the first month, however, the white bread was replaced by wormy cornbread. A fundraiser held in the region of the Lasithi Plateau came like a gift from above and provided the lepers with thirty five okes[13] of potatoes, which tided them over for a while longer. Money still circulated and was of value, so the patients managed to buy some oil, although it cost them a small fortune. However, the rapid rise in prices made them hesitate to purchase most supplies, no matter how crucial to their survival. According to testimonies, in order to avoid being taken advantage of and having to pay unreasonable prices for wild greens and herbs, they planted seasonal herbs in any part of the rocky island that had some soil. The lack of food and a curtailment of medical care led to a dramatic increase in the number of deaths, with even young people now numbering among the deceased. Photographs from that period show the residents of Spinalonga with eyes sunken and lifeless from malnutrition.

In March 1942, a system of bartering for foodstuffs was implemented, and this delivered a heavy blow to the poor lepers who had very few possessions to trade. They began by exchanging their Sunday clothes, unused beds, furniture, equipment, tools and anything else that could be traded for food. Couples that had married on the island and had two homes between them now stripped one of these homes of all furnishings to exchange for bare necessities. But despite these stop-gap measures, the situation soon came to a

[13] Approximately 45 kilos.

head. The patients got together for a lengthy discussion and came up with a plan: First, they would not allow the service boat to approach the island for the following days, since there was no food or medicine to be had anyway. Then, all the patients would lock themselves in their homes and refuse any help from the nurses and staff, thus giving the impression that the island was dead. If these actions went unanswered, they would then carry out the second phase of their plan, which would entail sending away the entire staff and all the healthy children born on Spinalonga to leprous parents.

Their first actions went unheeded, so they put all the healthy staff members and children on boats and forced them to depart, under threat of torching the island. Exasperated, they cried that they would rather take their own lives than endure the slow, painful death of starvation. The authorities were shocked by these developments and promised to deal with the matter within three days, while the Medical Officer urged them not to take any further action before receiving a response. Indeed, three days later, a motorboat arrived at Spinalonga bringing with it the authorities' decision. Their plan had worked: The following day, another boat transferred twenty kilograms of flour, two kilos of pasta, as well as some rice and sugar for every patient - provisions that had to last them for two months. This was the situation until the first trimester of 1943, when Italy surrendered to the Allies, again leaving the islanders at the mercy of fate. The Red Cross intervened, sending them some sacks of wheat, once again giving them a short respite. But the situation continued to worsen, and the patients had now sold almost everything movable on the island: beds, clothes, pots and pans... According to testimonies, even the staff of Spinalonga, who were public servants, went unpaid for at least 6 months. The patients' desperate cry for help was unavailing and their future bleak, since they had nothing more to barter. In their despair, they decided to turn two large roofs into salt pans. They filled them with seawater and in about two weeks' time, when the water had evaporated, they collected and cleaned the salt, distributed part of it to the patients and exchanged the rest for fruit that could be preserved - a process that was repeated once again during summer. The Metropolis of Petra also provided support, and its charitable work, in conjunction with the philanthropy of certain residents along the Gulf, played a key role in the survival of the lepers.

The waters surrounding the island were abundant in black gobies, a small fish currently avoided by consumers but considered a valuable commodity at the time. Using shells, limpets and crushed shellfish as bait, they would often end up with a good catch, since the outsized appetite of this little fish made it easy prey. With the passage of time, hunger, hardship and neglect debased the lives of the lepers. The toll of their disease and their constant need of clean clothes and dressings led them to create a detergent made of water, oil and ashes to wash their clothing and homemade bandages.

Their principal drink was *Haroubia*, which was made by crushing carob pods, soaking the resulting pulp in water for twenty-four hours, and then boiling it until all the water had evaporated and only a honey-like substance remained which they would scrape from the bottom of the pot and save in clay jars. Whenever they wanted something tasty to drink, they would simply dissolve a few teaspoons of the syrupy substance in water.

On 6 September 1944, the occupying forces withdrew from the area. The destruction they had caused to Spinalonga and the wider Gulf region, however, would prove difficult to repair. By the time they had withdrawn, more than 100 patients had died out of the 330 confined on Spinalonga - a massive number considering the normal mortality rate. This rapid decline in the number of patients was almost certainly the underlying factor behind the most horrific chapter in the history of the island.

Sitia, 1946

The rooster crowed, announcing to the village that it was five in the morning. Although it is still pitch-black outside, Pipina and Kostis have to get up, for they have work to do in the fields and two mouths to feed. If the fields are neglected or left untended, the land will soon revert to the wild and bear no fruit. And then what? What will become of them? With these thoughts in mind, Kostis dresses quickly. He splashes some water on his face from the pitcher beside the sink, pats his face dry with the towel hanging from the nail beside the makeshift mirror and then heads to the stable to prepare the donkey for its journey to the field. In the meantime, Pipina puts two pieces of wood in the fire to brew some milk-tea for her two little angels to drink when they wake up. Keeping in mind that they won't have anything else to eat until noon, she unfolds a cloth containing a piece of cheese and takes two *dakos* out of the earthenware jar to complete their breakfast.

'Children, rise and shine! It's time to get up!'

The more Pipina calls their names, the more deeply the children burrow under their blankets. All they want to do is to continue sleeping, and certainly not wake up at five in the morning on a cold winter day. Pipina's persistence finally pays off, and the two children grudgingly get out of bed.

Still half-asleep, they get dressed and listlessly wash their faces before sitting down at the *sofras* to eat their breakfast.

'Maria, have you said your morning prayers and crossed yourself?' Pipina asks her daughter, the older of the two.

'No, Mama,' she replies and immediately starts doing so.

'Never forget to cross yourselves before you eat, leave the house or go to bed at night, my children, if you want God to show you love and mercy!'

Pipina and Kostis may be illiterate, but they are also God-fearing and righteous people, who, despite their poverty and misfortunes, never neglect to thank the Lord for their family's health and the many blessings he provides them.

Kostis returns from the stable.

'Pipina, pour some water so I can rinse my hands.'

Pipina brings the pitcher from the sink and helps her husband wash his hands.

'You should eat something too before we go, Kostis.'

'Never mind me, Pipina; Let the children have it. I'll find something to eat on the way.'

'Maria!' Pipina shouts. 'Are you ready?'

'Yes, Mama!'

'And Giorgis?'

'Almost!'

'Tell him to hurry up, we've got to go! I'll drop you off at grandma Somarou's so she can take you to school.'

'I'll go on my own! It's only next door!'

'Oh, all right. Giorgis? What's taking so long?'

'I'm coming, Mama!'

Giorgis comes running down the stairs.

'Come let me help you get on the donkey,' his father says, grabbing him under the arms and lifting his little body onto the animal's back.

'Maria,' he says to his daughter, 'when you finish school at noon, go gather as much donkey dung as you can and bring it to the field, ok?'

'Ok, father.'

Her father, like most people back then, used donkey manure as fertiliser on their fields and vineyards to produce more and better fruit and vegetables. Moreover, the scarcity of arable land increased the need to fertilise their tiny holdings. Because their everyday lives were particularly harsh, everyone in the family did their part and contributed in many ways so the family could survive.

It is already five-thirty and they have to leave, for the working day begins early in the village. On the road they encounter many fellow-villagers also heading to their fields. The sun has yet to rise, so Pipina fastens the top button of Giorgis' shirt and tucks it into his pants to protect him from the cold wind. One of the reasons they leave for the fields so early is that it is still cool outside. Working in the sun is more tiring, so most of the work is always carried out during the early morning hours. In fact, there was a saying for lazy people in Crete back then: "Fat chance he'll feel the morning dew". The hours went by quickly, and it was soon time for a break. Pipina had a piece of cheese left over from the children's breakfast to give to Giorgis for a snack.

'Giorgis! Come, my child, take a break. That's enough for now. You can finish after you've eaten something.'

'I don't want to, Mama,' he replies. 'I ate a couple of pears from that tree over there.'

'All right then,' Pipina says. 'I'll leave it here for you. Have it when you're hungry.'

'Why don't we take a break too?' Kostis says to Pipina.

'You sit and have a rest, Kostis. I'll go pick some greens and herbs to make *horta* later.'

'Since you're going, Pipina, gather some grass and weeds so we can feed the animals when we get back. Just pile them up somewhere and I'll load them onto the donkey on the way home.'

Pipina carries many responsibilities on her shoulders; she not only helps her husband with all the fieldwork, but she is also a mother. Life is hard - not only for her but for everyone, but she would do anything for her beloved Kostis. They married for love, although his parents opposed the marriage. Pipina was four years older than Kostis, and he hadn't fulfilled his military obligations yet. But they were united by the kind of love that can move mountains, and he adored her too. Once he realised that his parents weren't likely to change their minds, he decided that they should elope. He hired a taxi-driver, and one night he "kidnapped" her without anyone suspecting a thing. Pervolaris, the sympathetic driver, discreetly drove them to the nearby village of Myrsini, where they took shelter for a few days while waiting for his parents to realise that they loved each other and couldn't possibly live apart.

But it was already too late for his parents to do anything other than give them their blessing. Back then, people paid great attention to a family's honour and good name. The social stigma caused by an affair or out-of-wedlock child had an impact on both families, but much more so on the woman's.

They believed that a girl should remain "undefiled" - a virgin - until she married. A woman who wasn't a virgin on her wedding day or had given birth to a child out of wedlock was completely marginalised; her life was basically ruined, and no one wanted to have anything to do with her. People lived by the saying "It's better to lose an eye than to gain a bad reputation", because the stain on a family's name and reputation was extremely difficult to expunge. As families grew and intermarried, they formed tightly knit communities, all strictly adhering to the customs, traditions and moral codes of Cretan society. Their pride and sense of shame kept them from doing anything that would give rise to gossip or censure.

Kostis' parents were simple people, like all the other villagers, but seeing how things were turning out, they finally agreed to the marriage. A year later, however, another event further complicated their lives and upended the world as they knew it. The Italians invaded Greece, and Kostis had to leave for the front at once, leaving Pipina behind, pregnant with their first child, Maria. Much time would pass before Kostis could return home...

The Battle of Crete - Dyo Aorakia, Heraklion.

A few years earlier...

Kostis' battalion was one of the first to be transferred to the village of Dyo Aorakia. Crete is under siege, and thousands of German paratroopers are dropping from the sky, their parachutes turning it from blue to white. The Greek soldiers, vastly outnumbered, are waiting in their trenches for the Germans to touch down, silently praying while waiting for the signal to attack. As the first Germans approach the ground, a voice yells *fire* and all hell breaks loose. The Cretans take aim at the falling paratroopers, most of whom are dead before they hit the ground. But more continue to drop in an endless rain, and the first living Germans manage to land, get clear of their chutes and begin to return fire. The Germans, armed with machine guns, open fire on the badly outnumbered Cretans, who fight bravely nonetheless. Chaos reigns; death is everywhere, and both sides suffer horrific casualties. The Greek army has left the trenches and is trying with all its might to prevent the inevitable. But soon they run out of bullets.

They are now left to fight the enemy with their bayonets, so Kostis and the other recruits engage in hand-to-hand combat. Although the battlefield is full of lifeless bodies, they fight on; death does not frighten them so much as losing their country.

At the same time, at home in Sitia, the sound of a baby's cry fills the air. Pipina has just brought their daughter into the world, but Kostis isn't there to hear her first cry...

As the battle drags on, the Germans slowly begin to gain the upper hand, and the Greeks, seeing that they are losing, sound the retreat. The situation has spiralled out of control: they have run out of ammunition; the paratroopers keep landing, and defeat is now certain. So there is nothing else to do but fall back, regroup and try to find a way to fight again. Kostis and some of his cohorts don't want to withdraw, but the others force them to follow them to safety.

Two days after the great battle, all those who fought are given a five-day leave. Kostis uses his time off to visit his family and hold his daughter in his arms for the first time.

The days pass quickly, and it is soon time for Kostis to rejoin his unit. But now he has one more reason to come home alive: their beautiful baby!

The months go by, and the baby is growing fast, but the battles in Crete are still raging, and Kostis has given no sign of life for months. His family is extremely anxious but can do nothing, and they too are struggling to survive. Terror and poverty overrun the land, and with all the able-bodied men and boys away fighting for their country, only the elderly, the women and children are left to manage everything else back home. One dark day, the church bells start ringing, sending the terrified villagers dashing from their homes. A voice rises above the clamour shouting: 'Hide, villagers! Run for your lives! The Germans are coming! Run, villagers! Hide!' The people, overcome by panic, hurriedly gather together the few essentials they can carry and flee with their elders and children to the mountain. A few days earlier, the Germans had burned two nearby villages to the ground, killing anyone they came upon. Certain that the same fate awaits them too, the villagers seek shelter in several *metochi*, small stone huts hidden deep in the folds and crevasses of the mountain. Pipina, holding her tightly swaddled baby, and with her mother by her side, seeks shelter at the *metochi* of one of her aunts. Kallio cautiously opens the door, and they see many of their fellow-villagers already sitting on the floor behind her.

'Auntie, can we come in?' Pipina asks anxiously.

'You brought the baby too?'

'Of course!' Pipina replies, taken aback. 'Where was I to leave her?'

'Pipina... I can't let you come in with the baby...'

'Please, Kallio,' Somarou intervenes. 'Let us in.'

'No. Not with the baby!'

'And where are we to go?'

'I don't know. But her crying might give us away!'

'But, please... Take pity on us!'

'I can't. Go somewhere else,' Kallio replies and closes the door in their faces.

Pipina bursts into tears. 'Oh, my dear child,' she cries to Maria.

Her mother puts her arm around her and tries to comfort her. Diamantoula, a fellow-villager, witnesses this scene from the doorway of her own nearby *metochi*.

'Pipina! Bring the child!' she shouts and signals them to come over to her.

The two women freeze and stare at her for a moment.

'Well, come on then!' Diamantoula continues.

Somarou and Pipina run to her doorway.

The old lady quickly pulls them inside, closes the door behind them, and they join the other villagers who have found shelter in her cabin.

'Come, Pipina, follow me! We'll put the baby in the back room. No one will hear her crying from there,' Diamantoula says.

Pipina follows her into a small room with thick walls and no windows. Diamantoula and her husband had built it as a shed and storage room, and it is filled with all sorts of food and assorted items: oil, straw, cheese, bread rusks, goatskins, etc. Diamantoula gathers an armful of straw, places it neatly in a corner, spreads a fleece on top and, voilà, the baby's bed is ready.

'Come, Pipina, lay her down over here,' Diamantoula says.

Pipina lays the baby down on the straw bed and Diamantoula covers her with another fleece for warmth. Two women and an innocent child are safe for the moment.

Shortly after, the bells ring again. The Germans have left the village, and it is time for the people to return to their homes and assess the damage. Many villagers have not been as lucky, including Kostis' mother, Eleni. They find her lying dead just outside the village, her body riddled with bullets. Over the coming days, the villagers will bury their dead, knit together the torn fabric of their lives and try to move on...

It has been more than a year since they last set eyes on Kostis. The Germans have fanned across Crete, and fierce battles are raging all over the land. Every night, Pipina cries herself to sleep and prays to God that her beloved husband might return to her safe and sound.

One day, there is a knock at the door. It is Kostis. Behind him a small crowd of children are chanting:

'Dead man! Dead man!' A rumour had quietly run through the village that Kostis had been killed in battle, but the villagers have kept it from reaching his wife. But now here he is, very much alive! His commander had given him a short leave during a lull in the fighting, and he immediately rushed to be with his family. After seeing that his wife and child are well, and, after mourning the loss of his mother, Kostis gets ready to leave again. Once more, he has to leave Pipina on her own, but now she would have to take care of *both* of their children - little Maria and the baby she would soon be carrying in her womb...

1943

The war was finally over, and the soldiers had returned to their homes and families. Pipina had given birth to their second child, a beautiful and healthy baby boy - the perfect addition to their family. And as with their first child, she gave birth to him with the aid of the village midwife and her mother on a handmade carpet laid over the dirt floor. But she didn't mind. The midwife cut the umbilical cord, cleaned the infant and placed him on Pipina's chest for her to nurse.

The young woman would breastfeed the little boy for quite a while, just as she did their first child. Besides, what else could she feed him? Food was scarce and not at all suitable for babies. The best she could do for him when he grew a little would be to chew his food before feeding it to him.

Born in 1912, Pipina was thirty-one years old. Maria, her first-born daughter, had just turned seven, while Giorgis was nearly five. Pipina wasn't disheartened by poverty and hardship; she felt happy and complete simply knowing that she had a loving family by her side and that all of them were in good health.

The only thing that worried her was Kostis' military obligations. He would soon have to leave them again, for Civil War had broken out, again sweeping up all the menfolk, and Kostis would have to report for duty when the time came.

She knew that she could count on her mother to help with the children. Even so, she would have to take on all her husband's chores while he was away: work the fields and care for the animals - their only livelihood. But she wasn't afraid; every time she began to feel discouraged, she would remember how hard she had already fought for her family, especially her two little angels. Then, she would brace herself and promise not to give up, no matter how difficult it might become. She would also take heart from her mother, Somarou, who was the only person she could turn to for help and the only family she had left. Her father and four brothers and sister had all been sent to Spinalonga, supposedly with Hansen's disease, so there was no chance of them ever returning - at least not alive. Every now and then, they would hear news of them from another leper who was on leave visiting relatives in the village. But that was a rare occurrence. A fresh outbreak of leprosy had made people especially fearful of contact; there was no effective treatment or cure, and it was thought to be highly contagious. The terrible physical deformities it caused made lepers look like otherworldly creatures, whose hideous appearance, combined with an acute fear of contracting the disease, led people to shun them. Patients needed a compelling reason to obtain two or three days' leave from the island. No signs of the disease could be visible on their body, and they should be judged certain to return as promised.

Spinalonga - Gulf of Mirabello, 1946

Nearly forty years had passed since the day the first patient set foot on the islet. With the wounds of the Occupation still fresh, the beginning of the Civil War in 1944 delivered another severe blow to the area, significantly hindering its recovery. The devastating effects of war left both lepers and residents of the Gulf struggling to rebuild their communities. Perhaps the only good thing to come out of the Occupation was that the residents of Spinalonga had developed strong ties of love and solidarity. Hardship, their common fate, and their survival instinct, had brought them together out of necessity. They had shared pain and sacrifice; they had given and received love, respect and recognition, all of which they needed dearly. It wasn't just the war that had brought them to their knees; they had all left behind children, spouses or relatives – almost certainly forever. Spinalonga had become their entire life and the place where they would breathe their last breath. Their bodies would be buried in nameless graves which their loved ones would likely never visit.

On this black rock, as they called it, they found the compassion and understanding missing in society at large. They were also united by their thirst for life, and that made them powerful. The era of idleness and dissipation had gone for good; they had seen better days, and they now wanted to restore the standard of living their community had enjoyed prior to the Occupation, at least until they could leave the island once and for all. With great effort they managed to accomplish this by 1946. However, nothing could bring back all the patients who had lost their lives during the war: in addition to the more than 100 patients who had died up to 1944, the Occupation continued to claim lives throughout much of 1946 due to the patients' weakened state after years of malnutrition. This resulted in a rapid decline in the number of inhabitants. At the same time on the opposite shore, the residents of the Gulf were starving once again, only surviving through their trade with the residents of Spinalonga. But just as things were beginning to improve, a new crisis appeared on the horizon: a proposal to close the leper colony. The news came as a bolt from the blue. The residents of the Gulf feared that if the leper colony ceased operation they would starve to death. Spinalonga was their main source of income, and they knew that they wouldn't survive without the lepers. To whom would they sell their produce and merchandise? How would they feed their families? Just the thought of closing the colony caused panic and led the desperate residents of the Gulf to seek a solution.

At the same time, Rasidakis, the Medical Officer of Spinalonga, was quietly observing these developments. This cunning and ambitious man had realised that this situation could help him achieve the big plans he had in mind. He knew how to watch his back, so the steps he took towards achieving his goals were always incremental, calculated and discreet. But what he probably did better than anything else was to deceive people. He knew what they were thinking and feeling; he could tell what they wanted to hear and what they really desired, and that made him extremely dangerous. His social status and education, in combination with his charitable works, kept everyone from suspecting his ulterior motives. He appeared to be a brilliant scientist with a heart of gold, but the truth was that he didn't think of anyone but himself. By earning people's trust, he could more easily influence them for his benefit. Another way for a person in a prominent position to gain influence was to form *koumbaria*[14]. By doing so, an ambitious man created powerful ties and enjoyed the lifelong support of his new relations. The more *koumbaria* someone had, the more their status grew. According to reports and records from the time, the Medical Officer formed approximately 2,000 *koumbaria* throughout the Prefecture of Lasithi.

Rasidakis was close friends with Alekos Platakis, an equally clever and ambitious doctor from Sitia. These two restless spirits shared many interests; Platakis, who had held the office of Senator in the past, never

[14] To become the best man at a wedding or the godparent to a couple's child, thus becoming an important member of their extended family.

ceased to plan bold and ambitious schemes. They were both stubborn, arrogant, greedy and had a tendency to claim the lead in any endeavour. Inevitably, their encounter would prove catastrophic...

Kostis' military service

The family is seated around the small table, but a silence lingers in the air. The day they had all been dreading has finally arrived; a paper has come ordering Kostis to report for immediate duty. The time has come. His wounded country needs him in the north, where fighting is raging, even between brothers. Pipina remains silent, fearing that a single word might reveal her devastation. She knew that this day would come but wasn't prepared for the pain she would feel. 'I will stay strong, my Kostis. I will manage...' she promises to herself. Kostis looks into her eyes, and although there are a million things he desperately wants to say to her, the words don't come. Finally, grandma Somarou turns to Kostis and breaks the heavy silence.

'Everything will be all right, my child. Don't be afraid. We won't leave Pipina alone. She can count on us for anything she needs. Besides, everyone has to go. Just take care of yourself and come back quickly.' Somarou then turns to Pipina.

'Don't be afraid, dear. We are your family, and we'll support you. Now get up, and let's go pack Kostis' things so he can be on his way.'

'Yes, Mama,' Pipina replies. 'We will get through this.'

Pipina knows how hard it is for the children to see their father leave again, so she tries to stay strong and not add to their pain.

Now in tears, Maria turns to Kostis.

'Daddy?'

'Yes, Maria dear?' he replies, wiping her cheeks with his hand.

'Why are you going away?' she asks, looking straight into his eyes.

'Because I have to, my child. But you have my word that I'll be back soon,' he replies reassuringly, even though he isn't at all sure if he will, in fact, return home again. The Civil War may not have greatly affected Crete, but in northern Greece the fighting is fierce.

In an effort to soothe and distract his daughter, Kostis strokes her head affectionately and sets her a task.

'While I'm away, Maria dear, I want you to do me a favour.'

'Anything, father!'

'Since you're the eldest, I want you to look after your mother and brother for me. Listen to your mother, and help her around the house so she doesn't get tired and discouraged.'

'All right, father. I'll look after her; you have my word. And if Giorgis disobeys or upsets her, he'll get the beating of his life!'

'I *never* disobey!' Giorgis interrupts. 'I'm the man of the house, and *I'll* take care of *you*! Fear nothing!' Giorgis says proudly, throwing back his shoulders and sitting up straight.

'That's my little man!' grandma Somarou exclaims. 'See, Pipina? You have nothing to fear with such children. But get up now because it's getting late.'

'Yes, Mama, let's get Kostis' things ready.'

The two women stand up from the table and go to the other room to pack Kostis' duffel bag, while the children sit beside their father.

Folding her husband's shirts, Pipina silently weeps. Somarou walks over to her, offers her a handkerchief to dry her eyes and whispers:

'Hush now, my child. This too will pass. Don't worry. I'll help you, and we'll get through this together. It pains me too, but they mustn't see our tears. Let's not make this more difficult than it already is. Kostis has to leave, and there is nothing we can do about it. Now dry your eyes, and show them the courage they need, because only you can do that.'

'You're right, Mama, I know. Give me a couple of minutes to pull myself together. I'll be right in.'

Kostis has to report for duty in just a few hours, and it is soon time to leave. He embraces his children, kisses them on the cheek and forehead - and takes a long, deep breath of their hair.

'Remember what we said now, ok? Take care of your mother! I'll come and see you at the first opportunity. Until then, I'll write you. Send me letters whenever you can, and don't forget me, ok?'

'Ok, father,' Giorgis and Maria reply, throwing themselves back into his arms. Finally, his two little angels can no longer hold back their tears and begin to cry.

'Will you still love us when you're away?' Giorgis demands.

'What do you think, my son? Could I stop loving you?'

'But what if you forget about us?' the boy continues.

'If you love someone, Giorgis, you can't possibly forget about them, no matter how far apart you are! Look after the women now, understand?'

'All right, father.'

'Dad?' Maria says.

'What is it, my child?'

'When you get there, tell them you have two children at home so they'll let you come back sooner.'

'All right, honey,' her father replies with a smile.

Kostis kisses the two children on the head and then turns to his mother-in-law.

'Goodbye, mother,' he says.

'Farewell, my boy. May God look over you and bring you back to your family soon'.

'Thank you, mother. Take good care of Pipina and the children for me.' He kisses her hand and receives her blessing.

Last was Pipina. They have no words to exchange, so they simply look into each other's eyes for a few seconds with perfect understanding. Kostis leans over and kisses her.

'I love you... Take care,' he whispers.

'I love you too; *you* take care and don't worry about me. I'll manage!'

'Kostis, hurry up!' a commanding voice is heard from outside. 'The car's about to leave! Come on!'

Kostis grabs his bag and rushes out of the house. As he descends the narrow road, he turns back towards his family, now huddled in the doorway, and waves a last goodbye.

'Farewell!' he shouts. 'I will write soon!'

Grandma Somarou, Pipina and the children watch the car drive slowly out of sight.

The meeting

Alekos Platakis has arranged a meeting with the Medical Officer to discuss a pressing matter, and it is time to put their friendship to the test. Once Rasidakis arrives, Alekos reveals his plan: He explains how he intends to stand for election and asks for his friend's support and help in devising a plan that will guarantee victory. The two men discuss the matter in detail, focussing on how to persuade voters to vote for Platakis when powerful opponents will also be running for the post. How will they convince people that he is the best man? After a lengthy discussion, the two men agree on a strategy.

The Medical Officer likes the idea of having a close friend in a powerful position because it will help him realise his own ambitions in the future. They come up with a brilliant scheme which will serve them both: Platakis will benefit in the short-term and Rasidakis later on.

Rasidakis had already informed Platakis about the situation in the Elounda area. Sending the first lepers to Spinalonga had led to a boom in trade, which hadn't made the residents of the Gulf wealthy but at least had given them a steady source of income. The fear of contracting leprosy was still a major concern, and the two friends knew that they could easily use it to persuade the residents of Elounda to vote for Platakis. But beyond fear, their plan relied on greed and self-interest as well, a winning combination. What did Spinalonga have that Elounda didn't? Allowance money - turning the patients into paying customers. And what would happen to the residents of Elounda if the leper colony closed? They would probably starve. So what could the two men promise in exchange for votes? An ongoing supply of clients, of course! That was their plan. They would keep on admitting new patients to Spinalonga so it would continue operating and ensure that the residents of the Gulf didn't lose their main source of income. It was a devious and deeply unethical scheme, but who could possibly suspect them? The mere suspicion that someone had leprosy was enough to condemn them to Spinalonga without a chance to defend themselves or prove otherwise – like Medieval witches, who were burned at the stake out of fear of what they supposedly had done or might do. But Platakis and Rasidakis believed that their ends justified any means and did not care about the harm they might cause or the innocent lives they might ruin along the way. Their ambition blinded them to the many injustices of their plan. Once they were convinced that it would produce the desired results and that no one would ever suspect them, they continued their meeting in an almost festive mood. Besides, who would dare expose them? Not the residents of the Gulf, who stood to lose their livelihoods, and no one would ever believe the victims themselves.

A few days later, the Medical Officer set the plan in motion and began to approach the residents of the Gulf one by one. He started each visit by confiding that he had information about lepers freely roaming the prefecture of Lasithi, and that the authorities knew about this but wanted to close the leper colony. He would then begin praising his good friend, Alexandros Platakis. Knowing that their soft spot was Spinalonga, he stressed Platakis' familiarity with the needs of the land and his opposition to closing the leper colony. 'They are sick', he would tell them, 'but why should you all die? Who cares about them? It's you folks - the healthy - who must figure out how to survive! Platakis is going to stand for election, and if you vote for him he will bring lots of patients to Spinalonga, and they will need even more supplies. No one will go hungry again if we elect this good man, and you have my word that you will all benefit. Rest assured!'

The Medical Officer was persuasive, and his visits were effective. His hosts were simple people, and, beyond the standard village tricks and cunning, none could imagine such a complex ruse, played out over such a wide area. All they could see was a clear and simple solution to their greatest problem. By voting for Platakis, new lepers would be rounded up and brought to the islet, and the increase in the number of patients would end all further discussion about closing the colony. In this way, the bonanza would continue uninterrupted, providing financial security to the people of the Gulf.

As I say and firmly believe:
Although money is alluring and sweet as honey,
it will run your life and make you worry.
It leads people to war, yet you need it to survive,
so everyone wants it; every single man alive.

The residents of Elounda were conditioned to trust doctors and other educated professionals and so were convinced that Rasidakis was being straightforward with them. The position he held as Director of Spinalonga also meant that he was an expert on anything having to do with the disease. Moreover, the Medical Officer had never given cause for gossip or rumours in the past. His actions were always well calculated, and he knew how to hide his true character and motives behind a friendly and professional manner. Rasidakis made the most of his position and the means at his disposal to help elect his friend, anticipating Platakis' favour and support in the future. He provided convincing reasons for people to vote for Platakis, and they soon gave him their answer. The deal was made.

In the upcoming elections, nearly all the residents of Elounda voted for Platakis. Even so, he didn't receive enough votes for a clear win. But a deal was a deal; the people had kept their end of the bargain and now their support had to be rewarded. A few days later, their plan was set in motion...

* It is clear from the election results that the residents of Elounda showed a clear preference for Platakis. He gathered the overwhelming majority of votes, even though some of the other candidates were powerful politicians of the time. Apart from that, we must also take into account the fact that Platakis had absolutely no connection or ties to Elounda, since he came from Sitia, while the absence of a road network or mass media made it extremely difficult to reach and sway the voting public.

Kostis' letter

The postman arrives at the village, and immediately a crowd forms around him. Apart from the radio, which broadcasts vague news from the front, the postman is the villagers' only link to their loved ones off at war. He opens his sack, takes out a bundle of letters and begins calling out names - while the villagers wait in silence, hoping that one of the envelopes is for them. Half-way through the bundle, he calls Pipina's name.

'That's me,' she cries, and with a 'Thank you', takes the letter and walks away.

Once she is a few paces away from the crowd, she tears open the envelope. Immediately recognising the handwriting, she stops, lost in her own world, and begins to read:

My dearest Pipina,

I am doing well, and I hope all of you are well too. I'm writing to share my latest news with you, and I don't want you to worry. I am in good health, and that's what matters. My dear, I was involved in an unfortunate incident, but with the help of God it all turned out well. Two weeks ago, I was shot in the right leg and was admitted to the military hospital where I have stayed until now. The attending doctor said that the bullet passed through soft tissue without hitting bone and that the wound was superficial. In all honesty, I can assure you that it has pretty much healed. I have now been discharged from hospital and have fourteen days' sick leave which I will use to come back home, so I'll be arriving in a couple of days. Please don't pass on the unpleasant news to mother and the children. May God watch over you.

See you soon.
Yours truly,
Kostis

Upset by the unexpected and frightening news but relieved by the outcome and the fact that her Kostis was alive, Pipina held the letter to her chest and let out a heavy sigh. She then put it in her pocket, but quickly recalled her husband's request not to share the news with the family. Maria could read and would surely open the letter if she came across it, so after a moment's deliberation she tore it up and threw away the pieces. Of course, she would tell them about Kostis' letter and upcoming visit, but if any of them asked to see the letter she would simply pretend to have misplaced it.

Sitia, April 1946

Two days have passed since Kostis came home, and after spending this time with his wife and children, he harnessed the donkey and went to the fields to take some work off Pipina's hands. It was still early morning, and Pipina was off looking for snails to cook for lunch. The Medical Officer's men, however, had been in the village since dawn, and it wasn't long before they showed up at their doorstep.

'Pipina?' a voice calls out. 'Pipina, where are you?'

'I'm down here! In the field,' Pipina replies.

'Come up here. I need to talk to you!' the man continues in a commanding voice.

'Hold on. Let me rinse my hands and I'll be right there.'

She quickly washes her hands, picks up her basket of snails and heads up to the house.

'Hello there!' she greets them cheerfully.

'Hello, Pipina', the men reply in unison.

'Who have you come for today?' she continues casually.

'Actually, Pipina, we've come for you...' the boldest one says after a pause.

'For me?' Pipina exclaims, startled. 'What do you mean? There's nothing wrong with me!'

'We're not saying there is. We've simply come to take you to Agios Nikolaos to get tested.'

'Tested? Why? I'm telling you again I'm perfectly healthy!'

'But, Pipina... aren't your siblings sick?'

'So what if they are? Does that mean that I am too? I haven't seen any of them in ages, so how can I possibly have the disease?'

'We're not saying you're sick. We just need you to have a standard check-up. Think of your children, Pipina. What if you *are* sick, and you pass it on to them? What's there to lose by getting tested and knowing for sure? What are you afraid of? If you're certain that you're healthy you have nothing to fear. You'll go, get tested at the Medical Centre, and if the results come back clean you'll return home with your chin up! Are we wrong? Everyone wins: If you're not sick you'll silence any suspicion, and if you are you can take steps to protect your family.'

Pipina knows they're right. She stares at them absent-mindedly for a few seconds and then says:

'Ok, I see your point, but I can't possibly leave before Kostis finishes his military service because the results won't come back for days. His leave is about to end and I want him to come with me.'

'But, Pipina; you'll know the results straight away. You'll get tested *and* leave on the same day.'

They had convinced her.

'Ok then. When do I have to go?' Pipina asks.

'Today.'

'What do you mean today? I've been working in the field. I can't go to the doctor in this state! Besides, Kostis won't be back until sundown.'

'Pipina, this is a serious matter. We can't afford to mess around with a health issue.'

'Yes, of course, I agree. But what can I do? I'm afraid to go all the way to Agios Nikolaos by myself.'

'There's nothing to be scared of. The doctors will perform a simple test. They're not going to eat you! Look, we're running out of time. The car's waiting for us, so send your son to call your husband and tell him to be quick! There are others waiting in the car for the examination.'

'Ok, I'll send him,' she says as she looks around for the boy.

'Giorgis? Giorgis, where are you, my boy?' she shouts.

'On the roof, Mama. What is it?'

'Come down here. I need you to go call your father!'

Giorgis comes running down the stairs straight to his mother.

'What is it, Mama?'

'Go tell your father that he needs to come home at once, because we have to leave right away.'

'Where are you going, Mama?'

'To Agios Nikolaos; they're going to perform some tests to see if I've got leprosy.'

'Leprosy? But you're fine!'

'I know, sweetie. It's just to be sure. So run as fast as you can and fetch your father because the car is about to leave.'

'I'm off, Mama!'

Giorgis takes a shortcut and reaches the family field within minutes.

'Dad!' he shouts. 'Dad, come quickly!'

'What's the matter, Giorgis?' his father asks in alarm.

'Some men have come to the house and want to take Mama away!'

'They want to do what?'

'To take Mama away! Run fast!'

'Take her where, my child? Who are they? Talk to me, Giorgis!'

'They're the men who gather the lepers and take them to Spinalonga! They want to take mummy! They said they're taking her to get tested in Agios Nikolaos to see if she's got the disease!'

'And what does your mother say?' Kostis asks, confused.

'She says that you need to get there right away and that she's scared to go on her own! That's why she sent me to call you! The car's about to leave!'

'Do they have to go today? I've still got work to do! I'm not finished.'

'Mama said that you definitely have to go today, but I think the men are pressuring her! I was watching them from the roof! Dad, please hurry and see what's going on; I didn't like how they were looking at her... They're up to something now...'

'Why do you say that, son?'

'Because when they were rounding up lepers the last time, none of the men explained anything. And if someone didn't want to go, they took them by force anyway.'

'And now? What do you mean, Giorgis?'

'I mean that they're trying to persuade Mama to go do this check-up, but they won't let her go when she wants. They're saying she has to go today! And besides that, you should have seen the look on their faces when they were talking to her...'

'What do you mean?'

'They weren't looking her in the eye, father. I don't know... I just don't think they're telling the truth. That's why! So please, dad, hurry up and see what's going on! Something's not right!'

'Ok, let's go; as long as your mother has me by her side, you needn't fear anything! I won't let anything happen to her, you know that!' he adds to reassure his son.

Once this decision is made, Kostis drops everything, saddles the donkey in a flash, lifts the boy onto its back and prepares to hurry back to the house.

'Hold on tight!' he tells Giorgis.

'Ok, father, let's go!'

Kostis uses a thorny stick to prod the donkey's rump so it will go faster. Every time the stick touches the jumpy animal, it dashes up the trail as if its tail is on fire, so they are soon home again.

'Hello there, strangers!' Kostis shouts. 'Let me tie the donkey and I'll be right there.'

Kostis takes the boy off the donkey and then leads it to the shed by its bridle. He then walks over to the men without hiding his agitation.

'So... what's going on here? My son says you've come to take my wife away.'

'That's right, Kostis,' the calmest one replies. 'We're here to take her to get tested.'

'Why's that necessary? My wife's fine! Can't you see that for yourselves? She hasn't so much as a pimple on her!'

'I understand, Kostis, but don't forget she has relatives with leprosy.'

'True, but she hasn't seen them in years.'

'Come on, Kostis; stop acting like a child. How can you be so certain she hasn't got the disease? You know how contagious it is. What if she has it and it's just not visible yet? Would you rather not know?'

'Yes, actually! I'll take that risk! My wife's clean, and I'm not blind!'

'Kostis, if she doesn't come with us willingly, she will by force.'

'What are you talking about?' he exclaims in shock, but the man has already turned to one of the others and says:

'Go get Pipina. If she refuses, you know what to do.'

'What did you just say, you miserable wretch?' Kostis yells furiously, but the crew ignore him and walk into the house.

'Pipina, get ready! We're leaving!' one of them calls out.

'What about my husband? Is he here?'

'Yes, he's downstairs.'

'Pipina, you're not going anywhere!' Kostis snaps, looking straight into her eyes as she comes down the stairs.

'Pipina, don't listen to him,' one of the crew interjects. 'If you're healthy - as you claim - you'll get tested just to be safe and be back home in no time at all.'

'Pipina, did you hear what I just said?' Kostis demands in a louder voice.

'If my husband says I can't go...' she mumbles and lowers her gaze.

All the commotion and yelling has now attracted the neighbours' attention, and people are literally everywhere: on roofs, in yards and on the street. Everyone is wondering why these normally peaceful people have risen up against the crew like this.

Although the Medical Officer is usually present when his crew is gathering "lepers" for Spinalonga, today is an exception. Even so, he has planned everything right down to the last detail to ensure that everything goes according to plan. They needed to gather a hundred so-called lepers in a very short period of time, so any resistance had to be dealt with quickly and decisively.

His men were well-instructed and knew exactly what to do when people resisted. They had a backup plan for such cases, and they put it into effect as soon as they saw how things were going with Pipina and Kostis.

'Pipina, I suppose you don't want to go for the examination because you're sick and hiding it from your fellow-villagers!' one of the men calls out in a loud voice meant to be overheard. 'And I bet your husband knows about it and is covering for you. That must be why he insists on not letting you come with us!'

The neighbours' jaws drop once they hear this news. They keep looking back and forth between Pipina and the crew, not knowing what to make of this accusation.

'How dare you!' Kostis explodes. 'Pipina is sick, and I'm covering for her? Are you blind? Can't you see she's perfectly healthy?' he yells, his eyes wide with anger.

'So what is it then? If she's not sick why won't you let her get tested? What are you afraid of?' the man asks in a calm tone.

'Ok! We'll go, and she'll get tested! But you... you should run and hide for insulting my wife and family!'

Calling someone a leper was a serious accusation, especially in a small community, so now, to clear their name, they had to take this test that they had been avoiding for so long - or else the stigma, and suspicion, would follow them for the rest of their lives.

'Get ready, Pipina, we're leaving!' Kostis tells her. 'Let's go get this damn test so they can see you're healthy and how they've wrongly accused you,' he continues, making an effort to control himself, even as his eyes fill with tears of anger and frustration over this sudden turn of events.

At that moment, Maria returns from school and sees the crowd gathered around their house and women on nearby rooftops staring in the same direction. Too far away to tell what the commotion is about, she starts pushing through the crowd, when she overhears two women talking in shocked voices:

'Poor children; losing their mother to the black island.'

Her heart begins to race as she strains to imagine who they are talking about, and suddenly she breaks into a run, frightened by the thought that has just struck her.

In the middle of the crowd she sees her parents, their faces white as sheets, the crew tightly ringed around them pushing them forward, and there's Giorgis sitting on the last step crying. No one had to explain what was happening; it's obvious the two women were talking about her own mother. Maria bursts into tears, and when Kostis sees her he starts crying as well. He takes her in his arms and strokes her hair, suddenly realising that if Pipina is actually sick she will never come home to them again. In his anguish, he unconsciously sings her favourite lullaby:

'Go, sweet child, ask your mother to put your dinner out; go, sweet child, ask your mother to comb your hair...'

The neighbours watch with tears in their eyes as the family members weep and embrace each other for a few moments more. Kostis and Pipina then climb into the car.

On the way to the Medical Centre

Pipina looked around her at the sullen faces of the other passengers; they all shared the same fate and were in the car simply because they had a relative, neighbour or close friend who was a leper. There was nothing to say, so everyone was silent, lost in thought. She noticed that none of the others had lesions on their faces or other exposed skin, but clearly that wasn't enough to convince the Medical Officer's men that they were healthy. The road to Agios Nikolaos was bumpy and full of potholes, which actually came as a welcome distraction because it momentarily took their minds off their dark thoughts and forced them to grab hold of something.

Pipina had a bad feeling; something wasn't right, but she didn't know what it was...

She feared she would never see her children again, and that something was warning her of what was to come. As she silently wept, she went over the events of that morning: the crew's claim that the examination was a "standard check-up", their humiliation in front of the other villagers, the accusation that she was a leper and that her husband was covering for her... It was all too much. The incident had left her an emotional wreck, but she was determined to uncover the truth. Besides, she could never face her neighbours again without the test results proving she wasn't sick. Healthy people didn't mingle with lepers; they felt sorry for them, but that was it. Pipina was a proud woman who had never given cause for gossip. She demanded respect, not pity. So the examination had now become her only hope to regain what, in a single morning, she had lost.

Pipina's innate sense of logic returned and dried her eyes. 'You have nothing to fear', she thought to herself. 'Everything will turn out well, and this examination will prove that you were wrongly accused...'

If only she knew what was coming...

* There were several other cases like Pipina's. According to various testimonies, the Medical Officer sometimes pretended to examine the people he had preselected for the island, and after finding a small mark or redness anywhere on their body, he would

instruct his crew to lead them to the boats waiting to ferry them to the islet. Furthermore, Rasidakis and his men didn't care how young or old their victims were because, according to law, minors sent to Spinalonga received the same allowance and enjoyed the same benefits as their adult counterparts.

Separation

The car slowly makes its way down the narrow streets of Agios Nikolaos. The locals have grown accustomed to the sight of service vehicles carrying lepers to the Medical Centre and boats ferrying them across to Spinalonga. Although the Medical Centre is up on a hill, the car is heading downhill towards the sea. Aware of the centre's location, the passengers exchange puzzled looks, unable to grasp the plot that was conceived behind their backs and is now unfolding before their eyes.

With the port now in sight, a man jumps to his feet and shouts at the driver:

'Hey! Where are you taking us? Why have you brought us to the port?'

None of the Medical Officer's men bother to reply. The car stops right next to the boat that ferries lepers to Spinalonga, and the crew jump out of the car, while

Pipina and the other passengers stay frozen in their seats with a look of terror and disbelief on their faces.

'Well, come on then! Get out!' one of the crew commands. 'Field trip's over!'

At that moment, the Medical Officer arrives.

'What's going on here?' he barks at his men. 'Why aren't they in the boat yet? Hurry up and get them out of the car! We're running late!'

'Ok, people, you heard the man! Out of the car now!' one of the crew shouts.

The people finally see what is happening but do their best to remain calm, still hoping they might be taken to the medical centre for examinations, even though they can see the boat just metres away. How can their rights be so flagrantly disregarded? As soon as the crew removes the last passenger from the car, the driver starts the engine and speeds out of sight.

'Hey! Where's he going?' someone cries.

'What do you care? His work's over,' one of the crew replies casually.

'What... what do you mean?' the man persists, but the Medical Officer interrupts them by turning to his men:

'Come on! What are you waiting for? Get it over with; get them in the boat already!'

'Boat? What are you talking about?' another man asks, but receives no reply.

Within a few minutes, reinforcements arrive, and the port is now full of guards and police officers who have come to help the crew carry out their task.

'Let's go! Let's go! Stop messing around and get them in the damn boat!' the Medical Officer yells again.

'But we're not lepers!' a man cries.

'Oh, yes you are!' the Medical Officer flatly replies.

The people see their world come crashing down around them.

Pipina finally snaps; she strides over to the Medical Officer, looks him straight in the eye and demands an explanation:

'Doctor, what are you trying to pull here? You know very well we're not lepers! You brought us here for a "check-up", but from what I can see, not only are we not getting tested, but you're sending us like lambs to the slaughter! What's going on? We're not sick! At least test us before you send us there so we can be certain we've really got the disease!'

'Oh, there's no need for that. Whether you get tested or not, you'll still end up in the same place,' he chuckles ironically.

Pipina and the others feel the walls closing in on them and burst into tears. Confinement on Spinalonga equals death, and everyone on the dock knows that no one has ever left the island alive. The officers and crew outnumber the people who, despite their resistance, are quickly bundled onto the boat. All their kicking and screaming has no effect on the healthy passersby who are enjoying a stroll by the sea. The medical people say they are lepers, and who would go near a leper? The passengers-turned-prisoners implore the onlookers to do something, insisting they are healthy and are unfairly being sent to Spinalonga without tests or proof; but their cries fall on deaf ears. Since the Medical Officer says they are lepers, then they are lepers. Besides, people are now accustomed to turning a blind eye to the Medical Officer's doings, since he has the power to destroy anyone who tries to thwart him.

Resistance soon gives way to despair, and their lamentations are enough to break even the hardest of hearts. Some even tear out clumps of their own hair. They have been condemned to a slow and tortuous death, and even if they don't have the disease now, they will surely contract it on Spinalonga. But what probably pains them even more is that they will never see their families again.

The Medical Officer accompanies them to the island, while Kostis, desperate to stay with Pipina, takes advantage of the commotion at the port to sneak on board as well.

The islet slowly begins to grow larger and more distinct, and the helpless passengers begin moving to the stern in search of something to hold on to. From the island the lepers take notice of the boat that is slowly approaching and begin descending to the pier, where the newcomers will disembark. They know the old hull too well; it isn't carrying food or supplies, nor is it bringing joy to the islanders. The cries of all the people it has carried still echo across the Gulf of Elounda and haunt the patients at night, reminding them of their own journey across the strait and the first time they set eyes on the islet.

The boat docks before the dozens of patients who are waiting at the pier, while the hideous appearance of some of the lepers sends tremors of revulsion through the newcomers.

'What are you waiting for? Get out!' the Medical Officer shouts. 'Or should I say *please?* Get out on your own, or you'll be dragged out like a sack of potatoes!'

The Medical Officer turns towards his men.

'Well, don't look at me! Get them out now!'

His words fill the passengers with fresh panic, and they begin frantically rushing every which way on the boat, trying to avoid the men. They know that if they are caught they'll be dragged ashore, and so they try to delay the inevitable as long as possible. Pipina buries her face against Kostis' chest...

'Oh, my dear Kostis... Don't leave me all alone! I can't stay here! I'm so afraid! Please don't let them take me!' she begs, crying inconsolably.

Two men grab her and try to pull her away from Kostis.

'Hurry up, lady. We haven't got all day!'

'No! Leave me alone! Please don't do this to me! I have two young children waiting for me at home. What will become of them? Have you no heart?' she screams and struggles against their grip. 'Let me go! Have you no soul? Can't you hear me?' she continues in vain.

Kostis tries to hold on to Pipina but sees that he is badly outnumbered and that this tug-of-war is only hurting her. He too begins to shout in anger, fear and grief - feeling his whole world being torn from his grasp. The family he has fought to create and defend is being destroyed: their two little angels will be motherless and hungry; their fields will be left to grow wild, and their animals will starve. Their home will cease to exist without Pipina. She is the heart and backbone of the family, especially with Kostis away on duty.

'Let her go! Leave her alone! She isn't sick! Don't do this to us! What will become of my children without their mother? Please, take pity on us! Have a heart!'

The Medical Officer and two others approach them.

'What are you doing here?' he asks Kostis angrily.

'Doctor, please...' he implores. 'Don't take her from me. She's all I have! What will become of our children?'

The Medical Officer looks him in the eye and says:

'She's sick. Why do you want her? She'll pass it on to your children.'

'She's not, Doctor, and you know it! Where are the test results? You should be ashamed!'

'Watch your words, young man... Aren't you a soldier?'

'Yes, I am.'

'Well, I suggest you pull yourself together, or I'll make sure you never see your children again! Let her go nice and easy, or just wait and see what I can do...'

'What... What are you talking about?' Kostis cries in distress.

'Don't say another word!' the Medical Officer snaps and turns to his men.

'Ok then. Drag her out if she won't come along willingly!'

Kostis' eyes fill with tears. He clenches his fists and grits his teeth in anger, while dark thoughts race through his mind. The sight of Pipina suffering makes him go mad, and if he could, he would kill them all one by one; slowly and painfully.

'No, my love,' he thinks to himself. 'This can't be happening to us... Oh, God, what should I do? Help me! Can't you hear me? What have we done to deserve this? What will become of our children? Oh, dear God, help me do the right thing... Please give me strength...'

Kostis is ready to explode, but his hands are tied. He knows that the Medical Officer and his friend Platakis have the power to make sure he never sees his family again.

He can't stand Pipina's pain anymore and steps back in shock as they pull her from his embrace. He feels empty and lost, and all he can do now is watch, unable to react. The men take Pipina ashore, and a few seconds later the boatman unties the mooring rope, and the craft begins to pull away from the pier. Pipina's final cry brings Kostis back to his senses.

'Kostis! Stay safe for our children!'

Kostis runs towards the stern and sees Pipina crying on her knees at the edge of the pier, her forehead pressed against the rough concrete.

'Pipina!' he shouts.

Pipina lifts her face, wet with tears, and looks imploringly at him.

'Pipina, I'll come for you! I'll get you out of here as soon as I can! As God is my witness, I promise! Be brave, my love!'

The boat gains speed, and they are soon separated from the island by a widening expanse of sea. Kostis sits in a corner apart from the others, his emotions running riot and his reason stymied: if he let his anger get the better of him he'd gut them every one and throw their bodies into the sea. But sense prevails and helps him find his way back to reality.

'You're a soldier,' he thinks. 'If you act out or challenge them they'll either kill you or send you into exile, and then what would become of Pipina and the children?'

With no more tears to cry and no more strength to scream, Pipina simply lets escape a long and rattling sigh.

'It's all over now,' she thinks to herself. She sits on the ground facing the sea, her knees pulled up to her chest, her face hidden behind her hands and her eyes tightly shut against this new reality.

She can sense a crowd gathering around her but continues to keep her eyes closed, overcome by fear. A woman approaches her.

'Welcome, dear,' she says warmly.

Pipina doesn't reply. She wants nothing to do with them. They're sick and might pass it on to her. Even the air she breaths chokes her with imagined disease. She fears looking at their ghastly faces and prefers to stay silent with her eyes shut tight. She hears heavy footsteps approaching and then a familiar male voice. She can tell that he is standing right over her but still doesn't dare open her eyes.

'Pipina? You too? But... why?' the man asks sadly.

Pipina knows this voice well, even though it's been years since she last heard it. She opens her eyes...

'Yiannis? Is that you? Oh, my dear brother... look at you!'

Pipina has just set eyes on her brother, who has been confined on Spinalonga for many years. Although his deformities are not life-threatening, they are certainly visible. She starts crying again at the sight of him and puts her hand over her mouth in an effort to restrain herself. Her brother knew her as a dynamic girl, undeterred by life's difficulties, and she doesn't want him to see her falling apart now.

'Come on, Pipina. Get up and I'll show you to your house.'

Yiannis would assume the task of helping Pipina adjust to life on Spinalonga. He was her brother, her blood and perhaps the only person she could trust. Pipina glances at the lepers who had gathered around her and notices that they were maintaining a respectful, compassionate distance. They understand her emotional state and realise she fears them and needs time. Pipina stands up and shyly brushes the dirt from her dress and knees.

'Where are we going?'

'To your house.'

'Yiannis, my house is in Sitia!'

'I know, honey. Think of it as your temporary house,' he replies to console her.

Pipina turns to fetch her belongings.

'Here, let me get that for you,' he says as he walks to her suitcase.

'No, Yiannis, I've got it,' she quickly replies. 'It's just one shabby old suitcase anyway.'

Although Pipina's suitcase is indeed light and easy to carry, the truth is that she doesn't want her brother touching it out of fear that she'll contract the disease. He may be her flesh and blood, but she has her children to think about, so she must be careful. They begin slowly walking up the cobbled road to the settlement. Residents greet her as she passes, but Pipina tries to ignore them and even holds her breath and lowers her gaze so she doesn't see their disfigured faces.

'Here we are. This is your home,' Yiannis says. 'It's got the basic necessities, but if you need anything else, my house is right across the street. You can knock on my door day or night.'

'Thank you for everything,' she says.

'And don't be afraid, little Sis; they decontaminated everything before you came. Besides, I'm here for you; whatever you need, just let me know, ok?'

'God bless you, Yiannis.'

'Ok then, I'll be off so you can settle in, but we'll talk later. Bye for now.'

'Goodbye, Yiannis. Thank you again.'

Yiannis steps out into the street and closes the door behind him, leaving Pipina alone in the empty, unfamiliar house that will be her prison for many days to come.

The first days on the island

The first days on Spinalonga were an absolute nightmare.

Pipina could hear people crying at night; sometimes they would weep quietly, and at other times they would surrender to loud and unrestrained sobbing. She kept her curtains drawn and the door locked and would let no one in apart from her brother, who would visit her now and then. She was going through a period of introversion, pain and fear - which every single person on the island had experienced. They were all tortured by the same questions, which no one could really answer: Why? Why did they have to get sick and be sent to this black rock instead of being with their families? Why were they being treated like criminals? Why must they die on Spinalonga?

Pipina had been neglecting herself, not eating well and spending the better part of her days crying, so no wonder she was feeling tired and weak.

There is a knock at the door.

'Who's there?' Pipina shouts.

'It's me, Yiannis. Open up!'

Pipina unlocks the door and lets Yiannis in.

'How are you?' he asks.

'Can't you see?'

'Have you been crying again? Didn't I say that we'll get through this together?'

'Get through *what*, Yiannis? It's all over,' Pipina replies sadly.

'Nothing is over unless you give up, Pipina. Have you had anything to eat?'

'Nothing goes down; nothing stays down.'

'The way you're going, you won't die from leprosy but from starvation. Wake up already! Life isn't over just because we're locked up here. Someday, we'll get back to the real world.'

'How? In a coffin?'

'Don't say that. We'll get out of here on our own two feet.'

'Yeah, right... Tell me, Yiannis, have you ever heard of anyone leaving the island alive?'

'Well... not so far. But they say they're close to a cure, so it won't be long now.'

'Yeah, right!' she says again with bitterness. 'The only way anyone leaves this place is in a coffin. Let me tell you another thing...'

'What's that?'

'You know what came to me when I was getting out of the boat?'

'No, what?'

'The people they threw to the lions in Rome. You know what they used to say to Caesar?'

Yiannis looks at her puzzled, hunches his shoulders and sticks out his lower lip to indicate he doesn't have a clue, so Pipina carries on.

'They said "Hail Caesar! We who are about to die salute you!" That's exactly how I felt; like I was being thrown to the lions. Why did they do this to me, Yiannis?'

'Do what, Pipina?'

'Why did they bring me here when I'm perfectly healthy?'

'That can't be, Pipina... The tests must have shown something.'

'But I was never tested!'

'What? That's impossible! Didn't you go to the Medical Centre?'

'I didn't go anywhere, and I was never tested!'

'Then how did this happen? Why did they bring you here if they weren't sure?'

'They came to my house and said they were taking me to Agios Nikolaos for a check up. You know... because father, you, our brothers and sister are all sick, I might be too.'

'Didn't you tell them you haven't seen any of us since the day they brought us here?'

'Of course I did, Yiannis, but they weren't listening! All they talked about was taking me for the test!'

'You mean they forced you to go?'

'Well, at first they tried to persuade me to go voluntarily, but when Kostis came back from the field he didn't want me to go. There was a big commotion, and all the villagers gathered around to see what was going on, and that's when the crew began to humiliate us.'

'What do you mean?'

'They spoke very loud so everyone could hear – and claimed that Kostis wasn't letting me go because I was sick, and he was covering for me. But nothing could be further from the truth. Kostis was telling them that I didn't have even a pimple on me, and he kept asking how they could claim I was a leper with no signs at all, no missing nose or fingers. He also didn't want me to go because he only had a few days left before returning to the fight, and if the tests came out positive, he wanted us to have time to look into the matter a little further.'

'I can't believe my ears!'

'Well, it's the truth. If they hadn't humiliated us like that, I wouldn't be here now. What were we to do with all our neighbours watching? Tell me, if they did that to you, wouldn't you have gone to get tested just to prove them wrong?'

'Of course. After all, it's better to lose an eye than to gain a bad reputation.'

'And that's the story... After that, Kostis changed his mind and started insisting we go for the test.'

'From the sounds of it, Pipina, he didn't have much of a choice. You know how frightened people are of leprosy, so would you prefer to be the talk of the village and have everyone turn their backs on you? Remember what happened with me? By the time they came to take me to Spinalonga, not a single person would talk to me and no one would go near me except mother and you all! I don't think you could go on living like that, so it's good you decided to go. But why didn't you get tested?'

'Well, that's the point! Once we reached Agios Nikolaos, instead of taking us to the centre, they took us down to the port, put us in the boat and brought us here! I don't know why, but I want to find out. And on top of everything else, they kept shouting that we were sick so the people in Plaka wouldn't get too close or interfere.'

'Jesus, Pipina! I don't know what to say!'

'It's true, every bit of it! See now why I'm crying and have lost my appetite?'

'What can I say, Pipina... Even so, you can't let yourself fall apart. I promise we'll figure something out, but until then you've got to stay strong. If you love me and don't want to upset me, eat something. Go outside and get some sun! You've grown so pale locked up in here all this time!'

'Right... go outside and get the disease...'

'What are you talking about? Not even the Medical Officer has contracted it, and he's touched and examined all of us. So why should you?'

'He hasn't? But how can that be? Leprosy's contagious!'

'Not always, dear; not always...'

'Even so, I don't want to. I'm afraid of them.'

'Who?'

'The lepers, of course!'

'Why? Because they're sick? What can they do about it? Do you think any of us wanted to get the disease? Besides, not all of them are that bad.'

'And what will I do if someone comes near me? Or if, God forbid, someone tries to touch me?'

'Don't worry; no one will go near you or touch you. They know you're afraid of them, and they'll give you your space.'

'How do they know?'

'Pipina, every single one of us went through what you're going through now, so believe me, they know how you feel. But they're good people, and they won't hurt you.'

'Yiannis, please, I'm not ready for that. For the time being, I think it would be best if I stayed here alone.'

'Ok, as you wish; no pressure. But don't forget you were the one who always told me to never give up! Anyway, I've got to go now, but I'll see you later,' Yiannis says as he gets up from the chair and walks to the door.

'Yiannis?'

'Yes?'

'Will you bring me some milk when you come again?'

'Only some? Honey, I'll bring you the whole goat! Thank God you've finally asked for something! Ok, I'm off now, but remember what we said... I want you to stay strong.'

'I'll try. Goodbye,' she says, seeing her brother out and locking the door behind him. She pulls the chair over to the window and looks at the closed curtain, embroidered from brightly coloured thread, wondering if what he said about the lepers is true.

She observes the curtain for a few moments and smiles at its vivid colours, then closes her eyes and runs her fingers over it, admiring its quality and marvelling at the love that so obviously went into its making.

'Why do they need nice things when they know they're dying?' she thinks, as the image of a grave springs to mind, beautiful on the outside, with disease and decay inside. She opens her eyes with a shudder.

'No! You have to deal with this and be strong if you want to go home. Yiannis said things aren't so bad. How has the Medical Officer not contracted it? If you're careful, why should you? You have to fight this, Pipina. You can't just sit back and wait to die.'

She looks at the curtain again and now notices a small rectangular lace pattern in the centre. It's a true masterpiece, clearly the work of a skilled embroiderer. Its dainty stitches form beautiful flowers that intertwine with one another, leaving a gap in the middle that allows beams of sunlight to penetrate her small "prison". She admires it a while longer, then begins to wonder about what is on the other side. Pipina moves her face close to the curtain and peers through the gap, her heart racing from fear and anguish. Her window looks out onto the main street, and it's not long before she sees two women passing by arm-in-arm in lovely dresses and striking hats, with no visible marks on their faces. As they walk by, Pipina draws her face even closer to get a better look, when suddenly one of them turns and looks directly at the window, revealing a face full of scars and open wounds! Shocked by the leper's unearthly appearance, and thinking that the woman has seen her too, Pipina quickly steps back from the window and presses her back against the wall, her heart racing. She stands still, fighting to remain calm, and holds her breath to hear their footsteps walking away. At that moment, she realises she can hear a strange melody. 'What's this now... Music?' she wonders.

She waits a few seconds more. 'They've probably left,' she thinks, still listening. This time she clearly hears children laughing and shouting, so, regaining something of her previous confidence and curiosity, she returns to the window and peeks outside again.

The women had left, but, to her surprise, she sees two little boys kicking a ball around. Shocked to discover children on the island, she quickly opens the curtain and stares at them with her mouth open. One of the boys is about the same age as her son Giorgis, while the other looks a year or two older. Their faces are spotless, and they don't seem to be sick. 'Why did they bring them here with all the lepers? What can they possibly have against these poor children?' She decides to talk to them and opens the window, but just as she smiles and is about to say hello, the children notice her and immediately take to their heels.

'Hey! Hold on! Where are you going?' Pipina calls after them.

She then hears the two little boys shouting at the top of their lungs:

'Hey, everybody, the new one opened her window! She's not afraid of us anymore!'

Shocked by their words, Pipina quickly closes the window and draws the curtains. She curls up on the bed and ponders the boys' words. 'Who did they mean by "us"? Have they got leprosy? And if so, where are their marks? How long have they been here to have integrated so well into leper society? Where are their parents to protect them?' With no one to answer her questions, Pipina falls into a troubled sleep.

* Apart from the children who were sent to Spinalonga with Hansen's disease, there were also several others who were born there to leprous parents. In fact, there are still people alive today - children of former patients - whose identity cards state "born to a leper father". The overwhelming majority of the children born on the island showed no signs of the disease, even when both parents were lepers. They say some were given up for adoption, others ended up in institutions, while only a few returned to their living relatives. According to the residents of Spinalonga, some of them remained on the islet until 1957, when the leper colony finally closed.

* The residents of Spinalonga had an abundance of material possessions. The monthly allowance they

received meant they were in high demand among merchants, and trading made them feel they were contributing members of society. Due to their habits of consumption – or over-consumption in many cases – they were frequently overcharged. And although they often lacked the simple commodities and foods they had often enjoyed in their former lives, such as the grapes they used to pluck from the arbours in their yards, they still enjoyed more security and material comfort than their healthy counterparts on the mainland, who faced such a struggle for their daily bread.

On the other hand, it isn't clear how business licenses were issued for the island. Some say that the authorities received commissions and kick-backs, but no one has dared publish specific cases or names.

The next morning, there was another knock at the door.

'Who is it?' Pipina asks anxiously.

'It's me, Yiannis. Open up.'

'Just a minute,' she says, wipes her hands on her apron and opens the door for him.

'Good morning! Look what I brought: fresh goat's milk! Drink up, it'll do you good!'

'Thank you, Yiannis dear. Have you had anything to drink?'

'No, I was in a hurry, but it's all right. I'll have some coffee later at the *kafenion.*'

'*Kafenion*?'

'Don't underestimate us, Sis. Aren't we entitled to a *kafenion*?'

'Sorry, I didn't know. Anyway, are you sure you don't want half of it?' Pipina says offering him the pot of milk.

'No, thanks. As I said, I'm going for a cup of coffee.'

'As you wish...'

'Let me know if you need anything else. In a few days, you'll get your allowance. There are grocery stores where you'll find all sorts of things, and then there's the daily outdoor market down by the pier, where merchants from across the way sell their merchandise. If you want something we don't have on Spinalonga, you can order it from them, and they'll bring it next time they come.'

'I don't want anything, Yiannis. I'm fine.'

'Ok. Tell me now... what happened yesterday? Is what I heard true?'

'What did you hear?'

'Someone said you opened your window. What brought about this miracle?'

'Well, I saw two children playing in the street, and I thought maybe they'd been brought here like me. I opened the window to ask them how they ended up here, but they ran off shouting.'

Yiannis bursts into laughter.

'And what were they shouting, Pipina?'

'Well, something that troubled me...'

'Meaning?'

'That the "new one", me, I guess, wasn't afraid of them anymore. What did they mean, Yiannis? How did these children end up on the island? Who brought them here?'

'No one *brought* them here. They were born here!'

'But... how? They looked healthy to me.'

'That's because they *are* healthy, Pipina! They were simply born to leprous parents who met and got married here. They're healthy leper-children, get it?'

'How's that possible? I haven't heard of sick parents having healthy children!'

'Well, I'm telling you it's true. You can ask anyone if you don't believe me, but they'll all say the same thing. Unfortunately, my dear Pipina, that's the way things are. It's not like that elsewhere, and even here in the past they were reluctant to permit marriages out of fear of spreading the disease, but somewhere along the way they started to allow it. Actually, many lepers want to come here so they can marry their beloved. In the other places they can't even have a relationship, let alone marry. You'll see other strange things if you ever decide to step outside! They're just people, Pipina; they want to live and have families. Actually, there are many children on the island.'

'Poor things!'

'So, how are your children, Pipina?'

'I'm not sure... I haven't heard any news at all,' she replies sadly.

'Who's looking after them now?'

'Mama is.'

'Mama Somarou... What would we ever do without her? She's been through the passions of Christ! Last time she came to see us, she was carrying all sorts of things. Imagine being her age and coming all the way from Sitia on foot with almost as much as a donkey can carry, just to see us. I admire her courage, but I've told her not to bother; that we're fine here. Besides, we brothers keep each other company, and if one of us needs something, the others compete to see who can fetch it first.'

'How's father doing, Yiannis?'

'Well... he's struggling. His health has taken a turn for the worse, so he doesn't leave the house much. He might go to the *kafenion* on Sundays to listen to a little lyre-playing, which you know he likes, but that's about it.'

'And our other brothers and sister? Are they doing well?'

'They're all fine. Well, so to speak! If they were really fine they wouldn't be here now, would they?'

'And how about your wife? I thought I saw her down at the port the day they brought me here.'

'She's ok too, poor thing.'

'Take good care of her, Yiannis; women like her are hard to come by nowadays. Name another woman who would willingly follow her husband to Spinalonga just to be with him? I sure can't think of any!'

'I know, Pipina. She loves me. The things she's been through... Do you know she washes all the patients' clothes and bed covers? I wonder at times if she isn't afraid of catching the disease. You should see the effort she puts into scrubbing the scabs off the covers!'

'Scabs? Why, is their skin falling off?'

'Well, that's how it is with people in the late stages of the disease. It makes the skin rot and fall off, but they don't feel any pain because the disease also destroys the nerves and limbs. That's why you see some missing a nose or an ear.'

'Oh, Yiannis, please stop! I'm going to throw up!' Pipina pleads, nauseated. 'Change the subject, I can't...'

Neither of them talk for a couple of seconds, and then Yiannis continues:

'So, how's Kostis?'

Pipina lets out a sigh and says:

'He's away on duty. They sent for him shortly after the Civil War broke out.'

'How long till he's discharged?'

'I'm not sure with everything that's been going on! I don't know who I should be more worried about: Kostis, the children or myself? I think I'm losing my mind! Anyway, he wrote to say he'll get a leave and come visit after he's seen the children. Poor things... they've been practically orphaned. What's mother to do? She can't possibly take care of everything.'

'It's a good thing we've got her.'

'Yes, Yiannis, she's a godsend. But it's not just the children; we've got fields and livestock. What will become of them? She found herself in the middle of it all; they're my children, but she's stuck with them. Oh, Yiannis, what I wouldn't give to see them again! I miss them and can't stand the thought of them suffering.'

'That's why I'm telling you, Pipina, you shouldn't give up! If you're healthy, as you claim, you have to get back on your feet so you can go home one day!'

'Oh, come on, Yiannis! How can I leave the island? Are you kidding me?'

'No, I'm not. You first need to be part of the community here.'

'Why do you say that?'

'You have to earn the authorities' trust. If you do, you'll get along fine and also gain some privileges. You look good, so that won't be an issue.'

'I don't follow. Where are you going with this?'

'If they're convinced you won't run away, they might give you a couple days' leave to go see your children. But your appearance is very important, I mean if you were disfigured you'd have no chance.'

'They give leaves?'

'Yes.'

'Ok, let's say I earn their trust and get a leave. How do I get to the village?'

'Slow down! First you have to be part of the community, earn their trust and get the leave. Getting to the village won't be a problem.'

Pipina looks at him thoughtfully.

'On another subject, they're putting on a play tonight. Will you come along?'

'Where? What kind of play?'

'A theatrical play. Come on, take the first step! We'll be together so there's nothing to worry about.'

Pipina looks at him in confusion. On the one hand, she badly wants to earn a leave, but on the other she is still afraid to go outside. She quickly weighs the pros and cons and makes up her mind. 'Is it better to sit here and mope? I'll go, and what's to be will be,' she thinks to herself and announces her decision.

'Ok, Yiannis, no more crying. I'm a strong woman, and I'll manage.'

'Way to go, Pipina! You've made the right decision. I'll pick you up at eight, and be sure to wear your best dress. Tonight, I'll escort you like the good old days! Remember when I used to take you to feasts and *kafenions*?'

'I do. But what dress are you talking about? I thought I was going to see a doctor so I only packed a nightdress, some towels and a pair of slippers!'

'That's ok, Pipina. I've got you covered. I'll be right back,' he says and runs out of the house without even saying goodbye. He quickly heads to the store and buys her the best dress he can find, then runs back to her house with the package under his arm.

'Look, little Sis! Look what I got for you!' he says, proudly unwrapping the dress. 'I think it'll fit. Ok, I'm off now, but I'll see you at eight!'

'Hold on! Hold on!' Pipina shouts after him. 'How can you possibly afford this? It looks expensive. Did you pay for it?'

'Down to the last penny! Our allowance is pretty decent; you'll see for yourself once you get it. All right, see you later! Be ready when I come!'

'Goodbye, Yiannis, and thank you!'

Yiannis leaves, and Pipina closes the door behind him, but this time she leaves it unlocked. She has started to accept that she must stand on her feet, face her fears and earn the authorities' trust so she can see her children again.

It is noon, and Spinalonga is resting. No music; no footsteps; no voices... 'They're probably sleeping,' she thinks. She nervously paces the room, wondering what she'll face at the theatre and whether she is really ready to deal with it. 'Don't be discouraged,' she thinks to herself. 'You can manage; you're strong. Besides, Yiannis said no one will come close or touch you.' With these thoughts in mind, Pipina gains some courage and calms down.

It is soon time for Pipina to get ready. 'God, give me strength,' she thinks.

At ten to eight there is a knock at the door, and Yiannis says:

'Come on, Pipina, open up!'

'It's open, Yiannis. Come in,' Pipina calls from inside.

Yiannis walks in with a surprised look on his face.

'You didn't lock the door?'

'Oh, come on Yiannis, don't tease me! I'm preparing to step into their "lair", so why should I worry about the door?'

'I must admit you look gorgeous!' he says after a brief pause.

'That's the last thing on my mind, but thank you, anyway,' she replies. 'What time do we have to be there?'

'We need to get there early to find seats, so... right away, actually! Let's go!'

'All right, all right! Let me fetch the key.'

Pipina is about to face the "outside world" which she has been carefully avoiding since her arrival.

It's late in the evening, but there is still enough light for her to make out her surroundings. They step out of the house, and Pipina locks the door, while praying and crossing herself at the same time. 'God, give me the strength and courage to face this. Protect me from evil. Guide me to do what is right and...'

'Oh, come on, Pipina!' Yiannis interrupts. 'Stop crossing yourself. We're not going to war but to a play, and we'll be late if we don't hurry.'

'Ok, I'm ready. Let's go.'

They start down the narrow street side by side. Pipina looks around her in astonishment, her eyes feasting on sights far removed from the horrid picture she had imagined: The houses were freshly whitewashed, with their yards full of flowers and aromatic plants. The smell of basil and peppermint fills the air, tickling her nose and lifting her spirits. Eucalyptuses and almond trees line the road, while grapevines are carefully trellised in yards. Children play in the streets, reminding her of carefree afternoons in the village. Yiannis breaks the silence and her reverie.

'Pipina, you'll meet many people tonight, and you'll see they're not the monsters you expect, but just people like you and me. However, I want you to promise me something...'

'What's that?' Pipina asks, looking into his eyes.

'If you happen to see someone with truly bad wounds, no matter how shocked you are, please don't let it show.'

'Why not?'

'Because they'll understand and become upset, and when they are upset their symptoms get worse.'

'So what should I do?'

'Just look away discreetly, as if everything is fine, or look at me.'

'I'll try, but I can't promise anything...'

'Ok, do your best, but think of me too. Whenever a newcomer looks at me all shocked, I hate it! On the one hand, I hate *them* for looking at me like that, and on the other I curse the day I got the disease. Then I curse God, myself, society and the people who brought me here. And then I end up crying at night with my face in the pillow. It's the only way I can calm down. So please don't put them through the same ordeal. If you can be strong for them, then do it; if not, try to pretend you can't see their problem. They're already in a difficult position, so try not to make it worse. If you need anything, let me know. I'll be beside you, and no one will touch you. All right?'

'All right,' Pipina replies solemnly, just as they come to the first *kafenion.*

'Yiannis! Yiannis!' someone shouts from inside. 'Come over here and let me buy you a coffee!'

'Thank you, Manolis, some other time.'

'Where are you off to?'

'To see the play. Aren't you coming?'

'I'll be there in a bit.'

'All right then, see you there,' Yiannis says and turns to Pipina.

'Did you see that man?'

'What man?' Pipina asks absent-mindedly.

'The man who just waved at us from the *kafenion.*'

'I didn't take a good look at him, why?'

'That was Manolis Kasapakis, our president. A very educated man and an important person here. I'll introduce you when he arrives.'

'And why is he such a grand figure?'

'Because he's educated. If it wasn't for him, we'd be lost.'

'Why?'

'He can talk to the authorities in their own language. He's a great unionist and the person who really pulls the strings on the island.'

'So he finished high school?'

'Think bigger. When he got sick he was a third-year law student! A great mind, I'm telling you. Everyone here respects his opinion.'

'He didn't look too good...'

'Well, that's true... but that doesn't mean his brain doesn't work; you'll see for yourself.'

'Ok, are we almost there?'

'In a couple of minutes. Remember what we talked about, ok? I want you to stay calm.'

Pipina doesn't answer. She simply bows her head and keeps walking.

'All right, here we are!' Yiannis says excitedly. 'Don't forget to act like...'

'I heard you the first two times!' Pipina interrupts, annoyed by the repetition. She then pauses for a moment, takes a deep breath and says:

'Let's go. I can do this.'

Pipina shyly looks around her at the large crowd. 'God, help me!' she thinks.

'Let's find a seat. Follow me,' her brother says.

Pipina follows Yiannis without hesitation. A man approaches them, and Yiannis stops to say hello.

'Good afternoon, Yiannis. How are you?'

'Still alive, so it could be worse. We've come to see the play. The talk around the *kafenion* this morning was that it's very good. Is that true?'

'That's why I came too. I heard it's really funny. We'll see... And the young miss?' the man asks looking at Pipina.

'Oh, I haven't introduced you.' Yiannis says, slapping his forehead. 'This is my sister, Pipina.'

'Very nice to meet you, miss.'

'Likewise,' she replies hesitantly, glancing from him to the ground. Under other circumstances she would have corrected him, saying "it's Madam", but she was in no mood to start a conversation.

'Has she just come to the island, Yiannis?'

'It's been about a month... a month and a half.'

'I'm sorry to pry, but I haven't seen her before.'

'That's all right. You know what the first days are like...'

'Yes, yes,' he replies, nodding his head. 'Anyway, let me know if you need anything, ok?'

'Bless you, my friend, thank you.'

'Thank you,' Pipina says too, remembering her brother's request to act normal.

The man walks away, and Yiannis heads towards two seats in the first row with Pipina following close behind.

He knows that it will be best for her to watch the play without the distraction of other people. If they sat in the back, her curiosity would compel her to look at the other audience members instead of the performance.

'So what's the name of the play, Yiannis?'

'"Sordina from Mirabello". You could do with a good laugh, so just relax and enjoy it. Tonight, you'll get a taste of our culture and see that we're not the savages many people think we are.'

A message of hope

There were many forms of entertainment on the island. Both cultural activities and social relations had developed enough to make the dry and isolated rock resemble a normal, healthy community, with radio, a satiric newspaper, cinema, billiards and various other modern amenities - all of which provide hours of entertainment and relaxation for the patients. But the pleasures of feasts and theatre, in particular, are unique because they involve laughter and human interaction.

Tonight, Spinalonga's troupe of actors is putting on a theatrical production called the "Sordina from Mirabello". The Sordina is a particular type of satire that has flourished in Crete for ages and has remained virtually unchanged till this very day. It addresses local socio-economic and political issues and presents them with humour. This type of variety show has its finger on the pulse of society and communicates social and moral messages, while addressing people's concerns in a way that makes the audience think. The actors often use sarcastic humour and make fun of themselves and each other. This teasing involves bawdy jokes with sexual innuendo, which almost always make the audience squirm in discomfort and then burst out laughing. Traditionally, the play takes the name of the place where it is presented, so if it was in Sitia it would be called "Sordina from Sitia". Since Spinalonga is part of Mirabello, the play tonight is called "Sordina from Mirabello".

The residents of Spinalonga love satire and the immediacy of theatre, and since one doesn't need to be either able-bodied or educated to watch a play, turnout is strong.

The play begins, and Pipina focuses on the stage, trying hard not to look around her. She has seen enough for one day and tries to keep her eyes on the actors, whose outstanding performance provides a welcome distraction from her dark thoughts.

The sketch is about War and Peace. In an effort to show the prosperity and well-being enjoyed during times of Peace, the actors portray two characters: an ambitious, belligerent king and his gentle brother, who is content with feasts and good company. The scene pictures the King returning to his palace after battle. The King is portrayed as a sickly, feeble man dressed in rags, while his fat, gentle brother is dressed in fine, clean clothes, his face flushed with wine and laughter.

The monarch staggers onstage with a prolonged groan, and the following dialogue takes place between the brothers:

Gentle brother:
Oh, brother, you are back!
How did you find the way?
I thought that you had died
A year ago today!

King:
Excuse me, but I thought,
You surely would have missed me.

Gentle brother:
Forgive me, my dear brother,
The wine has made me tipsy.

But tell me now, my brother

Why do you sulk and moan?
And where are all your men?
Have you come here all alone?

King:
Alas, my brother dear!
We have lost the battle!

Gentle brother:
That must indeed taste bitter
Go have yourself an apple!

King:
You dare to joke and laugh
As I ache and fall apart?

Gentle brother:
That can only happen
To those who have a heart!

The King falls to his knees and mourns the loss of his men:

I've lost my army! I've lost my men!
This day is just the worst!

His brother puts his hand on his enormous belly and replies with genuine concern:

And I've had way too much to eat,
I think I'm gonna burst!

The audience roars with laughter at the tragicomic state of the two brothers, and now that the sketch is over the audience - Pipina included - stand up, clapping and cheering. The ice is broken, and for the first time in ages Pipina laughs like a little child.

'Bravo! Bravo!' she shouts excitedly, as Yiannis looks at her with a smile on his face.

The lights go out, and the actors leave the stage, while dark figures hastily prepare the set for the next sketch.

Several more sketches follow, all well received by the audience. During intermission, the viewers head to a table with soft drinks, cigarettes and other goods, the proceeds from whose sale will be used to buy materials for the next play. Intermission is over, and the audience return to their seats. Knowing exactly what the patients crave, the performers have left a small and moving story for the finale. In a sarcastically humorous but *clear* Cretan dialect they will attempt to communicate serious messages which no one would dare utter under normal circumstances.

A few minutes later, the lights come back on, and a young Cretan lyre-player appears on stage. However, there is one major difference between this lyre-player and the other actors: He is obviously a leper. He walks to the centre of the stage, sits on a big "rock" that has been placed there, closes his eyes and holds his lyre firmly in both hands. He looks as if he is about to explode from rage and frustration, but he doesn't shed a tear. Cretans don't cry; instead, they make a song out of Death itself. The young man contemplates his lyre with a look of deepest sorrow, and to gain some relief he takes up the bow and starts playing a sad tune, while passionately singing a string of *mandinadas*:

Oh, Fate, what have I done,
And where did I go wrong
To deserve such awful pain
And sorrow for so long?

My body's full of wounds;
I couldn't feel more weak.
There's nothing to await;
The future seems so bleak.

I had a girlfriend once;
When I got sick she ran,
And now she seeks to find
A hale and hearty man.

Damn you, fickle Fate!
You'll never let me be.
Have you nothing else to do

Than always torment me?

He continues playing the sad tune, while a slender woman dressed in black, her face hidden by a hood, makes her appearance. She floats across the stage, stands next to the young lyre-player and says:

Well, young man,
Your accusations do surprise.

The lyre-player turns to her with a puzzled look, and the woman continues her *mandinada*:

It's me, your Fate!
Why don't you recognise!

The lyre-player gives her a dirty look and says ironically:

Well now, look who's here!
Why did you even bother?
Don't tell me you expected
A party in your honour!

Fate:
Oh, don't be cheeky now,
But show me some respect
Or life of constant woe
Is all you can expect.

Lyre-player:
You don't scare me anymore
Oh, dark and dreary Fate,
Your words are simply poison,
There's nothing to debate.

On this infertile isle
My body you've detained,
But never should you think
My mind can be restrained.

Fate:
And what, oh what, poor wretch,
Do you intend to try?
You'll be a dead man walking,
Until the day you die.

Lyre-player:
I am no dead man walking,
My dark and heavy Fate!
My *body* only falters;
My soul you underrate.

Fate:

And since your body's sick
What is it you can do?
Avoid me at your risk;
Your wasted time you'll rue.

Lyre-player:
You've never brought me joy,
So I've nothing to expect.
One thing you cannot kill
Is hope that I have left.

Hope is all I have;
There's nothing else, it's true.
But that is all I'll need
The day I come for you.

I'll fight the best I can,
And I'll defeat you, Fate.
Don't think that you can have
My future on a plate.

My family's back home;
They love and hold me dear
And cannot wait for the day,
They'll get to hold me near.

And Fate continues with her threats:
You'll not see them again,
Of that you can be sure.
This prison is your home;
Your problem has no cure.

Lyre-player:
A prison with *kafenions*,
And many sandy shores,
A variety of music
And lots of different stores!

Not sure if I'm a captive
Or a tourist on vacation...

Fate:
And yet you still complain
About your situation.

The lyre-player strokes his chin, lost in thought:
Of course, there is a problem
I've yet to figure out.
The sea that now surrounds us,
Confines me, there's no doubt.

No one comes to visit,
No ship approaches near
And the water is forbidding,
When moon and stars appear.

I know I can't escape,
Oh, dark and heavy Fate,
But I can play my lyre
And forget all that I hate.

The lyre-player starts singing again, more passionately this time.

Oh damn, oh damn you, Fate!
You've picked the proper place
To torture poor men's flesh
And their poor souls erase.

Fate:
You have a mouth on you
And pretend to be so brave.
I'll teach you now a thing or two
And show you who's my slave.

And even if your paltry soul
Is free of here one day,
The dirt of Spinalonga will
Your body soon decay.

Lyre-player:
A free man I was born,
And that is how I'll die
Who are you to strut and bark

And constantly decry?

Fate:
You really are quite miserable.
Do you want to start a war?
Show me honour and respect,
Or I'll hurt you even more.

Lyre-player:
I won't sit back when you
Are acting so unfair.
I'll fight you every step!
Be sure of it, I swear!

The furious lyre-player stomps off stage, while Fate watches him with a sarcastic grin on her face.

The lights go out for a couple of minutes, and when they come back on the set has changed completely.

Houses are being built; people dressed in nice clothes promenade the stage, and pots of colourful flowers are everywhere. The young lyre-player supervises all this activity, just like Kasapakis. He reaches for his beloved lyre again, sits on a half-built wall and starts singing.

Come on now, everyone,
Let's do the best we can
To make our island liveable

And worthy of a man.

Whitewash all the houses.
Plant flowers in the loam.
They think we live like savages;
Let's show them our new home!

The lyre-player admonishes a sad-looking craftsman:

And you there, mister craftsman,
Stop sulking! Do not mope!
It's time to get to work again.
Come on now, you can cope.

He then turns to the others:

The rest of you, don't look at me!
Get back to work in haste.
Don't let your skills and knowledge
Completely go to waste.

Women, start your weaving,
And brighten up the scene.
Make the finest garments
The world has ever seen.

Mothers, take your children;
Plant flowers everywhere,
And I will play my lyre
To drive away despair.

Our bodies may be sick,
But we're very much alive.
Don't just sit or stand there
Together we must strive.

Come on and let us build
Our very own society,
With commodities and goods
Of wonderful variety.

For in trouble we will be
If we ever leave this place
Without a skill to use against
The challenges we'll face.

If all of us forget
Our former occupations
We will deserve our Fate
And all our lamentations.

So, my friends, wake up!
And do your very best.
You've better things to do
Than walk around depressed.

Fate has been unjust,
But now we must consider
That we've the upper hand,
And not sit back and wither.

Although the years pass quickly
Make an effort to be strong.
Your children may be growing
But you'll see them before long.

The lights go out, and when they come back on the lyre-player is standing in a corner, admiring the result: Ruins have given way to clean whitewashed houses with flowers in their yards. A man sits at a table writing an article for the newspaper; two women display their embroidery, while a seamstress dances across the stage with a dazzling dress in her arms, which twirls as she moves. Two men, looking carefree and relaxed, enjoy a cup of coffee at the makeshift *kafenion*. The lyre-player, grinning broadly, starts playing a fast, cheerful melody and challenges Fate with provocative *mandinadas*.

Well, come on, Fate
Is that the best you've got?
I have my sweet revenge
Whether you like it or not.

Fate walks on stage, so agitated she can hardly stand still. She looks at the lyre-player and says:

You've got them all worked up,
And clearly had your fun,
But you should be ashamed
Of everything you've done.

Lyre-player:
You think I'm scared of you?
Well, think again, *m'amselle*
I told you not to mess with me,
Now you can go to hell.

I'm Cretan proud and bold;
My opinion carries weight.
I fight beside my fellow man
'Gainst everything I hate.

And even if, in the end,
It costs my precious life
You cannot force me to back down,
I'm ready for the strife.

Fate:
Beware, my foolish friend;
You're in over your head.
You're just a silly mortal
And just as good as dead.

Let's make a little bet to see,
Which one of us is right.
Harsh truths shall be uncovered
And all will end tonight.

Lyre-player:
The bet is on, my lady;
I told you I'm not scared.
I think, though, for defeat
You'd better be prepared.

The lyre-player looks to the side and shouts: 'Miss Message! Miss Message! Please come in!'

A beautiful young woman comes onstage and walks over to the lyre-player. He smiles at her and says:

Please introduce yourself
To this lady over here,
So she can see that I have been

Both truthful and sincere.

Miss Message curtsies to Fate and recites her own *mandinada:*

Hello there, I'm Miss Message,
And what I'm here to say
Will leave all of you islanders
Completely blown away.

Fate looks at her with suspicion and says:

And what is that, young lady,
You're holding in your hand?
I've never seen its like before,
Though I've travelled all the land.

Miss Message:
I present to you the cure,
For leprosy, my friends.
It's done with claiming lives;
Tonight the sorrow ends.

Astonished, Fate stares at the medicine in Miss Message's hands.

Fate:
Who gave this cure to you?
And who are now my foes?
Who dare to challenge Fate like this
And my will so foolishly oppose?

Miss Message:
The human brain, of course,
Which works all night and day
To solve man's many problems
And drive their woes away.

Not all of man's ideas,
Always go as planned
But the medicine we have right here
Will save many 'cross the land.

It's one of many benefits
That science brought about.
I hold right here the cure
We cannot do without.

The lyre-player looks at Fate and smiles:

See now how right I was?

I think you ought to know,
You've lost the game forever;
It's time for you to go.

So go and find yourself,
A weakling to control,
And maybe you'll regain again
The confidence I stole.

The lyre-player laughs at the sight of Fate struggling for words. She pauses, turns and quickly walks offstage in shame.

A great feast now takes place, and everyone celebrates their great victory and Fate's defeat. The lyre-player starts playing a rapid *pentozali*, his lyre ablaze. The lights go out, and the audience members rise as one and give the performers a standing ovation. The play's message of hope has obviously boosted their spirits and may even have changed how some view their lives.

It has bolstered their courage and patience, but most of all it has introduced hope...

The performers walk back onstage to take the customary bow, and the long applause indicates the play's success. They bow again and again before the audience, who cheer and rave. The play is over; the lights come back on, and the audience get ready to leave.

'Did you like it?' Yiannis asks Pipina.

'I loved it, Yiannis! We have to come again!'

'We will, Pipina. Can I buy you a cup of coffee?'

'Where?'

'At the *kafenion*, where else?'

'No, thanks. I think I'll call it a day, but you're welcome to come over if you want.'

'I'll go to the *kafenion* for a coffee, but I'll pass by your place tomorrow morning and bring you a pot of fresh milk.'

'That would be great, Yiannis.'

'Do you want me to walk you home?'

'No, I think I can find the way myself. You go along, and I'll see you tomorrow.'

'Ok, but if you need anything I'll be at the *kafenion* for the next hour or so. Sofia's at home so you can knock on our door any time, ok? See you tomorrow.'

'Ok, Yiannis dear. Goodnight.'

Pipina had her "baptism by fire" and has survived – and now walks along the narrow alleys of Spinalonga alone, her head discreetly bowed, but her spirits lifted high after the evening's performance. 'Yes, I can deal with it,' she thinks, as she cautiously glances about her. She hears music again - the same melody she heard from her house the other day - and lifts her gaze to find its source. To her surprise, she sees that the divine melody is coming from a wall-mounted loudspeaker. She pauses for a moment and stares at it, then bows her head again and continues on her way.

'Good evening!' a woman calls out.

Pipina looks at her hesitantly and returns the greeting but doesn't slow down.

Arriving home, she quickly unlocks the door and steps inside. She tidies up the small living room, kicks off her shoes and then lies down on the bed. 'What a day!' she thinks, as her mind strains to process all the images and information she has gathered during her first outing on the island. 'The first step...' she thinks and falls asleep with a bitter-sweet taste on her lips.

As the days went on, Pipina grew increasingly comfortable. She now thought of Spinalonga as her temporary home and was soon used to the sight of lepers. Her fear was further mitigated when she learned more about the disease. While talking to patients and staff, she discovered there were many healthy people on the island who, in spite of coming into direct contact with the lepers, had not contracted the disease. For instance, in a tremendous display of love and selflessness, many healthy people followed their leper spouses to Spinalonga. There they lived as husband and wife, shared the same bed and engaged in marital intercourse, yet the dreadful disease did not pass to the healthy spouses.

Yiannis brought her some flowers, which she planted in her yard. She also began fixing up her little house. She bought embroidery needles and thread, and even began teaching some of the younger girls how to knit and embroider. On Sundays, she went to Agios Panteleimonas – Spinalonga's little church – and after the Service they all went to the *kafenion* for the customary treat. Her evenings she spent alone on the northern shore of the island, and here she cried for her family and the life she had left behind. Pipina was a proud woman, who didn't want to give cause for gossip, so she avoided expressing her feelings openly in the presence of others. After her nightly tears had dried, Pipina would walk slowly home....

The first leave

Days turned into weeks and weeks into months. Pipina was slowly wasting away on the island, and although she had become a part of her new community, she missed her family more and more.

She had left behind two young children, a husband who was away on duty and a mother who was rapidly aging under the strain of all her responsibilities. Kostis would visit the island whenever he could - to boost her spirits and bring news from the family and village. He loved her with all his heart, but military service kept him from visiting more often. Pipina's eyes would light up with joy every time she saw him, and he was due to visit again today.

At noon, the boat arrives carrying her beloved Kostis, and a guard escorts him to Pipina's house. He knocks on the door, and the guard discreetly walks away. Kostis knows his way around and can be trusted to follow the rules: visits last half an hour, and visitors must remain where the guard leaves them.

Pipina opens the door.

'My Kostis!'

'How are you, my love?'

'I'm fine, more or less... Have you been by the village?'

'I was there last night, but I didn't stay long. I've only got three days off, and I've got to leave again tomorrow.'

'How are the kids?'

'Poor things... They didn't seem too well yesterday.'

'What's wrong with them?' Pipina asks in alarm.

'No, don't worry, they're both in good health, but there was something I didn't like... They seemed upset... maybe thinner... I can't quite put my finger on it.'

'I see... And Mama?'

'The same; she cries a lot. I don't know how much more she can take. I mean it's not just the children;

it's also the fields and animals. And the villagers have turned against her...'

'What? Why?'

'They want nothing to do with her because all the rest of the family are on Spinalonga. There was an incident the other day down by the stream; Mama went to wash some clothes, but when she got there the other women gathered up their clothes in a hurry and went farther upstream so they wouldn't have to wash in "contaminated" water. They were mean to her and said some pretty harsh words. Mama said if it wasn't for your aunt they wouldn't have let her wash there at all. Anyway, she asked me not to tell you because she didn't want you to get upset, so please don't mention anything when you see her.'

Pipina starts crying, shaking her head and murmuring to herself:

'Poor Mama... Who did you ever harm to deserve such misfortune?'

Kostis remains silent and simply strokes her hair.

'Kostis, I need to get a leave. I want to go to the village.'

'I know, dear, but will they give you one?'

'I don't see why not. I don't have any marks or sores, and I've never asked for anything before, so I think there's a good chance. Are you going back to the village again after here?'

'Yes. I've got to pick up some clothes I left with Mama to wash. Tomorrow, I'm going to Heraklion, so if you can get permission I'll take you with me today and bring you back tomorrow. Who do you have to ask?'

'The Medical Officer.'

'Is he here now?'

'I think so... Let me go see. You stay here in case the guard comes looking for you.'

'All right.'

A few minutes later, a smiling Pipina returns holding a document stating the terms of her first leave.

'I got it!' she announces excitedly.

'Great! Get ready to leave.'

Pipina heads to the kitchen to splash some water on her face but sees that the pitcher is empty.

'Oh, no! I'm out of water.'

'Where do you get your water?'

'The well.'

'Is it close by?'

'It's just a minute away; I'll be right back.'

'I'll come with you.'

'No, stay here in case the guard comes looking for you.'

'Never mind him; you shouldn't carry it.'

'Don't worry, I'm used to it. I just need a cloth...'

'What for?'

'For the rope... it's usually covered in blood.'

'Blood?'

'Yes. All of us get water from that well, and some of the lepers' hands have open wounds, so when they pull up the rope and bucket they often leave some blood and even skin behind. It's quite disgusting really.'

Troubled by the unsettling image, Kostis thinks for a couple of seconds and then says:

'Come on, Pipina, you know leprosy isn't contagious, let's go.'

Although the words come out of his mouth, deep down he doesn't believe them.

At the well, Pipina reaches for the rope, but Kostis intervenes.

'Let me do it, Pipina. You hold the pitcher.'

'But...'

'Just hold the pitcher.'

'At least take the cloth!'

'I don't need it.'

Kostis grabs the rope with his bare hands and starts pulling the bucket to the top, while the people in the nearby houses take notice and look at him with curiosity.

Kostis pulls the bucket out of the well then brings it straight to his mouth for a drink.

The onlookers' expressions change from curiosity to open wonder.

The sight of Kostis drinking from the "contaminated" bucket catches Pipina completely off guard, so it takes her a moment or two to react:

'Hey! What are you doing? Are you out of your mind? Don't drink from the bucket!'

'Why not? Don't you?' he asks calmly and turns to the others:

'Don't be afraid, my brothers! God watches over all of us!'

He then turns to Pipina again:

'Come on, hold the pitcher.'

An astonished Pipina does as she is told, and Kostis fills the pitcher.

Walking back from the well, they avoid discussing the incident, and when they arrive at Pipina's place she quickly packs her things, and they are soon on their way to Sitia.

It is late afternoon when the car comes to a stop at the village square. Pipina and Kostis sling their rucksacks over their shoulders and start walking home.

Two children playing in the square notice them approaching.

'Mama!' Maria and Giorgis shout in unison. They run to their mother and throw their arms around her.

Pipina, though, still worried that she might have contracted the disease, puts her hands behind her back and doesn't touch them, as tears run down her face. Although ecstatic to see them after all this time, she is appalled at their appearance: They are both terribly skinny and deeply grubby, dressed in filthy clothes which they have evidently been wearing for days, and only their sparkling eyes still seem bright and human. Pipina's heart sinks at the sight of them, but they banter excitedly for a couple of minutes and then start walking home.

On the way, Maria opens up to her mother.

'Mama, can I tell you something?'

'Of course, Maraki. What is it?'

'My friends won't play with me anymore.'

'Why not, sweetie?'

'Their mothers tell them not to. They say you're a dirty "lazar"' she blurts out and begins to cry.

'Don't listen to them, sweetie; and don't let them get to you. I'll be home before long, and we'll set these ladies straight for upsetting you. Just wait and see,' she tells Maria, and the little girl takes comfort in her mother's words.

'Where's grandma, honey?'

'Home.'

'Mama?' Pipina calls as she opens her mother's front door.

Although Somarou recognises the voice, she can't believe her ears and comes running.

'Oh, my sweet child, you're back!' she exclaims and hugs Pipina tightly in her arms as tears of joy stream down her face. 'Oh, how I longed for this day! Are you staying?'

'Only for tonight, Mama. I've missed you all so much, but tomorrow Kostis is taking me back to the island.'

'Oh, my dear child... What you've been through...' Somarou says in tears.

'Don't cry, Mama. I'm fine. How are you all doing?'

'It's been hard, dear... It's been hard...'

'Don't worry, everything will be all right.'

'I'm doing my best, but I can't keep up. You're on the island, Kostis is away, and the children are so young...'

'Doesn't Kostis help you when he's here?'

'Of course he does, poor man. He does everything he can, but he's changed from all the worrying.'

'What do you mean? He's not mistreating you, is he?'

'Oh no, no, no! On the contrary. He works all day long when he's here, but at night, instead of coming home to see the children, he goes to the *kafenion* and drinks too much. It's like he doesn't want to be here. You remember how he was when you were around; he'd come straight home from the fields. Not that he admits it, but he's clearly in pain, but please don't say I told you, ok?'

'You're talking about *my* Kostis, Mama?'

'I wish I wasn't.'

'It's so unlike him. And the children?'

'They're sad, Pipina. Everyone avoids them. They've no parents, and I can't always be there, what with the livestock and fields to tend to. What can they do? Thank God they've got each other,' she says nodding her head. 'Have you eaten?'

'Yes, Mama. We grabbed a bite on the way here. Tell me now, how can I help you? What do you need?'

'Nothing, my child. Tonight, just rest and be with the children.'

Pipina and her mother talk for a while and then go to bed.

The following morning, after getting Maria ready for school, Kostis and Pipina take the donkey to the fields, but they don't stay until sunset as they used to.

The car taking them back is leaving the village square in the afternoon. After returning to the house, they all have dinner together like in the good old days and enjoy each other's company, if only for a little while.

When the clock shows six, Kostis and Pipina prepare to leave. They say goodbye to Somarou and the children and then walk to the square, where the car is already waiting for them. They greet the driver, toss their bags in the trunk, get in quickly and drive away, while the village that holds everything they care about in the world soon disappears from sight.

Kostis accompanies Pipina to Spinalonga, where they say their goodbyes and plan the next meeting.

Kostis then leaves for Heraklion, and Pipina returns to her "prison".

Pipina's life on the island after the first leave

Pipina's visit to the village left its mark on her, while her children's appearance and her mother's tired face only made her stronger and more determined. She was no longer bothered by the lepers' unearthly appearance and had grown accustomed to the smell of their untreated wounds. She now faced her confinement on the island more calmly, and focussed on getting another leave to see her children again. To achieve this, she tried at all times to be on her best behaviour in order to gain the trust of the staff and show her solidarity with the other residents. She attended every event and participated in every activity: weddings, baptisms, feasts and even hunger strikes. She was a valuable member of the community, and the other islanders loved and respected her because she was compassionate and eager to help. Even though she dreaded contracting the disease, she didn't let it show and pretended, like a great actress, that everything was fine and normal. Yiannis' advice proved useful, and she followed it in all things. She became close friends with several patients and many of the merchants who supplied goods to the colony. It may have taken her several months, but she managed to stand on her feet again and get used to life on the island. Her dynamic character, neatness, reliability and liberal spirit charmed everyone who came in contact with her, and she tried to share her strength and natural optimism with the patients. Pipina persevered and even thrived because her survival instincts drove her to fight for herself and her family. More importantly, though, she managed to stay strong because she didn't have any marks on her; not even a pimple. Leprosy, a skin disease, causes horrific deformities, and if she had contracted it, surely there would be some evidence of it on her body. Pipina looked carefully every day, and the fact that she still found no sign of the disease gave her hope that somehow, someday, she would be vindicated.

The mirror

Pipina runs her fingertips lightly over her face, feeling her velvet-smooth skin for any signs of the disease.

It's been almost four months since she first set foot on the island, and her close contact with the lepers still worries her. A single thought occupies her mind day and night: 'Have I caught it?' She takes off her clothes one more time and carefully examines all of her body that she can see. She starts with her arms, stretching them out in front of her, turning her palms face up and then down. She does the same with her lower limbs, and soon confirms that her arms, legs and the front part of her torso bear no signs of the disease and that her skin is clear and smooth. Pipina can't see her face and back and must examine these as well in order to complete her self-diagnosis. 'A mirror... I need a mirror,' she mutters.

Pipina gets dressed and starts searching the room. 'There must be one somewhere...'

Her search takes longer than expected, but she doggedly continues. She finds it unimaginable to be in a house without a mirror when back home even the poorest household had at least a small mirror or fragment of a larger one. She looks everywhere: drawers, closet, the big chest... but comes up empty-handed. The house is now a complete mess, but Pipina carries on with her search. At that moment, there is a knock at the door.

'Who's there?' Pipina calls out.

'It's me, Yiannis. Can I come in?'

'Yes, it's open.'

Her brother walks in with a look of surprise on his face.

'What in heaven's name happened here? It looks like a bomb went off!'

'Oh come on, Yiannis, stop overreacting. Have a seat, and I'll be right with you.'

'What are you looking for?'

'A mirror... There's got to be one somewhere... How's Sofia?' she asks and continues searching.

'Sofia's fine... but you, dear, are wasting your time.'

Pipina stops and looks at him, puzzled.

'Why do you say that?'

'Because you're not going to find a mirror here. Come on, clean up this mess and make me a cup of coffee.'

'When you were furnishing this place for me, didn't you get a mirror?'

'To tell the truth, no...'

'Why not? Did you forget?'

'I don't think you understand where we are... This is Spinalonga, *not* the village. Come on, make us some coffee and I'll explain. You can put the things back first; I'm not in a hurry.'

'Never mind, I'll tidy up later.'

A few minutes later, Pipina serves Yiannis his coffee.

'Thanks. Aren't you having any?'

'I had one this morning; my stomach can't handle a second cup.'

'Well, if you want a mirror, I'll get you one,' he says, as he takes a sip of his coffee.

'Do you have a spare one home?'

'No, there are no mirrors in our house.'

'So where will you get it?'

'I'll order it from Alexandris, and he'll bring it from across. Actually, if I leave now we might have it by afternoon. Shall I go find him?'

'No, no! Drink your coffee. Tomorrow's fine.'

'What do you need it for, anyway?'

'Well... I want to see if there's any redness or blotches on my face and back. I can't feel anything with my fingers, but you can't exactly *feel* redness now, can you? Will you have a look, Yiannis?' she says, as she brings her face closer to his.

Yiannis scans her face for a couple of seconds and then says:

'You're spotless!'

'No redness? No marks?'

'I can't see anything.'

'Will you have a look at my back, too?' she asks and pulls down the collar of her dress to expose her shoulders and upper back.

Yiannis stands up, walks over to her and examines her back for any marks.

'Nothing here, either. This part of your back's clear.'

Pipina fixes her collar, and Yiannis sits back down.

'So the store doesn't sell mirrors?'

'No way.'

'You're telling me they don't have a single mirror for sale? Don't people buy mirrors?'

'Who's going to buy a mirror, Pipina?'

'Well, the patients, of course!'

'Just listen to yourself.'

'Why not, don't they care about grooming?'

'That's the last thing on their minds. Besides, they were the ones who decided to get rid of mirrors in the first place!'

'They were? Why?'

'Take a guess...'

'I don't know... Were they so upset at being brought here that they gave up caring about their appearance?'

'Bingo!' he says ironically.

'Ok, why then?'

'So they wouldn't have to see their wounds, Pipina!'

Pipina, lost for words, simply stares at her brother.

'You can search the entire island, but I bet you won't find more than one or two mirrors. Why do we need them? To see what we've become? *You* look perfectly fine, but just think how it is for patients who came here with only a little redness or a few sores and then started losing their limbs or body parts one by one: nose, ears, teeth, lips... Even if it's *you* you're looking at in the mirror, how can you possibly accept all these horrific changes? You think it's easy? Well, it's not! It's very hard, actually.'

'But, Yiannis, other people see you, so why don't you want to know how you look?'

'Even so, people here are too kind and discreet to comment on how you look. But watching ourselves gradually fall apart – in every way – is very depressing. We're already a mess, so we don't need constant reminders. Mirrors would just sap our strength and send us to an early grave.'

Pipina remains silent for nearly a full minute before replying.

'I see your point...'

'Anyway, I'll get you your mirror.'

'Yes, I'd like one if it's not too much bother.'

Yiannis stands up, but Pipina grabs his hand.

'Stay and finish your coffee.'

'I've had enough. I'll go catch Alexandris and order a mirror.'

Yiannis leaves Pipina's place in such a rush that he doesn't even say goodbye or close the door behind him.

Later in the afternoon, there is another knock at the door.

'Pipina, open up! I've got your order!'

After putting everything back in place and sweeping the floor, Pipina was taking a nap, but jumped out of bed at once.

'Hold on, Yiannis, I'm in my nightgown.'

'Don't bother getting dressed, I won't come in. Just come to the door.'

Pipina opens the door just wide enough for Yiannis to pass the mirror through.

'Thank you!' she says excitedly, taking it in her hands.

'It'll cost you a cup of coffee.'

'Do you want to come in?'

'No, I'd better head home; I've been out all day, and Sofia will be looking for me. I might come by tomorrow.'

'Ok, you're always welcome.'

'I know, dear. Bye for now.'

'Goodbye and thank you.'

Yiannis closes the door behind him, leaving Pipina alone with the mirror. The moment of truth has come; Pipina closes her eyes, takes a couple of deep breaths, holds the mirror to her face and looks long and carefully.

Although reassured by her unblemished face, Pipina's heart is still pounding because the examination is not yet finished. In the mirror, she sees a spotless, rosy face staring back at her, perfectly healthy in every respect. But she starts getting nervous again, thinking that a rash may appear on her back. She quickly removes her nightgown and looks for a place to put the mirror. She notices a nail in the wall, hangs the mirror on it and starts twisting her torso left and right to see her back and neck. Although she doesn't see anything alarming, she stands in front of the mirror for several minutes, scanning every inch of her skin to be absolutely certain. Once she has completed her examination, she gets dressed and hangs the mirror above the sink - where she used to hang it in the village. And as hope slowly awakens in her heart, a smile forms on Pipina's face.

Two sisters from Dories

A knock at the door.

'Who's there?' cries Pipina.

'Hey, neighbour, it's us!'

Pipina hurries to open the door and beholds the smiling faces of Argyro and Katina.

'Welcome! Come in! Come in!' she says, stepping aside to make way for them.

Pipina knew that the two sisters lived in a house nearby because several times she had seen them sitting in their yard. They had met in church a few weeks before but hadn't said much, and although she had several times invited them over, this was the first time they had taken her up on her invitation. She didn't know a lot about them; still they had never given her cause to doubt their sincerity and good will, and she could tell they were nice people because she discreetly observed all her neighbours and knew, more or less, what everyone was about. Pipina is now thrilled to have them over because she doesn't get many visitors, and although she knows most of the other islanders by sight, she hasn't really made any friends.

'Come in! Have a seat!' Pipina says excitedly. 'Would you like something to drink? A cup of coffee?'

'Yes, please, If it's not too much bother,' Argyro says.

'No bother whatsoever. How do you take it?'

'One sugar for me,' Katina replies.

'Two for me,' Argyro says.

'Ok. Give me two minutes, and I'll be right with you.'

Pipina takes a wooden tray from the cupboard and places it next to the *briki*[15]on the stone counter. While the coffee is heating, she opens a jar of her freshly made grape preserves and ladles some into two small, shallow dessert bowls. After serving the sisters their coffee and spoon sweets, she takes a chair and sits next to them.

'I hope I got it right. It's been a while since I last made coffee for a guest,' Pipina says anxiously.

'Don't worry, Pipina, it's just how I like it,' Katina says after taking a sip of her coffee.

'So is mine,' Argyro, the younger of the two, adds.

'So... What's new?' Pipina asks hesitantly.

---

[15]Small, long-handled brass coffee pot specifically used to make Greek coffee.

'What can possibly be new on this damn island? Same old stuff...' Katina replies wearily.

'How are you holding up? Have you got used to it here yet?' Argyro asks.

'Well, it's been hard... the isolation is quite challenging, but what can we do?'

'Where are you from, if you don't mind my asking?'

'Sitia.'

'Married?'

'Yes.'

'Children?' Katina asks.

'Two: Maria and Giorgis.'

'Perfect! One of each!'

'Yes, I'm blessed. How about you two? Are you married?'

'No... We never had the chance. We were still young when they locked us up here - curse the day!'

'How long have you been here?'

'Oh... It must be twenty years now,' Katina says, looking at her sister for confirmation.

'Sounds about right...' Argyro adds.

'And why did they bring you here?' Pipina asks curiously. 'Were you tested?'

'No, we were never tested! I know what you're going to say... that you weren't either,' Katina says.

'I wasn't! But how did you know?'

'Your sister-in-law told us your story. What a shame... I hope there's a special place in hell for them!'

'Look, Pipina,' Argyro says, as she lifts her skirt to reveal smooth, white skin. 'Katina, lift your skirt too, so Pipina can see your legs,' she then says to her sister, but instead of waiting for her to do so, she reaches over and lifts it for her.

'Hey! What are you doing?' Katina exclaims, startled by her sister's boldness.

'See? Neither of us have any marks,' Argyro continues, as she lets go of both their skirts and starts rolling up her sleeves. 'Nothing on our arms, body or face... Nowhere!' she adds.

Pipina starts rolling up her own sleeves to show them that her skin is in the same unblemished condition.

'No need to show us,' Argyro says, 'I know what I'll see...'

'Trust me, Pipina, if you were sick it would show,' Katina adds. 'So they didn't test you before bringing you here?'

'No!'

'Have you noticed any spots anywhere on your body?'

'Not even any redness; my skin is clear.'

'They probably brought her here for nothing, just like us,' Argyro says to Katina.

Wide-eyed, Pipina looks at Argyro and says:

'Hold on... Who sent you here?'

'Who else? The Medical Officer! But I think you're asking the wrong question... Why don't you ask Katina *why* he sent us here?'

Pipina looks over at Katina, who takes a deep breath and starts telling their story.

'Ok, let me start at the beginning... Argyro and I come from a big country family. We owned lots of fields and livestock, and we all loved and respected one another. Our father, however, didn't get along with one of his brothers, and they were always fighting over property and fields. One day, our uncle decided to take his revenge: He knew the Medical Officer well, so he arranged for the two of us to be brought here just to make our father suffer. So one fine morning, Rasidakis' crew came to the village and simply shoved us into a car. He claimed we were sick, even though we didn't have a mark on us.'

'Didn't they take you to get tested?' Pipina asks.

'Tested?' Argyro echoes. 'That's a good one! They just came and took us!'

Pipina is speechless.

'Why are you so surprised? Isn't that what happened to you?' Katina asks.

'Yes, yes... Remind me again who told you?'

'Oh, come on, everyone knows! It's not like we live in a big city! We all know a thing or two about our neighbours,' Argyro says.

'Did you have financial disputes with anyone?' Katina asks.

'No, my husband gets along well with everybody.'

'When I think it was our own uncle who sent us to this hell hole... Oh, if I could just get my hands on him...' Argyro says bitterly.

'This uncle of yours... why did he have such power over the Medical Officer? Were they very close?'

'You can't imagine what a slimeball he was... He would suck up to anyone who had even the slightest authority: send them oil, eggs, meat and do favours for them. If they accepted his gifts, they owed him, so when the time was right he'd call in the favours. The same with the Medical officer, but who knows exactly what dealings he had with him.'

'Judging by where we are now, I'd say he owed him a huge favour,' Katina says bitterly.

'I know relatives often fight over things like that, but still... why us? Or our poor mother?' Argyro says sadly.

'Change the subject, Argyro, the memories are too painful...' Katina intervenes.

'No, Katina. I'm going to tell the story, and I won't shut up until the whole world knows! Because of him, people think we're sick!'

She turns to Pipina again:

'Shortly before the crew came, we lost our eldest brother during the Occupation. And as if losing a child wasn't enough, our uncle delivered the final blow by having us sent here. Our father was devastated and lost his will to live. He gave up on everything: estates, assets, livestock... nothing mattered to him anymore. He became a drunkard, spent his days drinking at *kafenions* and never once came to see us. In the early days, our brothers would bring us news when they visited.'

'Don't they visit anymore?' Pipina asks.

'No... We haven't seen any of them in years,' Katina replies. 'We dragged them all down with us...'

'Your brothers? Why do you say that?'

'None of them ever married because no one wanted anything to do with our "leper family".'

'Anyway...' Argyro says in conclusion.

'I don't know what to say...' Pipina says, shaking her head. 'The point is we should have been tested.'

'In a perfect world, perhaps... But if everyone did the right thing, we wouldn't be here now, would we?' Katina says.

'Can't we ask them to take us to Agios Nikolaos for tests?' Pipina asks.

'Are you serious? Who's going to let you go there to get tested?' Argyro asks surprised.

'The Medical Officer...'

'You sure about that?'

'Why not? We've been here so long and we still don't have any marks, so why not go for the test to see if we've caught the disease?'

'You can't possibly be serious...' Katina says, laughing ironically.

'Of course I am. What's so funny?'

'You think the Medical Officer will let you get tested?'

'I don't see why not!'

'Come on, Pipina, do the math! He's the one who sent us here in the first place! He's the one who ordered the crew to drag us to the island without tests! Do you actually think he doesn't know we're healthy?'

'And don't forget - if he so much as senses your resistance, he'll make your life a living hell,' Argyro adds.

'I remember a while back there was a man who asked to go for tests because he suspected he was healthy - just like us. Not only did the Medical Officer not let him go, but he also never gave him another leave to visit his family. You should have seen him! Rasidakis was furious and kept shouting that the man had insulted him and that it wasn't his place to question his medical opinion!'

'So what happened? Didn't anyone back him up?' Pipina asks.

'Are you kidding? Who would dare? Let me explain it to you differently... Let's say you weren't locked up in here as a leper but were one of the staff – one of Rasidakis' favourites. If you had been there when the incident happened, and you didn't know the Medical Officer that well – because, as you know, he keeps to himself – who would you believe? The Doctor, who is a leprosy expert and knows the disease's symptoms better than anyone, or that poor man?'

'You're going about it all wrong,' Argyro interjects.

'What do you mean?'

'What would *any* of us have done under the circumstances? I know I, for one, would have kept my mouth shut.'

'So would I,' Katina concurs.

'Why? Aren't we allowed to have an opinion or speak our minds?' Pipina protests.

'Well, it's not written anywhere, but it's sure as hell implied... You think you can question the Medical Officer's decisions?' Katina says.

'Why not? Isn't he human? Doesn't he make mistakes?'

'I agree, Pipina, but why don't you ask the others who think he's some kind of God! I trust you've seen by now how powerful he is. He's a state within a state. He decides, orders and executes...'

'And who controls him?'

'No one,' Argyro says.

'Are there others on the island like us?'

'A few,' Katina replies.

Pipina scratches her head, puzzled.

'What are you thinking?' Argyro asks.

'Nothing in particular...'

'I know what you're thinking...' Katina intervenes.

'You do? Go on then; I'll tell you if you're right...'

'You're thinking we should organise a revolt, right?'

'How did you know?'

'We've all thought about it at some point.'

'Have you ever tried?'

'Well, there have been uprisings on the island, but not for that reason.'

'But why not? I mean, if we all rose up together he wouldn't be able to punish every one of us.'

'Waste of time; nothing will change.'

'How do you know if it's never been done before?'

'Think it through, Pipina! Who would give a damn? Rasidakis? He's the one who locked us up in here for no reason! The guards and staff? Last time I checked, they take orders from – and are paid by – the Medical Officer. And the other doctors and local authorities are his friends. Or do you think the people across will run to our rescue? They're disgusted by the mere sight of us and are only interested in our money. Wake up! Have you forgotten the day they put you on the boat?'

'I wish I could.'

'Well, did any of the onlookers help you?'

'No...'

'The same with us when the crew came to get us. Only our poor mother put up a fight and wouldn't let go of us. All the other villagers stood back in silence, watching the spectacle.'

Argyro, her head in her hands, mutters: 'It must have been our fate...'

'But that's not going to solve our problems, holding our heads and crying...' Pipina says.

'Argyro's right. We should be thanking the Lord for protecting us from the disease while we're here! I have faith that the rest will work itself out. Have you heard anything about a cure?'

'Even if they find a cure, we'll be long gone before it reaches us,' Argyro says.

'That's true, but I'm curious. Aren't there any other doctors who specialise in leprosy?' Pipina asks.

'Sure there are, just not in Lasithi,' Katina replies.

'So why don't we go to them?'

'How will we get there?'

'Well, where are they?'

'I'm not sure about the rest, but Markianos is in Athens.'

'Who's Markianos?'

'He's an expert in the field and has made quite a name for himself. Haven't you heard of him?' Argyro says.

'Can't say that I have...'

'They say he's the best leprosy doctor in the country, so his opinion carries great weight.'

'So he's the one who should examine us, but how?' Katina says.

'Getting a leave from Rasidakis to visit Markianos in Athens! That'll be the day! Nice one, Katina,' Argyro chuckles.

'Spare me the irony; I know he won't. It's just... Well, I'm just speculating...'

'Speculate all you like, it won't make any difference,' Argyro says, still laughing.

'Ok, go ahead and mock me; get it out of your system.'

'What if we sent him a letter telling him how we ended up here?' Pipina suggests.

'Trust me, it would never reach him,' Argyro says.

'Why not?'

'Do you take Rasidakis for a fool? Won't he know we're up to something the moment he sees Markianos' address on the envelope? And what if he opens it and reads that we're questioning his practice and badmouthing him to his superior? That'd be the end of us! Remember, all letters go through him.'

'You're right... I don't even want to think about it.'

'Anyway, I think we've said enough. We'll continue this discussion some other time,' Katina says, as she stands up and gives her younger sister a nudge on the shoulder.

'Come on, miss chatterbox, time to go. It's getting late, and we've got to make something for dinner. There's not much left from lunch.'

'Oh, come on; let's stay a little longer,' Argyro protests.

'Get up already! Pipina probably wants to rest. We've given her a headache!'

'No, really! Stay as long as you like. Besides, I get bored here all alone, and I enjoy the company. No one ever visits except my brother,' Pipina says solemnly. 'Shall I make us something to eat? It will be like the good old times back in the village: some days I'd go to my neighbour's house, and other days she'd come to mine; we'd chitchat, and the time would fly. So, please, stay! You're not keeping me from anything.'

'Well, how can we refuse when you put it like that? Don't bother making anything, though,' Katina says.

'Well, there's not much left from lunch; I don't make a lot because my brother eats at home. But Yiannis has brought me some fresh eggs, so we'll soak a couple of *dakos*, slice some tomatoes and have ourselves a royal feast! What do you say? Oh, and I almost forgot. There's also a piece of cheese my Mama brought last time she was here.'

'Come now, Pipina, don't go to all that trouble!'

'Well, I'm going to make it anyway, and you don't have to eat any if you don't want to.'

'Ok then, since we're all eating together, head over to our house, Argyro, and bring the pot with the kale and eggs,' Katina tells her sister.

'For Heaven's sake, there's no need, Argyro,' Pipina says.

'If you want us to feel at home, let me fetch the pot. Otherwise, we can all just eat our own food, end of story,' Argyro says.

'Fine, go along.'

Argyro leaves, and Pipina starts preparing their dinner.

'Now that we know each other better, we should spend more time together,' Katina says to Pipina.

'Of course. I'm glad I met you both because, from what I can tell, friendships don't always last very long on the island...'

'That's true, but what makes you say that?'

'Well, first of all, I've seen that not everyone here is that innocent. I get the feeling people try to take advantage of you any way they can.'

'Also true; well, not for everyone but for quite a few.'

'Then, there are those who are really deformed... No matter how hard you try not to be biased, you sort of avoid them instinctively - especially people like us, who aren't sure if they've got the disease. I know folks here think leprosy isn't contagious and always mention that couple - you know the woman who followed her sick husband to the island, and they've been living here together for thirty years, eating from the same plate, being together as a couple, and she still hasn't caught it... But what if that's only an exception? Would you take that risk, Katina?'

'No, I wouldn't...'

'And then, if a woman dares to befriend a man besides her husband or relatives, they immediately call her all sorts of names.'

'I agree, Pipina, but you can't live in isolation, either.'

'I don't. I talk to nearly everyone I meet, whether in church, at feasts or anywhere. It's just that I keep my distance, that's all. I've got enough on my plate and don't need new worries.'

'There are some people you're right to keep at a distance, especially people like our good neighbours across the street.'

'Why do you say that? What did they do to you?'

'To me? Nothing. Simply because I don't need them.'

'So who did they harm?'

'Remember Kyria Kalliopi, who used to live next door to them?'

'Of course! The sweetest person, but I haven't seen her in a while, actually. What happened to her?'

'Her health took a turn for the worse, and she's been bedridden for months. I went to visit her one day and... God Almighty!'

'Is she aware of her surroundings?'

'She understands everything, but can't see a thing or move a muscle.'

'Poor thing. Who's looking after her?'

'That's where our good neighbours come into the picture. Oh, how they love to play "good Christians" when people are looking!'

'What do you mean? Don't they take care of her?'

'Take care of her? They treat her like a dog! They give her a piece of stale bread to eat and just let her wail!'

'What about her allowance? She gets one, doesn't she?'

'Yes. The state sends her an allowance, but they collect it since they're her caretakers. They've found themselves the goose that lays the golden eggs, while Kyria Kalliopi lives off their scraps.'

'That's outrageous!'

'Oh, and what's more, all of her furniture and belongings have vanished into thin air!'

'Did they move them to their house?'

'Worse... When I was there, I commented on how the house looked quite empty, and they didn't even try to hide it: "We sold everything. What use is furniture to the old lady?" they said. That was the end of the discussion; I didn't even have to ask who got the money.'

'Shame on them!'

'That's how some people make money here. It's the law of the jungle: your death, my life.'

'But that's not how everyone thinks.'

'I'm sure it isn't, but you need to be careful if you want to survive.'

Their conversation is interrupted by a knock at the door.

'Open up, it's me!' Argyro shouts from outside.

'It's open, come in,' Pipina replies.

Argyro fiddles with the knob for couple of seconds.

'I can't open it... Katina,' she shouts.

Katina rushes to the door, and Argyro walks in holding a hot clay pot with two cloths. She runs to the kitchen in search of a place to set it.

'Pipina,' she says out of breath, 'quick, put a tea towel on the table, hurry!'

Pipina spreads a towel on the table, and Argyro leaves the pot on it.

'Phew! Thank God! I burned my fingers and thought I'd drop it!'

'I'll set the table so we can eat,' Pipina says.

'Argyro, have we got any wine at home?' Katina asks.

'Yes, shall I go get it?'

'Would you mind?'

'No need, Argyro. I've got wine - from Sitia, as a matter of fact.'

'Sit down then, Argyro, we don't drink much anyway; just a glass for a toast.'

Argyro sits in her chair while Pipina sets the table and then takes a seat beside them. Two more hours go by as the three women eat dinner, chat and discover they have many things in common. After finishing their meal, they all clear the table together; then Argyro and Katina thank Pipina and say goodnight, giving her a warm hug and arranging to meet again the following Sunday in church.

* Argyro and Katina's names have been changed, but their story is true. Many others have shared similar stories, dating all the way back to the leper colony's early years: stories of revenge, properties and possessions seized, and even healthy people

voluntarily admitting themselves to the leper colony in order to survive.

Sunday Service

Six-thirty on Sunday morning, and the ringing church bell of Agios Panteleimonas calls the faithful to worship.

Pipina, like most of the islanders, is dressed in her Sunday clothes. She has washed her face, combed her hair and is patiently waiting for the church bells. Her religion says her body and soul must be clean when she receives communion, so she hasn't had coffee yet. When the bell rings for the second time, she starts walking up the cobbled road to the small church.

Service has already started when she quietly enters the back of the church. She puts a coin in the box and takes three candles from the stand. She kneels before the icon of Saint Panteleimonas, then lights the candles one by one and, with a short prayer, places them next to the small forest of other flickering candles in the round container of sand by the icons. Crossing herself, she walks down the left aisle of the chapel and finds an empty seat among the other women. The rhythmic drone of the priest's words immediately soothes her soul and takes her back to simpler times. Remembering Sunday mornings in the village when she would rush to get Maria and Giorgis ready for church, a bitter-sweet smile forms on her face. A hollow cough brings her back to reality, and she discreetly tries to pinpoint its source. Although she no longer dreads catching the disease as much as she used to, she is still anxious about it. As she shyly lifts her gaze to scan the nave, she sees her brother in the men's section on the opposite side and then spots his wife sitting two rows in front of her. This separation of men and women in church has long been observed in Crete. Women sit on the left side, and men on the right. The people who ended up on Spinalonga - sick or healthy - brought with them their own customs and traditions. Their families and communities had all passed certain principles down to them, and this became who they were, guided by certain standards and expectations and following a set of spoken and unspoken rules.

Church, for people back then, was a holy place filled with love and acceptance. Priests were respectful of others, performed their duties selflessly, and opened their arms to embrace their flock without discrimination: drunks, fools, crooks and the sick all found a place beside their simple and righteous neighbours. Spinalonga's priest set an example of Christian patience; he gave those who were undisciplined and confused the time they needed to engage in sincere self-examination, understand themselves better, repent where needed and, finally, figure out what they really wanted. With the patients, he used comforting and encouraging words to strengthen their faith, urged them to pray, and presented prayers to help them heal their bodies and souls. The priest knew how to listen without judging, so the confession that followed Sunday Service was a liberating ritual. The presence of a man who truly cared about them and was willing to listen to their problems made all the difference. This wise and righteous man, who loved people simply and wholeheartedly, wasn't the only one to perform the sacraments at Agios Panteleimonas. Many other priests had held the position before him with the same dedication, love and self-sacrifice.

And self-sacrifice it was. None of the priests who served at the church of Spinalonga were sick. It was their choice to accept or decline the position offered by the Bishop, and although no one exerted pressure to accept the post, none of them had hesitated. They weren't afraid to shoulder such an ominous responsibility at a time when being around lepers was the last thing anyone might want. For the second time in the history of Spinalonga, the Church stood by those who were most in need.

Service is nearly over, and the members of the congregation who are going to receive communion start moving towards the altar – "the Beautiful Gate".

Pipina stays in her seat because, as much as she wants to, she won't be receiving communion.

In devout concentration, the priest blesses the communion chalice and then turns towards the communicants again, holding the chalice in his hands. 'With fear of God, faith and love, draw nigh...'

With these words he invites the faithful to receive the Body and Blood of Christ. The communicants form a line and one by one receive communion, all from the same silver spoon, cross themselves and move towards the exit where there is a basket filled with pieces of communion bread. After the last one receives communion, the priest holds the chalice to his lips and drinks the rest of the wine. Pipina has seen him drinking straight from the chalice several times, but no matter how many times she sees him doing so, the sight still leaves her in awe. Although the Church says that priests must consume the contents of the chalice at the end of the Service and that it is forbidden to waste a single drop, Pipina still marvels that they hold fast to this rule against all common sense, since the communicants in this case are lepers, suffering from a highly contagious and serious disease. She hasn't heard of any priests getting sick, but then again, she hasn't been on the island very long. Conflicting thoughts now pass through her mind: On the one hand, the priest's example gives her courage, but a voice in her head urges her not to let down her guard - and to be careful.

Service is over, and the faithful are now standing in the courtyard of the church in small clusters of two or three, quietly talking and laughing. Pipina is chatting with the two sisters when Yiannis steps up to them.

'Ladies, coffee's on me!'

'Where?' Pipina asks.

'At the *kafenion*. Come on, I won't take no for an answer.'

'If Argyro and Katina come along, I might think about it,' Pipina says with a smile.

'Well? Will you do me the honour?' Yiannis asks the sisters.

'What do you think? Shall we go?' Argyro asks Katina.

'Sure, why not.'

At the *kafenion*

The *kafenion* is crowded, and dozens of voices fill the air. Sunday is the busiest day of the week because everyone heads there directly after Service. It is also the only day of the week one can see women there, but whether they are young or old, beautiful or ugly, they are all accompanied by a husband or male relative. Traditionally, men escort their wives and children to the nearest *kafenion* after church and treat them to some Turkish delight, an orange juice, a cup of coffee or whatever else strikes their fancy.

Pipina, Yiannis and the two sisters sit at a corner table. The other customers stare at them because they aren't used to seeing the sisters with Pipina. The three women, however, do their best to ignore the stares. Besides, the general appearance of the clientele is appalling, to say the least. Most of them are sick – and quite visibly so. Their missing limbs and the stench coming from their wounds and the various salves and antiseptics applied to them keep the healthier residents at a discreet distance. And regarding the men - Yiannis had described the situation on the island and had warned her to be extremely cautious. Many men were either single or divorced, since confinement on Spinalonga had cost some of the older ones their families and prevented the younger ones from having a relationship. This made them dangerous when their romantic urges got out of hand. However, there were only so many women on the island who were both young and able-bodied. Lepers who entered into a relationship would often get married, and after the wedding the newlyweds would choose which of their two houses they would inhabit. Moreover, couples enjoyed two allowances between them, and that made for an easier life. They also often had children, which, sick or healthy, gave them a sense of normalcy and fulfilment and usually made them better people. Marriage helped them deal with their problems, while sexual relations also contributed to their psychological health. Married couples could experience the unique feeling of wholeness that lovemaking offers; it boosted their self-confidence and self-esteem and made them stronger. Single patients, on the other hand, were often quarrelsome and hot-tempered and frequently disturbed the peace in the colony. Their desperate need to live, love and be loved often drove them to near-madness. They yearned for a normal life filled with affection and intimacy, but the scarcity of women on the island meant that single men always outnumbered their married counterparts.

At Pipina's

Pipina has woken up early to get some housework done. She washes her black dress and scarf and pegs them on the line to dry, then starts the fire for lunch and starts sweeping the floor. After the cleaning, she'll boil the beans Yiannis brought her with some chopped tomatoes and olive oil. Her house is small, like most houses on Spinalonga, but always neat and tidy.

There's a knock at the door, and a cheerful voice calls out:

'Pipina, open up! It's me, Sofia!'

Pipina lets the broom fall to the floor, runs to open the door and beholds a woman she hasn't seen in years.

'Sofia!' she cries, not believing her eyes, as she throws her arms around her and holds her tight.

The two women stand there, just holding each other for a minute before Pipina invites her in and offers her a seat.

'Thank you,' Sofia says, sitting down.

'What would you like to drink?'

'Nothing, thank you.'

'Something to eat then?'

'No, I'm fine. If I want anything I'll tell you. Come, sit for a minute, and let me look at you.'

'Is my brother coming?' Pipina asks, as she sits down next to her.

'No, he was going to the *kafenion*, and he'll probably stay a while. Did he bring you the beans yesterday?'

'Yes, thank you. As a matter of fact, I was just getting ready to cook them.'

'Yiannis and I were talking the other day, and he mentioned something that surprised me...'

'What was that?'

'That you refuse to accept your allowance.'

'That's right. I don't want it.'

'Why not? You're entitled to it.'

'I don't want their money.'

'And what will you live on? It goes without saying that we're here for you and will help you with anything you need, but still, why won't you accept it?'

'Because I'm not sick. I don't want their money; they should give it to someone who needs it.'

'Pipina, there are others who aren't sick but still collect their allowance. Do you think they're stupid? Besides, the allowance is sent in your name so even if you refuse to collect it, the money will only return to the state. It's not as if they'll give it to someone else who needs it more.'

'And I'm telling you again that I don't want that kind of money.'

'Is it better to just leave it with the state? Go get it and give it to a patient or send it to your children back home.'

'There's no way I'm sending them contaminated money. You go get it if you want.'

'When the postman comes again, I'll tell Yiannis to go and collect it for you.'

'Tell him not to bring it anywhere near me.'

'All right... We'll figure something out till then. So... what else is new?'

'Nothing really.'

'Have you seen Zisis yet?'

'No. I asked Yiannis to arrange for us to meet the other day, but Zisis wouldn't hear of it. Do you know why he won't see me?'

'I do... Well, it's kind of hard in his condition. Your brother cut himself off from us a while ago.'

'Why?'

'Because of the disease, of course.'

'Isn't he doing well?'

'The truth is he's in the final stages, and he lost his sight a little while ago.'

Pipina's eyes fill with tears, while Sofia carries on.

'It's been a year or so since he first started avoiding us. He never leaves the house and doesn't let anyone in apart from the woman who looks after him.'

'So if we went by...?'

'He wouldn't open the door for us. Leave him be; he's got the right to be left alone if he wants.'

'How about my father? Have you seen him?'

'He's not doing so well, either. He's bedridden and not really in touch with his surroundings.'

'But Yiannis said he goes out every now and then.'

'He used to, but not anymore; not since he got worse.'

'Can we at least visit him?'

'Sure. I'll tell Yiannis to get the keys from his caretaker.'

Pipina nods in assent, looking anxiously at Sofia.

'Sofia, what happened to my other brothers and sister? Manolis, Vangelis and Stamatoula? I keep asking Yiannis, but he won't tell me.'

'Oh, Pipina... They weren't doing so well...'

'What do you mean?' Pipina whispers, as her beautiful eyes fill with tears again.

'I'm afraid...'

'No! Don't tell me... they're gone?'

'Yes...'

Pipina can't take any more bad news and bursts into tears.

'Oh, Mama, where are you to mourn your children? Where are you to mourn your precious angels? You thought you'd see them again when they left the village... Vangelis and Manolis, my dear brothers; Stamatoula, my sweet sister... You never deserved this... Damn Spinalonga and the man who discovered it! Oh, my loves, how will I ever get over losing you? How will I tell my poor Mama that her children are gone, that she's never going to see you again? How can a mother endure such pain? Damn you, disease! Damn you for doing this to our family!'

Pipina sobs inconsolably for several minutes, while Sofia puts her arms around her and tries to comfort her. Yiannis and his wife are practically all the family she has left on Spinalonga, out of six originally. Sofia lets her sobbing run its course, dabbing Pipina's cheek with a handkerchief every now and then until finally she runs out of tears.

'Better now?'

'Yes...' she replies, blowing her nose into a tissue.

'So, now you know...'

'I'd rather have died and never heard the awful news.'

'At least their children are all grown and can take care of themselves. It would be different if they were your age and left young children behind.

'Where are their children now? They didn't go back to the village.'

'They were sent to boarding school and got a good education, but we lost track of them. We never heard from them again after their parents passed away.'

'Where are they buried?' Pipina asks solemnly.

'In the cemetery here.'

'Will you take me there?'

'What for?'

'I'd like to light a candle in their memory.'

'I can take you, but I don't know which graves are theirs.'

'Weren't you at their funerals?'

'No. Yiannis doesn't handle death all that well, especially relatives. All three times he was a real mess - going on about how it should have been him because he was the eldest. He was hallucinating and having conversations with them! It was just too much for him...'

'Won't we find their graves if we go to the cemetery?'

'No.'

'Why not?'

'All the graves are unmarked.'

'But why?'

'Well, they wouldn't know where to start... So many people have died here, and continue to die, but it's only a small cemetery. Besides, surviving friends and relatives pretty much know where their loved ones are buried, so names aren't really necessary. And just think how depressed people would be if they started counting all the people who have died on the island. Plus, it's forbidden for mainlanders to come here for a memorial service, and even if it wasn't, I think people mostly want to forget.'

Pipina looks at Sofia, near tears again.

'Come on, Pipina. Don't start again. It's over, and there's nothing we can do about it. Don't forget you still have Yiannis, and he mustn't see you upset; it's not good for him.'

Pipina wipes her eyes, and the two of them talk for a little longer about the good times they had back in the village. They laugh, cry, and exchange advice and opinions just like they used to. It is nearly noon, however, and Sofia has to return home to cook for Yiannis. She says goodbye to Pipina, and the two of them arrange to meet again in about ten days.

The allowance

The postman arrives at the pier carrying envelopes with the patients' monthly allowance. He starts calling out names, and, one by one, the patients step forward, sign a receipt and collect their envelopes. He calls Pipina's name, and Yiannis steps forward.

'Who are you?' the postman asks.

'I'm her brother.'

'Your name?'

'Yiannis Solidakis.'

The postman stares at him for a couple of seconds trying to figure out if he's telling the truth.

'Why didn't she come herself?'

'She's sick.'

'Ok, then; sign here,' he says, handing over the envelope.

Yiannis signs, takes the envelope and, after receiving his own, he starts walking up the road to the market. Sofia has given him a list with everything she figures Pipina will need. Half an hour later, he arrives at Pipina's laden with all kinds of goods.

'What's all this?' Pipina asks in surprise.

'Supplies to get you through the month.'

'I told you not to spend your money on me.'

'I didn't; you paid for it.'

'What are you talking about? I didn't give you any money!'

'With your allowance, Pipina.'

'What allowance? I didn't collect any allowance.'

'I know. I went and collected it for you and bought you these groceries because I know how stubborn you can be.'

Pipina looks hesitantly at the bags on the table.

'Don't look like that! It's food, and it's clean. Sofia said that this should do, but if you need anything else just say the word. All right?'

'Ok, Yiannis, but you didn't have to go to all this trouble.'

'I kind of did... I'm off now; Apostolis has been waiting for me since morning to help him build a wall. If you need anything, Sofia's home.'

Pipina thanks him and sees him out. Although she isn't pleased that the groceries were bought with her allowance, she keeps them to survive.

Irene

A beautiful woman walks into the *kafenion*, immediately causing a stir among the male customers, who start arguing over where she will sit.

'Irene!' one of them cries, jumping out of his chair. 'Come join us!'

'She sat with you last Sunday!' another shouts from a table in the back. 'It's our turn today! Come here, honey. Anything you want is on us today. Hey, waiter! The lady would like to order.'

Irene looks at the first fellow and shrugs her shoulders, indicating that she doesn't have a choice, and then sits down with the other man and his friends.

With Yiannis deep in conversation with a man at the next table, Pipina and the two sisters indulge in a little gossip.

'What a stunning woman!' Pipina comments.

'Who?' Argyro asks.

'The one who just walked in. Where's she from?'

'How should I know? But wherever she's from, her fellow-villagers must be *very* proud...'

'Why do you say that?'

'Because she's a whore!'

'Why do you call her that? What has she done to you?'

'She's actually a whore! What am I *supposed* to call her? She's slept with more men than you can count!'

'Is that true?' Pipina asks, astonished.

'Back me up here, Katina. Didn't she pretend to be your friend when she and her husband first came to the island?'

'That's right, Pipina. There's something really wrong with her...'

'And who does she have sex with? Not the patients, of course?'

'Who else is there?' Argyro replies.

'Is she sick?'

'No, she's as healthy as can be! Can't you tell?'

'I can; I'm just checking.'

'Oh, she's fine! It's us who should worry,' Katina adds.

'And what is she doing here if she's not sick?'

'She's helping to "take care of" people...'

Yiannis finishes his conversation and turns towards them again, abruptly ending the women's exchange of vital information. Pipina glances at Irene every now and then and can't get over how beautiful she is. 'She's like an angel. I wonder if what Katina and Argyro say is true,' she thinks to herself. After finishing their coffee, Yiannis pays the bill, and the four of them leave the *kafenion* together.

Upon arriving at Pipina's door, the two sisters thank Yiannis and Pipina for their company and continue up the street together. Yiannis says goodbye to Pipina and turns to walk away, but Pipina, curious to know more, grabs him by the arm and pulls him into the house.

'Stay for a couple of minutes, won't you?'

'What for?'

'I want you to tell me something.'

'Go on then. I haven't got all day.'

'Who was that gorgeous woman who came to the *kafenion* today?'

'Who are you talking about? Irene?'

'Yes, that's her! Tell me, why is she here? Is she sick?'

'No. Not that I know of, at least.'

'So what's she doing here?'

'She's trying to survive...'

'By prostituting herself?'

'Oh, I see. Your friends made sure to fill you in... What did they say?'

'That she's a whore, but I have my doubts, that's why I'm asking. It seems so strange.'

'Don't listen to people's cruel comments, Sis. She's just unhappy, that's all. What did those sharp-tongued spinsters have to say?'

'That she came here with her husband, but she's been sleeping around... That sort of thing.'

'Ok, I'll tell you a few things about Irene because I see that your friends have quite conveniently misinformed you, and I hate it when people distort the truth.'

'What reason do they have to lie?'

'They didn't exactly lie, but they only told you half the story.'

'That's just as bad. So I'm asking you again, what reason could they possibly have to lie to me?'

'Well, I can think of one...'

'I'm listening...'

'Why would *any* woman badmouth another woman?'

'Why?'

'Take a guess... Hmm, jealousy perhaps?'

'You mean they envy her?'

'Do you find that so strange? You saw her with your own eyes. Would you call her ugly?'

'On the contrary, I think she's beautiful.'

'See? That could be one reason right there!'

'Hold on, Yiannis. They said she has sex with lepers; even ones in the late stages!'

'She'll have sex with anyone who can pay. But the point isn't who she sleeps with, but why.'

'So Argyro and Katina were right to call her a whore.'

'Oh my God! Can you just put that aside for a minute and listen? It's not good to purposely turn a blind eye to the truth. First hear what I have to say, and then draw your own conclusions. Grab a chair.'

Pipina sits down, and Yiannis stands in front of her.

'Ok, little Sis, here's the story: Irene was very poor, downright destitute actually. She met a man, fell in love, got married and moved into a small house in their village. Her husband was also poor, no property or fortune, nothing really except the shirt on his back. He worked at whatever odd jobs he could find, but they still struggled to make ends meet. Shortly after their wedding, he got sick, and the doctors ordered his transfer to Spinalonga. But Irene loved him too much to let him go and was determined to follow him to the island. Besides, staying in the village wasn't really an option, since she didn't have any means of support and no relatives who could help her financially or provide food. The odds of her remarrying were slim, because no one wants a woman who was previously married to a leper. So she decided to follow him here. At first, the authorities refused to let her stay, but she put up a fight and wouldn't give up. Finally, when they saw that no matter what they did they couldn't keep her away, they gave in and let her stay.'

'So she's married...'

'Hold on, let me finish. When they came to the island, her husband began receiving his allowance, so they slowly furnished their house and settled in. Oh, you should have seen their place, Pipina! She made it really beautiful, always clean and tidy. But I'm getting sidetracked... Anyway, she was well liked among the islanders. Gradually, however, her husband's health worsened, and his lesions spread. During his final days, Irene took care of him like a baby. She could easily have cheated on him or simply left him when he was no longer conscious of his surroundings. But she was a lady; she honoured her vows and never left his side until the very end. When he died, she was left absolutely penniless. All she had was her house and the few things her husband had bought when he was alive, and, as a widow, Irene wasn't entitled to her husband's allowance. The law's clear on that point: Only *patients* receive an allowance. *No one else*. But Irene had lived here for so long and wouldn't have been accepted anywhere else. She was part of Spinalonga. The island was now her home, and all of us had become her friends and family. So she decided to stay on, hoping that people here would be merciful and generous - and not let her starve. I'm ashamed to say that people's compassion didn't last very long. When they got tired of providing for her, the "vultures" started circling. Most of them had had their eye on her since the day she first set foot on the island. They were jealous of her husband and secretly pleased when he began to get worse. They could hardly wait for him to die so that one of them could take his place. But they were careful; they didn't approach her straight away after his death. Instead, they waited – and when she ran out of food and money and could no longer count on the other islanders for help, one by one they made their move and approached her with money. You can imagine what they wanted in return... At first, she rejected them all. She held out for as long as she could, but when she was on the verge of starvation she started a relationship with one of the patients and went on to marry him. She never loved him, but she was grateful to him for saving her from certain death, so she stood by him during his sickness. He, on the other hand, after so many years on the island without a woman, had only one thing in mind... But his health went downhill fast, and so Irene gave up being a wife and lover and became a nurse again. She managed his allowance and made sure to always buy the best food she could find in the market to try to help him recover. That cost her a lot of money and didn't do any good. When he died, she returned to her first husband's house because the authorities said that one house was enough for her since she wasn't sick. Her second marriage was a further blow to her standing in the community. You know how it is in the village when a woman remarries after her first husband's death - she's considered a whore. That's what happened to Irene; it seems like her one great sin was getting married again. This bothered a lot of people, so they shunned her. But it wasn't her fault. Just imagine how it must be to live in a community which has rejected you. After a certain point, we couldn't help her either. Her reputation was damaged beyond repair, and people assumed that whoever so much as talked to her was only looking for sex. She then married another man just to survive, and history repeated itself for the third time. And when *he* died, no one would take her seriously. She now had two choices left: to either starve to death or start selling herself – and who wants to die?'

'Poor thing. Now I feel sorry for her.'

'I know. Now, of course, they all line up outside her house.'

'Who do you mean?'

'All those "righteous" men who badmouthed her when she was married. But of course... They only did that because they couldn't have her.'

'You've troubled me now...'

'Why? Which part don't you understand?'

'I understood everything; it's just that Katina and Argyro told the story differently.'

'Everyone's free to say what they want, but just think about those two. Don't you find it odd that they've been here so many years and still not found anyone?'

'Oh, stop it, Yiannis. You're talking nonsense.'

'Why? Isn't that what we're meant for? To meet someone and start a family? Wouldn't they be better with some intimacy in their lives?'

'Ok then, Yiannis, since you have all the answers, let's assume they do want to have families... Who here's a suitable match for them?'

'You know there are many unmarried men on the island.'

'Are they able-bodied and healthy?'

'Some are only in the first stages of the disease, so they don't have any visible marks on them.'

'But they're still sick!'

'What's your point?'

'Katina and Argyro aren't sick!'

'Oh, yeah? And how do you know?'

'Well... I can't be positive, but I think they're like me. So tell me, in all honesty, if you were healthy and brought here without tests proving otherwise, would you go marry a woman who had leprosy?'

'Perhaps not.'

'I'm sure you wouldn't; no one in their right mind would.'

'Anyway, it's getting late, and Sofia will be wondering where I am. We'll continue this discussion some other time.'

Yiannis says goodbye and leaves in a hurry, while Pipina pulls her chair over to the window, gets out her knitting needles and wool and starts knitting. Thinking of Irene in the hours that follow, she keeps dropping stitches and starting all over again.

Markogiannakis

The Medical Officer is furiously marching towards the pier with a dozen guards behind him trying to keep up. One of them catches up to him and whispers something in his ear.

'Markogiannakis is it?' the Medical Officer snarls, and the young guard nods in assent.

Rasidakis grits his teeth in anger and continues on his way, walking even faster than before.

'Sir, stay calm,' one of the men hesitantly offers.

The Medical Officer stops at once and pivots to face the young guard with a murderous look:

'Shut your mouth or you'll be sorry!' he hisses, and the guard immediately drops his head in silent embarrassment. Rasidakis is clearly not kidding, and his men know that the next one to say anything will regret it bitterly. But the loud voices heard from his office just minutes earlier have aroused the curiosity of the islanders, who now stand in front of their houses, silent and solemn. The braver ones, Yiannis included, follow the procession down to the pier, where they soon face a disheartening scene: A patient is lying on the ground with two guards kneeling on his legs and two more holding his arms. He is desperately trying to escape their grip, and his screams resound across the gulf. The islanders form a circle around them and watch the scene with puzzled looks. It doesn't take them long to figure out what has happened, but even then, no one dares step forward to help the poor man, who is fighting the guards tooth and nail. The crowd starts speculating about his punishment, but they fall silent when they see Rasidakis approaching.

'Well, Markogiannakis, what's going on here? Did you suddenly decide you needed a change of scenery?' he adds sarcastically, patting the young man on the shoulder.

Markogiannakis remains silent with his eyes fixed on the ground, while the people around them hold their breath, anxiously anticipating Rasidakis' next move.

'Bring him to my office. Now!' the Medical Officer barks at his guards. He turns his back to them and starts heading towards his office in the sanatorium and, as soon as he's out of earshot, the islanders start murmuring again. The guards grab his arms, lift the young man to his feet and start dragging him to the sanatorium. The crowd follows them to the hospital entrance, but the medical staff stop them from going inside. It isn't long before they hear Rasidakis shouting, and, overcome with curiosity, they decide they mustn't miss the "show". They sneak to the back of the sanatorium, which offers a direct view into the doctor's office, and when they get there, they discover that in the commotion the doctor has forgotten to close the window. Now they can both see and hear what is going on inside.

The onlookers soon notice that the scene playing out before them is a kind of interrogation: Markogiannakis is sitting in a chair in the middle of the high-ceiling room, his head bowed and his arms crossed, while Rasidakis is angrily pacing around him.

'Well, Markogiannakis? Why do you keep doing it? Do you want to get us into to trouble?' Rasidakis asks, but receives no answer. 'Cat got your tongue? I asked you a question!'

Markogiannakis looks at his tormentor but remains silent.

'Didn't we talk about this the last time you ran off? Didn't we agree that you've got to behave if you want to have a good time on the island? Why did you run off again? Don't we have fun here?'

Markogiannakis meets the sarcasm in Rasidakis' voice with sullen silence. It is obvious that he's making a determined effort not to respond to the man who has condemned him to live the rest of his life here, with only death to look forward to. His silence irritates the Medical Officer even further, and his pacing and gestures grow more agitated.

'Ok, Markogiannakis, I'll do the talking. You think you can do whatever you please and not be held accountable? Well you've got it all wrong, you miserable little man! This is my island, and I'm in charge here! You have to inform me before you do *anything*. Got it? You had the entire Gendarmerie out looking for you, for God's sake!'

A desperate Markogiannakis finally breaks his silence.

'Is it my fault? I asked for a leave, but you didn't give it to me!'

'Where on earth do you want to go in your condition, you poor fool? Do you want to scare everyone you meet?'

'You're the one who scares people with your behaviour, but *you* still walk around a free man.'

'Don't you dare disrespect me like that!'

'You've no idea how things are or what's fair.'

'No idea, eh? Well, Markogiannakis, as one of nature's mistakes, I guess you know best. But if you were truly human, your family would want you, but even they can't stand you! How long has it been since you last had a visitor?'

'That's not why they won't come to see me. They're afraid of catching the disease. You've convinced people we're monsters!'

'You seem to be forgetting something, Markogiannakis: you're sick. Instead of being grateful to us for providing food and medicine and putting a roof over your head, all you do is complain! Is that your way of saying "thank you?"'

'That won't work with me, Doctor.'

'What's *that* supposed to mean?'

'You know damn well what I mean... Anyway...'

'No, no, by all means, go ahead! We're all dying to hear what you have to say!'

'Forget it. I suspect you don't want the truth out there, Doctor. It's not in your interest...'

'Stop talking in riddles, Markogiannakis! Go on and finish what you were saying. Right here, man to man, what do you mean?'

'All right then, you asked for it. I'll tell you straight out what I mean because you seem to take us for idiots.'

'Just get to the point.'

'How long have I been here, Doctor?'

Rasidakis shrugs his shoulders, looks over to one of the guards and says:

'How long has he been here, son?'

'About twelve years, Sir.'

'You heard the man; twelve years. That means I've got twelve years' worth of dirt on you...' adds Markogiannakis.

'I'm running out of patience...'

'Ok, Doctor. First question: Is everyone on Spinalonga a leper?'

'Of course they are!'

'Are you sure, Doctor? I'm going to ask you again in case you didn't understand me the first time... Do *all* of us on the island have the disease?'

'Where are you going with this, Markogiannakis?' the Medical Officer asks with a look of icy menace. 'Are you implying that you are being wrongfully detained here?'

'No. I was sick. But were all the *other* people you brought here sick?'

'Of course they were!'

'And where are the tests to prove it?'

'How do you know who has or hasn't been tested? Are you my secretary? Everyone here's sick.'

'That's not what I've heard... A little bird told me that not everyone has been tested.'

'Seems like this little bird of yours has a pretty big mouth...'

'It's an open secret, Doctor. And that's not all it has to say...'

'Oh? Go on then. What else does it say?'

'That some of them ended up here because you were trying to get that friend of yours elected - the one from Sitia - and that you rounded up others so their relatives could get their hands on their money and land. I hear you've had others committed as favours to friends looking for revenge, and, apart from lepers, you've also brought people here with tuberculosis, hepatitis, syphilis and other contagious diseases that'll send the rest of us to an even earlier grave.'

'This little bird of yours seems to have a lot to say...'

The onlookers outside the window are following the scene with their mouths agape – not that these charges are exactly news to them, but no one has ever had the courage to stand up to the Medical Officer before and say these things to his face, which is turning increasingly red as these accusations multiply. Although Rasidakis hasn't noticed the crowd of people outside his window, he is certain that the guards and medical staff are listening outside the door, so he moves swiftly to limit the damage.

'Don't think I don't know what you're trying to do here, Markogiannakis... You're only making these accusations because we didn't simply step aside and let you escape. But let's say, for the sake of argument, that such rumours are circulating. Why haven't any of you ever asked to see your tests or demand to know why you're here? If you were actually healthy, I think you'd have the courage to come forward and speak up.'

'No one dares because they're afraid of you!'

'Me? Why would they be afraid of me?'

'Because you're the one who grants or refuses our leaves of absence. They're afraid to open their mouth or they'll never get to see their families again.'

'Markogiannakis, you know that the ones who don't get leaves are in really bad shape or so deformed they'd scare people. There's also the matter of public safety. We can't let people with open lesions mingle with healthy people. As far as the others who are denied leaves, well, they're usually people like you: misfits and troublemakers.'

'Why am I a misfit? Because I want my freedom? What would you do if you were exiled on a tiny island? You're wrong, Doctor. I'm sorry to say this, but...'

'But, what?'

'I may be sick, but I am well aware of my condition, and all I want is to be free. So if that makes me a troublemaker, how will you treat someone who comes to you claiming you've wrongfully detained them? If you refuse to give *me* a leave, then what will you do to them? Kill them? I don't have any children or family waiting for me back home, and because of you they've even erased my name from the record books in my village! As far as my fellow-villagers go, I never even existed! So do what you want with me; I'm not afraid of you. But you should know this: even if you never give me another leave again, I'm *still* going to leave.'

'Guards!' Rasidakis shouts, 'Get him out of my sight! And, you, Markogiannakis, mark my words: next time you try anything foolish again, I won't go so easy on you.'

Markogiannakis leaves the Director's office with a guard holding each arm, but before he's out the door he turns again to Rasidakis and says in a voice seething with rage:

'You, Doctor! Remember... I'm leaving this place...'

'Get lost, you bum!' Rasidakis shouts, as the guards drag the patient out of sight. The crowd now runs to the sanatorium entrance, curious to observe the outcome and hear the story first hand. They arrive at the front of the building just in time to see the guards throwing Markogiannakis out of the building like a sack of garbage. Markogiannakis loses his balance and tumbles to the ground, while the other patients rush to help him to his feet.

'Let go of me!' he shouts, pushing their hands away and brushing the dirt off his trousers. 'I'm fine.'

'What did Rasidakis say?' one of them asks.

'The usual rubbish; that he won't give me another leave.'

'So what're you going to do now?'

'I'm going to leave.'

'Aren't you worried?'

'No. Not anymore.'

'And what if they catch you?'

'They won't... Not this time,' he says in a calm and even voice. He then starts limping slowly in the direction of his house, leaving the crowd behind more intrigued and confused than before.

Freedom

'No!!!' a woman screams, sending shock waves through the island community and making everyone's blood run cold. People stop what they are doing and stand silently to try to pinpoint the source of the cry; then they throw on anything they can find and pour into the street, joining a river of people running towards the sound of the scream. Although none of them knows exactly what has happened, they can tell that it is something terrible. This anxious torrent rushes to the northern edge of the island, where a handful of neighbours are trying to restrain Markogiannakis' sister Violetta, who is hysterically struggling to break free.

'Let me go! Let me go!' she cries desperately, and, although they keep a firm grip on her, her frantic momentum drags them all forward.

When they reach the wall which marks the northern edge of Spinalonga, the islanders face a macabre scene: Markogiannakis has fled the island once and for all, and now no one can drag him back in chains. Like so many others before him, he has ended his life by leaping to the shore below, adding his name to a long and doleful list of desperate lepers.

His body lies on the rocks by the sea, like a ship washed ashore in a gale. The height of the fortress walls above, combined with the jagged rocks below, have left him almost unrecognisable, but death, at least, had been mercifully swift.

The islanders stand silent and tearful by the wall, while a service boat slowly makes its way to the scene carrying three guards, a nurse and two patients who have volunteered to assist the staff in its gruesome task. Unable to endure the shock, Violetta passes out shortly before reaching her brother's body, and some neighbours carry her home and call for a nurse. Violetta and her brother, just children when they showed the first signs of disease and were sent to Spinalonga, were thereafter shunned by family and relatives. Violetta, now in her forties, found comfort in the company of her brother and never married, not wanting to inflict such a curse on future generations.

On hearing the news, neighbours rush to Violetta's house to be with her in her hour of need, and when she begins to come around, the nurse injects her with a sedative as a precaution.

'Where am I?' she asks weakly.

'You're home, dear,' the nurse replies.

'And my brother?'

'I'm afraid...' the nurse whispers, but is unable to complete her sentence. Violetta, however, understands, and her eyes fill with tears and loss. But no mother is there to hold her and share her pain, to stroke her hair or whisper words of comfort. Violetta suddenly realises that she is all alone in the world; a stranger among strangers. She cries silently, rivers of tears streaming down her face, and although she is looking straight at the nurse and neighbours, her thoughts are miles away.

'Where have they taken him?' she whispers and then drifts into a sedated sleep.

Another nurse, wearing medical gloves, walks carefully over the jagged rocks to Markogiannakis' body. She bends over him and tries to find a pulse, while the Medical Director's crew stand a few steps behind her, waiting for the verdict. After checking both radial and carotid arteries, she turns towards them and solemnly shakes her head. The two patients who are present remove their caps as a sign of respect, while one of the guards wades to the boat for a white sheet to cover the body. A wooden stretcher and this white sheet will now be the vessel carrying the deceased to his freedom.

Four strong men lift the stretcher and lead a silent procession of islanders back by land towards Markogiannakis' house so that people can say their final goodbye.

His front door and windows are open wide, while his friends and neighbours are waiting outside in the yard. When the procession arrives, several of his closest friends take the body from the stretcher-bearers and begin preparing it for burial. After laying him on the bed, three women start washing the body. They plunge clean cloths into buckets of water and scrub away the drying blood, while the men turn the body to the left or right as needed. The sight of the battered corpse and the combined odour of death and leprous decay cause one of the women to put her hand over her mouth to keep from vomiting.

'Are you ok?' the others ask.

'I'm fine; it's nothing,' she quickly replies.

After Markogiannakis' body has been cleaned and dried, one of the women takes a small bottle of myrrh out of her apron pocket and sprinkles it over him. When she's done, two men take his arms and legs and lift him up so the women can replace the bloody sheets with fresh linen from the wooden chest across the room. Then the men gently lay him back on the bed. Now that he's clean, they all help to dress him in his Sunday clothes – to look his best when he meets his Creator.

Two more things remain to be done before Markogiannakis is ready to receive the friends and fellow-patients who have come to pay their last respects. One of the men who have been helping prepare the body folds Markogiannakis' arms across his stomach, wraps a white scarf around his wrists and secures it with a knot. He then seals his mouth with wax and ties a second scarf around the head to close the lower jaw and prevent the mouth from opening. Now nothing more is needed, and Markogiannakis is ready for his final journey.

The encounter

It's a great day. The sun is shining, and there's not a cloud in sight. Pipina looks up and marvels at the clear blue sky, thinking she mustn't waste such a lovely day indoors. She brings a chair out into the yard and places it in the sun, then heads back inside to fetch her embroidery needles and white thread. She had started knitting a doily for Maria's dowry a few days before but had laid it aside because of the poor lighting inside the house and the intense concentration it requires. This bright and sunny day, however, seemed like an excellent opportunity for her to continue. Whatever Pipina embroiders is so delicate and fine that it catches the eye and instant admiration of any visitor. Back in the village, between the children and Kostis, her mother and the fields, she never had time to knit or embroider. On Spinalonga, however, her chores and obligations were minimal, and her newfound spare time was now filled with needle-work, which helped her relax and forget her troubles.

Neighbours pass by and occasionally stop to say hello. She politely returns such greetings while continuing her embroidery. Time passes, and Pipina is absorbed in her work, but at some point she realises that there is a woman standing at the gate, silently watching her. She lifts her gaze to find Irene gazing fixedly at the doily in her lap.

'Good morning, Pipina,' Irene says with a slight smile.

'Good morning,' Pipina hesitantly replies, surprised that Irene has ventured to talk to her. 'You know my name...?'

'Of course; everyone does. That's very pretty,' she says, indicating the doily.

'Thank you.'

'So? How about some coffee?'

Pipina is taken by surprise and quickly weighs the pros and cons of letting her in. 'What will people say if they see her walking into my house? Everyone will know about it tomorrow! On the other hand, she's done me no harm so it would be very rude of me not to invite her in,' she thinks to herself.

'Of course,' she says, after a slight pause.

And in this moment she makes a conscious decision not to let people dictate her life and tell her who she can and cannot see. She always tries to give people a chance, and, although much has been said about Irene, she plans to draw her own conclusions after speaking with her over coffee. If she discovers that people are right about her, she won't see her again. But she must find out for herself and not simply shun her because of malicious gossip.

'Shall we sit outside?'

'I don't mind; wherever you want.'

'It's too nice a day to stay indoors, don't you think? Hold on; I'll bring a chair.'

Pipina brings out another chair and places it next to her own. 'How do you take your coffee?' she then asks.

'Two sugars, please.'

'Ok. Here, have a seat and I'll be right with you.'

Pipina comes back out carrying a small coffee table for their cups, and then heads back inside to make the coffee. When it's ready, Pipina pours the coffee from the *briki* into two small cups, which she places on a tray with two glasses of water and then returns to her visitor.

'Thank you,' Irene says, taking her cup in her hand.

'Tell me if it's ok.'

'It's fine,' she says after taking a ladylike sip.

A few moments of awkward silence go by, and Pipina attempts to break the ice.

'Lovely weather, isn't it?'

'Yes, yes...' Irene replies, looking up at the sky.

'I'm sorry, I'm not very good with names... It's Irene, right?'

'That's right.'

'I'm Pipina,' she says, extending her hand. 'We haven't been formally introduced.'

'It's nice to meet you, Pipina. Where are you from?'

'Sitia.'

'Are you married?'

'Yes, with two children.'

'I'm sure you've heard about *me...*'

'Well, I'm new here, so I don't know much about anyone,' Pipina lies in an effort to avoid embarrassment and give her guest the opportunity to tell her own version of events. 'I don't really know that many people here.'

'That's probably better, Pipina. Most of them pretend to be your friends, but they'll stab you in the back first chance they get. So be careful. Where are your husband and children now?'

'The children are in the village with my mother, and my husband's at the front.'

'He's fighting, eh?'

'Yes, yes... As if the Germans and the Italians didn't do enough damage, we had to go and start a civil war! Anyway... How about you? Are you married?'

'Well, I married three times, but I was unlucky with all three. They all passed away.'

'Three times? But you're so young!'

'Young, but unlucky.'

'You poor thing. My brother mentioned something the other day. I'm sorry to pry, but you're not sick, are you?'

'No, I'm perfectly healthy.'

'Sorry, again, but weren't your husbands lepers?'

'You don't need to apologise. I'll tell you anything you want to know. To answer your question: yes, they were, all three.'

'How did you manage not to catch it?'

'Well, leprosy's not contagious - at least not the kind we have here.'

'I keep hearing that on the island, but why do they send people to Spinalonga and other institutions if it isn't contagious?'

'Well, you *can* contract it, but you've got to be extremely unlucky.'

'Even so, why do they quarantine us in leper colonies if it's *that* hard to catch?'

'For money, perhaps?'

'What money?'

'Don't you get an allowance?'

'I do.'

'Where do you shop?'

'The boatmen and the stores. Actually, Yiannis shops for me.'

'And where do the boatmen and stores get their supplies?'

'The Gulf.'

'Have you heard anything about the financial situation of the people over there before they opened this colony?'

'Nothing specific.'

'That's all right; I'll fill you in. Before Spinalonga became a leper colony, they were completely destitute, wandering the nearby villages begging for food. Ok, and another thing... how many people work here: staff, guards, cleaners, nurses, etc.?'

'I don't know; fifty? Sixty?'

'More than that. Where do they all come from, Pipina?'

'How should I know?'

'They're all from nearby villages. Before the colony opened, they were all poor farmers or housekeepers. And look at them now: public servants with a regular salary! Do you think any of them would be here if it wasn't for us? I very much doubt it...'

'I hadn't really thought of how many families live off the island. What will happen to them if the leper colony closes?'

'Oh, that will never happen!'

'How do you know? What if they find the cure?'

'Haven't you heard? The cure's already been found!'

'It has? When?' Pipina asks, her eyes flashing with sudden excitement.

'It's been a while now, but they haven't brought it to Greece yet.'

'Why? What on earth are they waiting for?' she cries, excitement giving way to disappointment.

'Perhaps they're waiting for our staff to find other employment.'

'You're kidding, right?'

'Of course I'm kidding! How should I know what they're waiting for?'

'Well, if they *do* bring the medicine, they'll have to let us go.'

'That's true, but I doubt they'll ever do that.'

'How do you know? Did someone tell you?'

'Well, there's a patient here from Athens who regularly corresponds with his sister. She told him in her last letter. Apparently it's been in all the papers.'

'Oh, dear God, let's hope it's true so we can finally get our lives back!' Pipina says, crossing herself.

'Don't go crossing yourself for nothing. You'd better pray that God guides them to do the right thing.'

'Who?'

'The politicians and bureaucrats. If they refuse to license the medicine, there's not an earthly chance it'll ever reach us here. On another topic, you're Yiannis' sister, aren't you?'

'That's right. You know my brother?'

'I do... He's a good man your brother. We used to talk until a couple of months ago, but then we stopped.'

'Why?'

'His wife had the impression that I was also going to steal him away from her. But that's not what I'm like. I've never come between couples, and despite what I do for a living no one has ever left their wife because of me. I imagine they told you that much, didn't they?'

'Tell me what?'

'That I'm a prostitute. It's one of the first things people learn when they arrive.'

'I had heard, to be honest.'

'And doesn't it bother you?'

'Why should it bother me? You've done me no harm.'

'It's just that it disturbs most people here; especially the women.'

'Why?'

'They're afraid I'm going to steal their husbands. If they weren't so close-minded, they'd see that I'm no danger to them.'

'I'm sorry to ask this, and you don't have to answer if you don't want to: Do you sleep with lepers?'

'I sleep with anyone who can pay.'

'Yes... My brother said so.'

'I've had many long conversations with Yiannis about this. It's not that I like what I do for a living, it's just that I don't have any other way to support myself.'

'I understand,' Pipina says, nodding sadly. 'But... how do you stand them?'

'Oh, I'm used to them now. All men are the same, basically, with only one thing in mind...'

'Come on now, I think you're exaggerating. They're not *all* the same!'

'Why am I exaggerating? Men aren't like women, Pipina. They don't have to have feelings for someone to have sex with them. All they care about is satisfying their desires, so any woman will do.'

'Well, I disagree. I think it depends on the person. There are good and bad men, as there are good and bad women, and I'm talking about character, not reputation.'

'Ok, if you put it like that, I'll give you another example: Let's say for some reason the cure never comes to Greece.'

'Don't say that!'

'Hear me out, just for the sake of argument. So no cure - no chance of ever leaving the island.'

'Ok...'

'So you're forced to stay on Spinalonga.'

'Go on...'

'How old is your husband, Pipina?'

'In his early thirties.'

'If he found out that you'll probably never leave the island again, don't you think he'd eventually start over with someone new?'

'No, I don't think so. He loves me.'

'For how long? You know what they say, Pipina: Out of sight, out of mind...'

Pipina silently ponders Irene's words.

'Where's your husband now, anyway?'

'At the front.'

'So you're lucky, so to speak. At least he's surrounded by just men. But what will you do when he returns?'

'I hope I'll be out of here by then.'

'How are you going to do that?'

'I don't know yet. But, I'm not sick; or at least I don't think I am.'

'Oh, yes, Yiannis had mentioned something... They brought you here without tests, right? Didn't you say anything when they came to take you away?'

'What could I say? They knew very well I hadn't been tested, and that's where I thought we were going – to the Medical Centre for testing!'

'Oh, my! It's different with me, I came here by choice, but you... you poor thing! When did you get here, anyway?'

'Oh, when was it?' Pipina says, scratching her head. 'I can't remember the exact date, but it was some time after the elections.'

'After the elections? Are you sure?'

'Of course I'm sure. I voted at the village!'

Irene falls silent and looks Pipina in the eye.

'What are you thinking?'

'There's something fishy going on here...'

'What do you mean?'

'Well, I'm not really sure, but I think they brought a *lot* of people here after the elections.'

'Yes, that's true. There were a lot of us from Sitia.'

'Not just from Sitia! They brought them from everywhere!' Irene says, lost again in thought.

'Hey! Where have you drifted off to?'

'Give me a minute, I'm thinking about something.'

'Ok, sorry. I'm just going to get a glass of water, and I'll be right back,' Pipina says, as she heads inside with her empty glass.

A lightning bolt of insight makes Irene spring from her chair and run inside after Pipina.

'Pipina! 'Pipina!' she calls, waving her arms up and down.

'What's the matter? Have you gone mad?' Pipina asks in bewilderment.

'You'll go mad too when I tell you!'

'Tell me what?'

'Have you filled your glass?'

'I have...'

'Ok, let's go back outside,' Irene says, taking Pipina's hand and leading her out into the yard. 'Sit down.'

'Why? Can't I hear the news standing up?'

'Trust me, you'll want to hear this sitting down,' Irene says, gently pushing Pipina into her chair. She then puts her hands behind her back and starts pacing the yard slowly, like a doctor about to announce the results of a medical test.

'Well, my dear Pipina, we may not know each other that well, but there's something about you I find very likeable,' she states seriously.

Pipina laughs at the tone of Irene's pronouncement.

'Please don't interrupt me. And stop laughing!'

'Whatever you say, doctor,' she says, covering her mouth with her hand and trying to restrain herself.

'All right, now. Please don't interrupt me again because I'm about to tell you something I think you'd like to know...'

'What's that?' Pipina asks, still amused.

'Why they brought you here!'

Pipina's smile immediately vanishes, and she stands up, reaches for Irene's hand and gently pushes her into her chair. Still holding Irene's hand as if afraid to lose her, she pulls her own chair closer so their knees are almost touching. 'Go on,' she whispers anxiously.

'I'll tell you everything, but first you need to calm down.'

'Don't tell me to calm down! I'm about to explode, so go on!'

'Ok, ok... You said they brought you here *after* the elections, right?'

'Right.'

'Well, in addition to your fellow-villagers, they also brought a number of other new people during the same period.'

'I already told you I don't know about that.'

'Well, I do.'

'Ok, so? Where are you going with this?'

'I'm just pointing out that many new patients were admitted during that period.'

'How do you know we're patients?'

'You're missing the point! Weren't you brought here as patients?'

'Yes.'

'Weren't you each given a house and an allowance?'

'I suppose...'

'Those devils!' Irene hisses to herself.

'Who?'

'The people in charge!'

'Don't keep me waiting! What did they do?'

'Well, by bringing all you newcomers here they put an end to any talk of closing the leper colony.'

'Why, was that ever an issue?'

'Of course it was! It was all people could talk about at the time.'

'Why did they want to close it?'

'Because there weren't enough patients. Lepers were so completely neglected during the Occupation that most of the weaker ones died.'

'How many?'

'Well, here on Spinalonga... more than a hundred. Oh, those bastards! In order to keep their jobs and continue making money, they dragged healthy people here and destroyed their lives and families!'

'This is too much; let me think a minute. Is there any way we can verify this?'

'Don't you worry... One of my clients is a snitch for the Medical Officer. He's always around him, so he must know something.'

'How will you find him?'

'He'll be coming to see me in a few days. He's like clockwork.'

'So what'll you say to him?'

'Oh, I have my ways and little tricks, and he'll tell me everything.'

'What if he figures out what you're up to and tells Rasidakis?'

'If he was clever, dear, he wouldn't be so obvious about being a snitch.'

'Does he actually go round telling people he's Rasidakis' snitch?'

'No, but even the children have figured it out by the way he behaves.'

'Ok, good. When are you expecting him?'

'I bet he'll come to see me by Saturday. I really hope I'm wrong, but I think you were simply pawns in their grand scheme.'

'We'll just have to wait and see,' Pipina says, nodding her head.

'What time is it?'

'It must be around two.'

'Oh, my! It's late, I've got to go,' Irene says, rising from her chair and giving Pipina a quick kiss on the cheek. 'Bye for now, and thanks for the coffee. I'll let you know when I've got some news, ok?'

* According to medical records, patient testimonies and the 1946 election records, most of those brought to the islet without being tested were admitted *after* those elections. The admission of "healthy" lepers continued through the first months of 1947, probably to bring the colony back up to full strength following the mass mortality of the Occupation years and to end talk of closing the leper colony once and for all.

Feast at the *kafenion*

The musicians have been at the *kafenion* since early afternoon, helping Kyrios Stamatis prepare the place for the festivities later that evening. Kyrios Stamatis is busy removing chairs from the area that will be used as a dance floor. He has already set up a makeshift stage across from the entrance: three large planks spanning a few bulky cinder blocks, the whole thing covered with a colourful woven carpet. Since it's his turn to host the feast, Kyrios Stamatis has borrowed some chairs from the other two *kafenions* on the island. When the musicians start playing, the others will close for the night, and their staff will join in the celebrations. It's been a while since the *kafenion*-keepers last fought about anything; rotating the feast among them has benefited everyone, and since they all make the same money now none of them have any reason to complain.

The lyre-player turns towards Kyrios Stamatis: 'Hey! Have you forgotten about us?'

'Oh, I'm terribly sorry. I've got a lot on my mind...' he mumbles, slapping his forehead. He quickly carries three chairs onto the stage and arranges them to face the dance floor. 'Ok, we're ready. Come on up,' he calls to them.

The three musicians who comprise the Cretan band of Spinalonga step onto the stage carrying a lyre, tabor and mandolin, take their seats and start tuning their instruments. The lyre and tabor players, who each suffer from a different disease, had brought their instruments with them when they were sent to the island, while the mandolin player bought his instrument on the islet as a way to escape his pain and suffering. Disease was eating away at their bodies, but it had left their limbs intact and their sight and hearing unimpaired. And so they continued playing together - one of the few pleasures they had left - and managed to bring a measure of joy to the patients' dull lives. After the musicians finish tuning their instruments, they rehearse for a while and then return to their homes for a few hours of rest before the feast.

Argyro and Katina are waiting for Pipina outside her door. They've made plans to meet at eight and then accompany Yiannis and Sofia to the feast.

Pipina comes out and locks the door behind her. 'Ready. Shall we go?'

'Finally! How long does it take you to get dressed, for heaven's sake?' Argyro exclaims.

'Sorry, I lay down for a nap early in the afternoon, and I must have overslept.'

'Early in the afternoon? But it's dark now!' Katina exclaims, looking up at the night sky.

'Anyway, where's your brother? Isn't he coming?' Argyro interjects, not giving Pipina time to answer.

'He said he'll meet us there.'

'Did you tell him to save us a seat?'

'We just said that whoever gets there first will save seats for the rest.'

'All right. Can we please leave now? We'll be the last ones there!'

The streetlamps along the cobbled road flicker to life as the three of them walk arm-in-arm in the direction of the *kafenion*.

When they arrive, they pause at the door and scan the customers' faces for Yiannis and Sofia.

'I can't see them,' Katina says after a few seconds.

'I'm sure they'll be here any minute,' Pipina reassures them.

'Where shall we sit?' Argyro asks, searching for the best place among the crowded tables.

'There?' Katina says, pointing to an empty table in the back.

'Yes, that looks good,' Argyro agrees. The three of them slowly make their way to the empty table, but when they reach it they notice that there are only four chairs.

'We'll ask Kyrios Stamatis for another chair,' Pipina says.

'We're lucky we found a table. Don't worry about a chair; Kyrios Stamatis always has plenty in reserve.'

'What shall we drink?' Katina asks the others.

'Yiannis drinks *raki*,' Pipina says.

'I don't! It's way too strong for me. How about some wine?' Argyro proposes.

'That sounds good. What about you, Katina?'

'I'll have wine, too. It's not as if we drink much anyway.'

'Let's order a small carafe to begin with, ok?' Argyro says, and the other two agree.

Kyrios Stamatis comes over to take their order.

'Good afternoon, ladies!' and the three women return the greeting in unison. 'Will it be just the three of you?'

'No, my brother and his wife will be joining us, so could you bring us one more chair?'

'No problem,' he says, turning towards the customers at the next table and asking them if they need their empty chair. They shake their heads, so he lifts it over their heads and places it next to the three women.

'Thank you,' Pipina says.

'It's nothing. So, what will it be, ladies?'

'We'll have a half litre of wine to start.'

'White or red?'

'White,' Pipina says, looking at the others for confirmation.

Argyro and Katina nod in assent, and Kyrios Stamatis marks the order on his pad and repeats: 'Half a litre of white wine... Anything to eat?'

'Are you hungry, girls?' Pipina asks the others.

'How about something to go with the wine?'

'Yes, we shouldn't drink on empty stomachs,' Katina adds.

'What's good, Kyrios Stamatis? Argyro asks.

Kyrios Stamatis recites the menu from memory: 'Wild green salad, snails *boubouristi*[16], *dakos* with tomatoes, split pea spread, cabbage with vinegar, boiled fava beans, *xigalo*[17], fried pickerel - caught just this morning in Elounda - chips... I can also whip you up an omelette...'

'All right... We'll have the wild greens, the *dakos*, chips... Girls, what else?'

'How about a *xigalo*?' Pipina suggests.

'And a *xigalo*,' Argyro repeats.

---

[16] A Cretan delicacy: The snails, still in their shells, are salted, floured and sautéed (opening face down) in olive oil, vinegar and rosemary.

[17] Soft Cretan cheese traditionally made from goat's milk, sheep's milk or a combination of the two.

'And snails!' Katina cries. 'Kyrios Stamatis' wife makes the best snails! She adds a lot of vinegar and rosemary, and you can't stop eating them!'

Kyrios Stamatis, repeating the orders to himself, adds the snails and looks up: 'and one portion of snails... Is that all?'

'Yes, Kyrios Stamatis, thank you.'

'Thank *you*, ladies!' he cries cheerfully, tearing their order from his pad before returning it to the pocket of his white apron. He then places the pencil behind his ear and gracefully navigates the crowded room back to the kitchen.

Seeing the pencil nearly graze the open sores on his face, Pipina is suddenly overcome by panic. She had momentarily forgotten they were on Spinalonga and that the food they had just ordered would be prepared by lepers. Argyro sees she is lost in thought and tries to bring her back to reality by waving her hand in front of her face.

'Hey! Where are you?'

'Nowhere, nowhere! I'm right here,' Pipina quickly replies, straightening up in her chair.

'I can see you're *physically* here, but your mind seems miles away. What were you thinking about just then?'

'Nothing in particular...'

'Come on, tell us!'

'Actually, I was thinking that maybe we shouldn't have ordered any food...'

'Why not? His prices are reasonable,' Katina reassures her.

'I know. That's not what I mean...'

'What then?'

'Because the people who will cook our food are sick...'

'So? What are you afraid of? Catching the disease?'

'Am I wrong to be scared? We've got to be careful, haven't we?'

'Don't be afraid,' Katina says reassuringly. 'Argyro and I have been coming here for longer than I can remember, and look at us: we're both healthy.'

'She's right, Pipina. Besides, we've told you this a million times: Leprosy's not contagious! Not the kind we have here anyway.'

'If it isn't contagious, as you say, why are so many people sick?'

'It's really quite simple when you think about it, Pipina,' Katina says, followed by Argyro:

'When do epidemics break out?'

'When people are suffering and in bad shape,' Katina adds.

'That's right. When they're starving, working too hard...'

'Or have no access to medicine,' Katina completes her sister's sentence.

'In short, Pipina, when living conditions are bad, all sorts of diseases break out,' Argyro concludes.

'I see...' Pipina says, mulling over the sisters' words.

'And I see you're as clueless as can be...'

'Of course I'm clueless! No one has ever explained it to me! Whenever I try to learn more about the disease, people always change the subject! Come on, girls; since we're on the subject, enlighten me, please!'

'Ok, I'll tell you a couple of things so people won't take you for a complete fool,' Katina says. 'All right, pay attention now. I don't know about the rest of Greece, but leprosy arrived in Crete with the Saracen pirates.'

'When was that?'

'Oh! Way back. Before the fifteenth century.'

'A.D.?'

'Yes, Pipina,' Katina replies with a smile.

'So, it's been around a long time.'

'What did you think? That it's a new disease? It's been around for centuries! Anyway, leprous pirates arrived in Crete...'

'Yes, but they didn't stay, did they? And then came the Venetians, right? And then the Turks, and, finally, the Germans and Italians.'

'Don't confuse the facts. Just listen: The Saracen pirates didn't leave straight away. They stayed for quite a while and mingled with our people.'

'So?'

'They were the ones who originally transmitted leprosy to the Cretans!'

'So why didn't people get sick back then? And why are there still lepers today?'

'Of course they got sick. There have been cases of leprosy in Crete since the pirates were here. Haven't you heard of Meskinia in Heraklion or the exiled lepers of Ierapetra?' Argyro asks.

'That's right. There are lots of stories about them,' Katina adds.

'Yes, but...'

'But, what?'

'Ok, there are stories, but you don't hear about masses of cases.'

'You mean outbreaks?' Katina asks.

'Exactly.'

'Listen: The Saracens brought the disease to Crete. They were the ones who transmitted it to the native Cretans. All right so far?'

'Go on.'

'As you know, there are many different types of leprosy. In this particular type we're dealing with here on Spinalonga, people can be carriers and still go their entire life without ever realising they're infected.'

'That's what I'm talking about! Why weren't there so many people sick back then? Why did an epidemic suddenly hit Crete?'

'And that's what I'm trying to explain!' Argyro exclaims. 'In order for a disease to spread and become an epidemic, certain conditions have to be present. Our people were resistant to the disease, but over time and after everything they went through they became weaker and more vulnerable. Do you understand?'

'Who came to Crete after the Saracens, Pipina?' Katina asks.

'The Venetians.'

'And what were they to us?'

'Invaders, conquerors.'

'And don't forget that after the Venetians came the Turks, who enslaved us.'

'Ok.'

'So think about it: Cretans have been enslaved by one conqueror after another from the fourteenth century until 1900 when the Turks left.'

'So? What are you trying to say?'

'Isn't it obvious, Pipina? People who suffer like this are bound to come down with physical *and* mental illnesses at some point. Remember what year it was when they first started worrying about the disease and started to take measures to prevent it from spreading?'

'Wasn't it during the time of the Cretan State? Under Prince George?'

'What was the year?'

'Oh, I don't know.'

'It was shortly before the Turks withdrew from Crete. The Turks arrived in 1669, and they pillaged, slaughtered and enslaved the natives. Just think that the Turks alone had us enslaved for two hundred and fifty years! Our people were starving and forced to work like slaves on land that used to be theirs - and to hand over most of their harvest to masters who considered them animals for field work.'

'How much more could they take? It was just a matter of time before they succumbed to the inevitable,' Argyro adds.

'And then the Great Powers came to our rescue like a gift from above.'

'Again during the time of the Cretan State, right?'

'Yes.'

'So, what happened then?'

'I won't go into detail because that's not the point. When the Great Powers intervened and Crete became an independent state, most - but not all - of the Ottomans left the island. Have you seen the Cretan State's flag? Three blue squares and one red square with a white star in the middle?'

'Yes?'

'Do you know what that little red square with the star stands for?'

'No.'

'It stands for the Sultan's dominion on the island.'

'The Sultan wasn't Cretan, of course,' Argyro interjects.

'I know that much. I'm not stupid!'

'Anyway, after the Cretans managed to drive the Turks off the island, they sent lepers to Spinalonga to scare the remaining Ottomans away.' Katina continues.

'I bet the Turks are still talking about that.' Argyro says with a giggle, glancing at her sister.

'Why?' Pipina asks.

'French troops were stationed on the islet to protect the Turks from the Christians, so the cunning politicians came up with a plan: They sent the first lepers to Spinalonga so the Turks would leave *voluntarily*, and since they left voluntarily the French had no reason to intervene,' Argyro says.

'Then what?'

'Then, the Cretans began rebuilding. In 1913, the island was united with Greece, and, as you know, things began looking up. Until the Occupation,' Katina explains.

'The Germans and the Italians,' Argyro adds.

'And then it happened all over again: misery, hunger, hardship... What are people to do when they suffer one misfortune after another?'

'I understand,' Pipina says sadly.

'Anyway, after the Occupying forces left, the Civil War breaks out,' Katina continues.

'To finish us off...' Argyro adds. 'Do you know how long we went without an allowance at the beginning of the Civil War?'

Pipina shakes her head.

'Almost six months!'

'Six months? How did you survive? Were you allowed to leave the islet?'

'That's a good one, Pipina. As if they'd ever let us leave this place.' Katina chuckles.

'God bless the residents of the Gulf for taking pity on us and bringing us something to eat every now and then...' Argyro says.

'And the Metropolis of Petra. God bless their souls!' Katina adds.

'Yes, of course... and don't forget the fundraisers in Lasithi. How many times did they send potatoes and other supplies?'

'Forget? If it wasn't for them, we'd all be dead!'

'Thank you for telling me all this,' Pipina says, breathing a sigh of relief. 'I feel as if a weight has been lifted off my chest.'

'So, you'll eat something, right?' Argyro asks with a smile.

'I will. And I think Katina's right: If it *was* contagious, you'd both be sick since you've been eating here all these years. Now that I think about it, it's the same with Sofia: Yiannis is a leper, and although they live in the same house, share the same bed and eat together, she's still fine.'

'Exactly! So don't be afraid. I think they're using leprosy to scare people.' Katina states.

Just then, Kyrios Stamatis arrives at their table balancing a large tray crowded with dishes.

'Here we are, ladies!' he announces with a flourish.

'Thank you, Kyrios Stamatis,' Argyro says.

He then begins serving their food, announcing each dish as he places it on the table:

'Snails *boubouristi*, split pea spread, *dakos*... and your wine. All right, ladies?'

'There are no forks. Do we eat with our hands?' Katina jokes, wiggling her fingers before his eyes.

'Oh, my goodness, I forgot!' he cries, putting his hand over his mouth. 'Just a second...' he adds and dashes off, his shocked expression sending the three of them into giggles. Unintentionally, Kyrios Stamatis has lightened their mood and helped them relax.

'Good afternoon!' Yiannis calls to no one in particular as he enters the *kafenion*.

'Hi there, Yiannis, come join us!' one of the customers shouts back, gesturing to an empty chair beside him.

'Thank you, my friend, but my sister's expecting me,' Yiannis replies politely, walking toward Pipina's table with Sofia in tow. 'Hello, girls,' he greets the three women with a smile.

'Finally! Come, have a seat,' Pipina says.

'Good afternoon,' Argyro and Katina cry in unison, as Yiannis and Sofia take their seats.

It's getting late; the *kafenion* is crowded, and any minute now the musicians will take the stage and start playing.

'What will you have to drink, Yiannis?' Pipina asks her brother.

'I'll have *raki*. Sofia?' he asks, turning to his wife.

'Wine for me, Pipina.'

'Yiannis, tell Kyrios Stamatis that we need another glass and some more wine,' Pipina tells her brother.

'Kyrios Stamatis!' Yiannis calls out to *kafenion*-keeper: 'Bring us a small carafe of *raki*, some more wine and a couple of glasses!'

'Coming right up!' Kyrios Stamatis shouts from across the room.

The three musicians walk into the *kafenion* and are immediately greeted by an enthusiastic audience, most of whom are already tipsy after hours of drinking *raki*. The lyre-player is a cheerful and dynamic man who knows exactly what his audience wants to hear. He is also extremely good-looking and has no physical deformities, since he doesn't have leprosy but a venereal disease instead. A misdiagnosis brought him to the islet, but in time he grew to love his new home and become a part of the community.

The musicians don't take long to settle in and begin playing a *sigano*, while reciting *mandinadas*. Most of the customers know the tune, and many rise from their seats to dance one dance after another: *syrtos, pentozali* and *maleviziotis*. The islanders continue to drink, sing and dance through the night – until their legs can take no more. Then, they bid goodnight to their neighbours and in the grey light of dawn unsteadily weave their way back home - spirits somewhat lifted, and hearts somewhat warmed.

Menelaos

It's late at night, and heavy darkness covers the cobbled roads of Spinalonga. The form of a man, a shadow within the darkness, moves swiftly and stealthily to one of the shuttered houses. The islanders are fast asleep, and the breeze that was brushing the treetops all afternoon is now still, allowing even the faintest sound to echo between the stone walls of the houses. The shadow arrives at Irene's house, knocks twice, pauses for a moment, then knocks again. Irene recognises the knock and hurries to the door.

'Menelaos!' she exclaims in surprise.

'Hiya, baby-doll!'

'Did anyone see you?' she whispers, looking right and left over his shoulder.

'I don't think so...'

'Come in,' she says, quickly pulling him inside and locking the door behind him. 'Where have you been, honey?'

'I couldn't come any sooner; I was too busy,' Menelaos replies, wrapping his arms around her from behind.

'Shall I pour us a glass of wine?' Irene proposes, trying to escape his oily embrace.

'I'm not here for the wine... It's you I want,' he says, his voice thick with desire.

'You'll get what you want, honey, but first let's have a glass of wine. Come on... Just for me,' Irene says in her most alluring voice, turning around and looking him straight in the eye.

Although Menelaos can't wait to get her clothes off, he makes this small sacrifice to keep her happy.

'You know I can't refuse you. Go on then, pour us a glass.'

Irene pours two glasses of wine, with Menelaos still clinging to her.

'Come on... Stop it!' she giggles. 'Take your wine. Here's to us,' she toasts, raising her glass with a seductive wink.

Menelaos grabs the glass and, to hasten the moment when he will have the voluptuous Irene in his embrace, downs the wine in one gulp. Annoyed by his haste, Irene comes up with a new strategy.

'Oh, honey... Don't let me drink all by myself... I'll pour you another glass so you can keep me company while I drink mine. I want to enjoy our time together,' she says, taking the glass from his hands and gently presses a finger against his lips to prevent him from protesting. She then pours him a second glass:

'Here you are, my love. Good health!'

'Here's to you, baby-doll,' Menelaos says and downs the second glass in one go. Irene pretends to be drinking, but she's really only just wetting her lips.

'Oh, honey! Did you finish already? Didn't we say we'd drink it together? I'm pouring you another one...'

'But...'

'No, we said we'd have a glass of wine *together*!' Irene declares, taking his glass and filling it a third time.

Helpless before her charms, Menelaos again has a full glass of strong wine in his hand, and he is already starting to feel dizzy.

'Nice wine, but strong, eh?' Menelaos comments.

'Don't tell me that a strong and virile man like yourself can't handle a couple glasses of wine,' Irene teases, knowing for sure she'll touch a nerve.

Not wanting her to think less of him, Menelaos raises the glass to his lips and quaffs his third glass with an air of Cretan machismo.

'Here, pour me another,' he then adds in his manliest voice.

'Haven't you had enough?'

'I can hold my liquor. Another!' he shouts, gesturing at his empty glass.

Irene brings the pitcher over to Menelaos, and he refills his glass.

'Better not have any more, honey; it's quite strong...'

Menelaos, seriously tipsy now, can't restrain himself.

'Here's to you, gorgeous!'

'Irene clinks her glass against his, but doesn't drink – observing him slowly approaching the desired level of inebriation. She urges him to stop drinking twice more, but he doesn't listen and she doesn't insist, fearing he'll start shouting and wake the neighbours.

After several more glasses of wine, Menelaos is clearly and utterly drunk. Having overestimated his ability to hold his liquor, Menelaos has blindly fallen into Irene's trap and is now at the mercy of his beautiful temptress. Irene puts his arm around her neck and raises him out of the chair where he has collapsed. She then slowly leads him over to the divan, while he serenades her drunkenly and out of tune.

'Shhh! Be quiet, for heaven's sake! You'll wake the whole neighbourhood! Come, let's sit down and get comfortable,' she coos.

'Let go! Where are you taking me?' he protests.

'Come, sweetie, let's sit over here so you can lie in my lap.'

'Yes... That sounds nice...' he mumbles.

Irene manages to drag him across the room, undrapes her drunken burden, and begins to lower him onto the divan. Too drunk to support himself, however, Menelaos sprawls backward into the cushions.

'Come here, you...' he slurs, throwing open his arms.

'Hold on; let me bring another pillow for our backs.'

'Quick!'

Irene fetches a pillow, props it against the corner of the divan and sits down. She gently pulls him up to her, nestling his head between her breasts. She wraps her arms around him, tenderly strokes his face and runs her fingers through his hair. Menelaos closes his eyes and surrenders himself to her caresses, while Irene starts whispering to him in a soft, sing-song voice:

'My baby came to see me and got drunk drunk drunk...'

'I'm not drunk; jus' a little dizzy...' he protests, without opening his eyes.

'Where have you been all these days? I've been waiting for you...'

'Oh, I couldn't come.'

'Why not?'

'Too much work...'

'You mean for the Medical Officer?'

'You could say that...'

'And you forgot your girl?'

'I couldn't forget you if I wanted to, baby-doll...'

'Anyway, I'm just happy you finally made it.'

Menelaos followed Rasidakis around everywhere, and Rasidakis, in turn, kept him close because Menelaos told him all the local news and gossip. Rasidakis thought of him as an extra pair of eyes and ears. And now here he was: as drunk as can be in Irene's embrace. Irene is observing him carefully, trying to figure out the best way to proceed, knowing that in his present condition it won't be difficult to get information out of him. Her cunning mind is spinning, and she begins to ask questions cloaked in praise so he doesn't catch on.

'Oh, honey, I'm worried you're exhausting yourself working for that man. He has you running all sorts of errands for him.'

'I know...'

'But he must really care for you, don't you think?'

'Hmm... Why do you say that?'

'You're together all day, every day. If he didn't care about you, he wouldn't keep you so close.'

'You're right. He thinks a lot of me,' Menelaos replies after a moment's thought, his eyes still shut. 'But I do a lot for him, too.'

Irene decides to pursue another course.

'He's a good man, the Medical Officer. Just look how much he's done for us.'

'Yeah, I know.'

'My case, for instance: I wasn't entitled to a house, but he intervened and made sure I got it.'

'He's a decent man.'

'When I think that they planned to close the colony, send everyone to other institutions and toss me out like a sack of rubbish... I get the shivers.'

'Spinalonga was never gonna close, baby-doll.'

'It wasn't? Didn't they say there weren't enough patients for the colony to stay open?'

'They did...'

'That's what I'm saying; just the thought of being homeless...'

'There was no chance of that ever happening.'

'What do you mean?'

'Rasidakis took care of it.'

'Poor man. I can only imagine how stressed he must have been with that whole business, worrying about the colony closing and all. It's not easy losing your job after so many years.'

'Why would he be stressed? The colony was never going to close.'

'But everyone heard it was.'

'It wasn't going to close... It wasn't going to close...' Menelaos starts singing into Irene's chest, over and over again.

'Why not?'

'Because he'd bring more lepers.'

'So there'd be enough lepers to stay open?'

'Exactly.'

'Bless his soul! I couldn't stand it if they took my house away! But... where'd he find so many lepers?'

'From the patients' relatives and friends.'

'Did he go round asking people if they had relatives?'

'No.'

'How then?'

'He keeps all of our records in his office, everything: the year we were admitted, where we're from, how old we are...'

'That's very clever... Then again, the doctor's a clever man.'

'*That* he is...'

'Then what?'

'What d'you mean?'

'What did he do after checking the records and finding out where everyone's from?'

'He sent his crew to round up their relatives, one village at a time. They were here the next day.'

'You mean they took them to get tested the next day? I know that takes at least a day or two...'

'Tests?' he echoes ironically, letting out a muffled laugh. 'If the doctor says they're lepers, that's good enough.'

'Naturally. He's been a doctor for God-knows how many years, so he should know better than us.'

'He also had his friend.'

'What friend?'

'The one who was running for election. You know, the one Rasidakis supported.'

'Yes, I remember. What about him?'

'Spinalonga had to stay open.'

'Or else?'

'He'd lose credibility from everyone around Elounda. He promised them the leper colony'd stay open; promised them he'd bring more people here to ensure that.'

'You mean, if they voted for him?'

'You got it, baby-doll...' Menelaos murmurs with a slight smile, before drifting off to sleep wrapped in Irene's embrace. Irene slowly lifts his head off her lap, slides out from under him and gently lays him out on the divan - a smile of satisfaction playing across her lips. She covers him with a blanket and lets him sleep. Shortly before sunrise, Menelaos wakes up and sees Irene fast asleep in a chair across from him. His head throbbing and his mouth like a dry towel – and utterly unable to recall anything from the previous night – Menelaos takes a couple of banknotes out of his pocket and leaves them on the table with a smile, certain that he was the cause of Irene's apparent exhaustion. He finds his jacket, opens the door, and, without making a sound, leaves as he had come: a shadow in the darkness.

The following day

It's noon, and Pipina is knitting in her yard when a familiar voice calls from the gate:

'Open up. I've got news!'

'Irene! What news?' she asks and runs to open the gate.

'Startling news, actually. I found out why they locked you up here...'

'How did you manage that?'

'The Medical Officer's snitch - the one I told you about – he came by my house last night.

'And? Have a seat, and tell me everything.'

'I'd better not. Someone might see us and get suspicious, although he was so drunk, I doubt he'll remember any of the questions I asked him. Well, do you know why you people were sent to Spinalonga?'

'You mean everyone from Sitia, or just me?'

'All of you! It's not just you, Pipina; others came here the same time.'

'From Sitia?'

'From all over Lasithi! And what's worse is that it was all women, children and old people. More than a hundred of you were sent here then, and none of you have any symptoms or were ever tested!'

'How can that be?'

'You were the "exchange" promised to the residents of the Gulf if they voted for the Medical Officer's friend.'

'We were? How? I don't understand...'

'The Medical Officer promised them that if they voted for his friend he'd bring in more lepers to keep the colony open. May I have some water?'

'Of course, but I don't understand what those elections have to do with us being here...'

'Get me a glass of water, and I'll explain...'

Pipina comes back out with Irene's water, and the two of them continue their conversation. What Pipina hears leaves her deeply troubled...

Father

Yiannis walks quickly to Pipina's with the keys to their father's house in his pocket, as promised. Today's the day they're going to visit him - a day

Pipina has been looking forward to with great anticipation. Their father was a good man, who loved them dearly when he was young and healthy and lived with them at home in the village. And when he first got sick and was sent to Spinalonga, he wrote to them regularly, but now it's been five years since he last communicated with anyone. Yiannis arrives at Pipina's to find her waiting anxiously by the gate.

'Ready?'

'Yes.'

'Ok, let's go.'

The two of them start climbing the road to their father's house, which sits on a hill close to the hospital. When they arrive, Yiannis puts the key in the lock but pauses before turning it.

'Are you sure you want to go in?'

'Yes.'

'Father's in pretty bad shape...'

Pipina gently pushes him aside, turns the key and slowly opens the door.

Her eyes take a few moments to adjust to the darkness inside, and at first she can only see the outlines of the man lying in the low bed across the room. But even in this scant light, Pipina comprehends a change so profound that no amount of imagining could have prepared her. Tears immediately burst from her eyes and start streaming down her cheeks, even before his face comes fully into focus. It has been many years since she last saw him, but even allowing for the normal depredations of age, her father's appearance, so far from the image she has carried in her mind these many years, causes her so great a shock and so much anguish that it takes a full minute before Pipina can compose herself enough to move. She walks over to the bed and slowly stretches out her hand – but then hesitates. Drawing back and clenching her hands tightly to her chest, she silently cries. Her once-strong and sturdy father now lies in bed, oblivious of his surroundings, his skin quilted with lesions and purulent wounds reeking of formalin.

'Father, father!' Pipina cries, reaching now to touch his arm.

'He can't hear you, Pipina,' Yiannis says quietly, wrapping his arm around her shoulders. 'Come on, let's go,' he adds, and starts walking her to the door. With one final glance backward at the man lying motionless in the shadows, they step back into the open air, lock the door and start walking in silence down the cobbled road to their own homes. Pipina is deeply shocked by her father's condition, and in the days to come his image will bring her hours of sorrow and will haunt her dreams at night.

Insecurity

Confinement on Spinalonga had taken its toll on Pipina's self-esteem and self-confidence, and she was often overcome with guilt. She felt unfit as a mother for not protecting her children; incompetent as a wife for not supporting her husband while he was away fighting; and a burden on her mother. This wasn't the life she had pictured for herself and her loved ones. She blamed herself for the hardships her family now had to face and the permanent stain on their name. She spent hours every day dwelling on the problems her absence had caused, struggling to find a solution, but to no avail. Not only had the islet deprived her of her freedom, but it had also tied her hands. The only thing she could do for her loved ones was to write to them regularly with love, encouragement and advice. And although she could express her feelings through her humble letters, her family needed her there *in person*. After so many months in confinement, she was beginning to abandon all hope of ever getting out. She kept thinking how unfair it was for her to be locked up without proof or tests but, much more, how unfair it was for four other innocent people to suffer because of her. Pipina also spent countless hours thinking of Kostis, her beloved husband, who had fought so hard to be with her. And now, unintentionally, she had entangled him in a mess which seemed to have no solution. A young man with two small children, his wife on Spinalonga, his wounded country asking him to kill his fellow-Greeks... 'Is there a God?' Pipina kept wondering. 'Why did this happen to us?' Under these circumstances, Pipina's absence from home was even more noticeable. Before Kostis had gone off to war, she had promised that she'd take care of their family at all costs. But she had failed. And even though it wasn't her fault, it still hurt her deeply. Every time such thoughts entered her mind, Pipina would begin to cry. 'Why does Kostis want me anyway? I have nothing to offer. What good am I?' As one dark thought followed another, she would succumb to fear and imagined Kostis finding a replacement for her. Her husband was still a young man; he had his whole life ahead of him, and their children needed a mother. 'What if I never get out? What if they test me and discover I'm sick? Oh, God, what will I do then?' Pipina couldn't stop thinking that Kostis might fall in love again and marry another woman who could offer him everything he was now missing - a fear intensified by Irene's cynicism: "Men will be men... They can only go so long without satisfying their needs..." 'Will he cheat on me?' she wondered. 'No, don't think like that. He loves you! But what if they continue to hold me here? I have to get out before he comes back, but... how? Oh, he's just a man... How long can he go on like this? He hasn't got time to think about our life together with the war and all, but what if he comes back and I'm still here?

He's young and good looking, too... Will he wait, even with other women approaching him, all those young war-widows...? Oh, God, what should I do? What if a stranger ends up raising my children?' Pipina bursts into tears, wringing her hands and pacing the floor. She stares at the curtain and unconsciously starts picking up objects and putting them back down again. 'I need a pen and paper,' she mumbles as she walks over to the table, sits down and starts writing:

My beloved Kostis,

I am doing well, and I hope you are well too. A few days ago I received a letter from Mama, saying the children are both in good health. You haven't written in days, and we're worried about you, so please send us a letter. I constantly ask God to watch over you. Without you, my love, my loneliness is unbearable. This island is so cold and foreign. I long for your return, so please take care of yourself. I love and honour you. Please don't neglect to visit me first chance you get, for seeing you brings me great joy. I love you and think of you every day. I hope you do too...

Faithfully,
Your Pipina.

The letter is sprinkled with Pipina's tears, so she pats it dry, trying not to smudge the ink, then folds it carefully and puts it in an envelope. Come morning, she'll give it to the postman and will wait with increasing impatience for a reply.

Black rock

There's a commotion on the island, and people are striding up and down the streets in agitation, their faces serious and preoccupied. Early in the morning, Kasapakis sent four Fraternity members to gather all the island's men at the large *kafenion*. At ten-thirty, they are sipping their coffees, anxiously waiting for Kasapakis. He arrives fifteen minutes later with a thick sheaf of papers in hand and the rest of the board members in tow. Everyone stands as he enters.

'Good morning,' he says briskly, dropping the pile of papers onto one of the tables. 'Sit down,' he then adds, and they all take their seats. 'Well... we have a serious problem here,' he continues and starts pacing the floor, while his listeners remain silent. 'We received the Ministry's reply today... And what do you think they said?'

'What, Sir?' one of the men asks anxiously.

'That we already have enough; that we cost them too much as it is, and there's absolutely no question of increasing our allowances.'

His words cause instant consternation, and everyone begins talking at once.

'Quiet down, my friends,' he urges in a commanding voice, again focusing their attention.

'I'm sure you all remember our request for a permanent doctor and a couple of women to take care of the bedridden?' he asks, and the men all nod in assent.

'Well, apparently we don't deserve that, either! *They* turned us into outcasts; *they* condemned us to a slow death; and yet *they* won't let us live out the rest of our lives with dignity! If they allowed us to leave the island, things would be different; we'd have more choices. But they've deprived us of even the simplest things, like sage and dittany. *Sage and dittany*, for God's sake, which we used to pick with our own hands in the mountains! We're deprived of our freedom; deprived of our families and loved ones. And what for? To protect the health of the fat cats and their friends, who fear we'll give them the disease. What do they know about disease? What do they know about confinement? About oblivion, isolation and stigma? They know nothing! They sit in the comfort of their homes and believe that everything in this world is just fine. But *they've* never had relatives reject them; *they've* never had their names - their very existence – wiped off the town records! So how, my brothers, can they possibly understand our problems? But we're not animals; we're not asking for riches. We haven't requested a doctor and nurses for our amusement. We *need* them! It's not enough that they mistreat us; they won't even let us go! They want us here - on this God-forsaken dry rock of a place. They actually believe they're fulfilling their entire duty by sending us this miserable pittance of an allowance. And these are the same people who only show their faces once every four years just before the elections to enhance their image - without actually listening to our problems. These are the same people who don't dare visit us to see how miserable our everyday lives really are. One must be courageous to live on Spinalonga, brothers! *They* buy whatever they need from their neighbourhood stores, but *we* buy these things from the Gulf – at two or three times the cost! But what can we do about it? Stop eating? We're sick, so we need food even more than healthy people do. And not just any food, but food that's right for sick people! Are we to stop dressing? We have to wash our clothes so often they fall apart in no time at all. We didn't *choose* to be covered in sores; we didn't *choose* to be here. That was *their* choice; *they* chose to isolate us here, so *they* have to make provisions for our survival. Brothers, I believe we have come to the end of our rope. They are quickly leading us to extinction, but we can't let them think that this is fair. Brothers, we must rise up and make them take notice! As long as we sit back and do nothing, things will stay the same or get worse... and lead to one thing: our death.'

The men cheer, but Kasapakis continues:

'Once again, my brothers, I'm afraid there's but one solution: a strike. We will go on strike, and if our death is what they want, then so be it. But we'll end our lives with dignity; with our heads held high. We're not livestock. They don't own us, but they have a responsibility to us. They can either accept this responsibility and give us proper care, or we can force them to live out the rest of their lives in guilt, knowing that they sent three hundred and thirty of their helpless fellow Greeks to an early grave. There's no middle ground here, brothers!' he cries, pounding the table with his fist. 'Who's with me?' he shouts, as all the men rise to their feet and cheer.

'Good,' Kasapakis says with satisfaction. 'The strike starts tomorrow, so go on now and inform the women. Petros, Nektarios and Sophocles will make a banner saying "Black Rock" in big, black letters. Aristides and Yiannis will make another saying "Strike". You, Antonis, go inform the guards and staff that we're going on strike tomorrow. Iasonas, tell the women to gather warm clothes and blankets. Come tomorrow, we'll be sleeping at the port. I'll inform the Director.'

Kasapakis takes his hat from the table and heads for the door, but one of the Fraternity men stops him.

'Sir, should we come with you?'

'No, I'd better go alone. You get organised,' he replies and leaves, absorbed in thought.

Over the next twenty four hours, the islanders work hard to prepare for their strike. Seeing how determined they are, the Medical Officer doesn't stand in their way. After finishing his work in the afternoon, he locks his office, boards the service boat with the rest of the staff and leaves. The islanders gather wood, prepare banners, pile plenty of blankets by the gate, and wait for nightfall. They don't want the residents of the Gulf to suspect anything until the next morning, when their strike will hit them like a bolt from the blue. Once darkness falls, they set to work: They suspend a large white banner with thick letters saying "Black Rock" over the main gate, where it will be visible from across the narrow Gulf, and hang a second banner saying "Strike" a few metres from the first. They make flags by cutting black clothes into rectangles and sewing them onto wooden poles, some of which they set up at the port, while mounting others atop the island walls. They carry wood down to the pier and arrange it in neat piles. They lock the grocery stores, close the *kafenions* and secure the public buildings. Wearing their warmest clothes, they descend to the port. Pipina moves in with Yiannis and Sofia, while her other brother, Zisis, stays with their bedridden father. They also will be participating in the strike, but from home, as their condition is too serious to risk long exposure to the cold. They and other patients in the later stages of the disease are even exempt from the fasting that is a necessary part of the strike - but they too are willing to starve if necessary.

Dawn finds the islanders gathered at the port in groups of twenty to thirty people huddled around a dozen fires. Children are asleep in their mothers' arms, but every now and then a cry interrupts the early-morning stillness. Knowing what to expect from the authorities and residents of the Gulf, they wait quietly, saving their strength, lost in thought and prayer.

When the first boat appears in the distance, one of the men jumps to his feet.

'Someone's coming!' he shouts, and heads toward the sea.

'Let them come...' another murmurs, stirring the fire.

'It's one of the merchants,' another man shouts from the edge of the pier. 'And another one's right behind!'

'Stay strong now, my friends,' Kasapakis says, rising to his feet.

A few minutes later, the first merchants approach the pier, coming to sell their wares to the islanders, as they do every day. When they draw closer, however, they face a new situation: The gates are wide open; no guard is there to meet them, and the employee normally in charge of disinfecting the lepers' money is nowhere to be seen - only banners and black flags, and patients scattered here and there.

A small crowd of islanders have gathered at the pier to prevent the merchants from docking, and Kasapakis, making his way through the crowd to the edge of the pier, speaks to the puzzled merchants sitting in their boats. He tells them about the strike, politely requests them to leave, and asks them to inform their fellow-merchants and other residents along the Gulf. He tells them that the patients have decided not to accept any form of help, neither food nor medicine, and that no doctor or employee is to set foot on the island - *indefinitely*. His message is clear, and the merchants turn their boats around and leave the port in frustration.

The patients' strike immediately begins to cause a stir and affect the local economy. The residents of the Gulf are poor people who only manage to get by thanks to what they earn selling things to Spinalonga. If the lepers stop buying, how will they survive? Rowing back across the Gulf, the merchants decide to make a stop in Plaka to meet with the Medical Director. After tying up at the pier, they walk together to the Director's office and beg him to find a way to end the strike. Even though Rasidakis has dealt with numerous strikes before and knows that the best solution is to let them run their course, this time he decides to go to the islet. He calls for two of his guards, and they board the service boat.

The approach of that particular boat is greeted by the islanders with apprehension and fear.

'Stay calm now,' Kasapakis urges them and heads back to the pier to meet the boat.

Rasidakis stands and informs the boatman and guards that they won't be docking or getting off at the islet, knowing that this would only enrage the strikers and harden their stance. He tells the pilot to steer as close as possible, and when almost touching the dock

Kyrios Alekos turns off the small engine and drops anchor.

Rasidakis is now standing in the stern less than two metres from the pier, where Kasapakis is standing with a look on his face that says he's ready for war.

'What's this now, Kasapakis? Are you at it again?' Rasidakis asks, looking around at the crowd.

'We told you yesterday. You should have informed them,' Kasapakis calmly replies.

'I understand why you're striking, but what have the people of the Gulf done to you?'

'We have nothing against them.'

'Then why don't you let them dock?'

'Because that's the way it must be.'

'Kasapakis, they're poor people; they need to live, too.'

'On our backs!'

'What do you mean?'

'They live off us! But we've got to survive, too. You think if we die they'll find anyone else to buy their merchandise? You and the rest of the staff will go somewhere else and continue working, but they'll share our fate: misery and death!'

'That's enough, Kasapakis,' Rasidakis hisses.

'No, it isn't! If you want to be responsible for so many deaths, then I have nothing more to say... But know this: If you don't talk to the authorities and get them to give us what we're entitled to, then no one will be allowed on the island again, and we'll all starve to death. We're ready and determined. So, if getting rid of us is your plan, then I suggest you come back in a week or two to bury us.'

'Kasapakis, stop talking nonsense. Go home, and tomorrow morning we'll draft a new petition together and send it to the Ministry.'

'To hell with petitions! How many papers and petitions have we sent them already? Have you seen any results, because we sure haven't. So what do you think will change this time? No more petitions.'

'What exactly do you expect me to do then, Kasapakis?'

'Go find the Prefect.'

'The Prefect?'

'Yes, the Prefect.'

'What do you want with him?'

'Have *him* call the Ministry himself. Enough is enough! They can either treat us like humans, or we might as well just die. Do you understand? Tell him that!'

Rasidakis stands there for a moment, agitated and thoughtful at the same time, but soon realises he doesn't have any choice.

'You're putting me on the spot here, Kasapakis... All right, Alekos, let's go,' he says to the boatman, who starts the engine, hoists the anchor and slowly pulls away from the pier. The two men maintain a steely eye contact as the boat picks up speed and heads for the opposite shore.

The following day finds the islanders in a weakened state: Hungry children are crying everywhere, and the rancid smell of pus-stained bedding fills the air. Without their daily medication, moreover, a number of the patients have begun to experience new or aggravated symptoms, pain and even nausea. Only the bedridden patients who depend completely on others are given their medicine. Oblivious, for the most part, to their surroundings, and unaware of the strike, these poor souls have not been forced to partake of the others' deliberate suffering. Even so, the absence of medical staff is a growing threat to their survival.

The islanders' bodies are cold and sore after sleeping on the hard concrete, and several of them stayed awake all night in shifts to guard against the authorities trying to end their strike by sending over the Gendarmerie under cover of darkness.

But now it is noon, and no one has yet approached the island. No merchants, no staff. Fortunately, the weather is on their side today, with the winter sun high in the sky, shining its warming rays down on them. A woman walks between the seated strikers and approaches Kasapakis with a sleeping child in her arms.

'Sir, can I give him something to eat?'

'No, Eftaxia,' he replies calmly.

'But he's only a baby...'

'Be patient. We shall be vindicated,' he replies, and the woman walks away with tears in her eyes.

Evening comes and is followed by the night, and still no one visits the island.

Spinalonga, day five

A boat carrying the Medical Officer, the Prefect and the colony staff is motoring towards the islet, but the semi-conscious and exhausted strikers are barely aware of its approach. Rasidakis is standing at the bow, excitedly waving a piece of paper back and forth.

'We got it!' he cries, as those islanders who are still able rise to their feet and run to the pier.

'Help us tie the boat,' Rasidakis shouts again, and the men grab the mooring rope, tie it to the bollard, and help Rasidakis and the others on to dry land.

'Here, Kasapakis, read it out loud.' Rasidakis says, as Kasapakis grabs the paper from his hands, reads it once over quickly and then turns towards the others.

'We've been vindicated, my friends!' he exclaims with joy. 'Our allowance will be increased next month, and they'll send us three caretakers for the bedridden!'

A wave of excitement spreads among the strikers, who start cheering and hugging each other with the little strength they have left.

'All right, my friends, gather your things. Strike's over! We're going home!' Kasapakis cries, and then walks over to the Medical Officer.

'Thank you,' he says sincerely. 'Thank you for helping us.'

'Don't thank me; thank the Prefect,' Rasidakis replies, gesturing to the man beside him.

'Thank you very much, Sir,' Kasapakis says.

'I did my best. But don't do it again, because I don't know if I'll be able to help you a second time. It was very difficult.'

'I understand, Sir, but it was something we had to do.'

The other islanders thank him warmly, gather up their belongings and head to their houses with smiles on their faces. There was no celebration following this victory, however. Instead, the strikers simply received some much-needed medical care and then buried three of their own, including Pipina's father...

Two equal one

It's Saturday, and all the islanders have been invited to the wedding of Panagiotis and Amalia, which will be held at the small church of Agios Panteleimonas at six in the afternoon. Panagiotis and Amalia met on Spinalonga. They are both lepers, assigned by fate to this infertile islet. But even though sick, they still possess abundant hopes, needs and dreams, and today, before God and man, they shall unite their lives. Amalia and Panagiotis are the perfect example of a leper couple: Panagiotis has lived on Spinalonga for many years and has made it his home, with a nice little house and a monthly allowance. They decided to get married, not so much out of love, but to improve their everyday lives. Panagiotis has lost both of his hands to the dreadful disease, and while all of Amalia's limbs are intact, she is blind. Even so, she can take care of herself: she cooks, does the washing, mingles with the other patients and tries to do everything a healthy woman can do. But because she cannot see, some of the merchants take advantage of her and sell her spoiled or faulty goods. Panagiotis, with his vision, will become her protector in these matters, while she can do the cooking and washing, feed and dress him and even scratch his back when it itches. Their union is a classic marriage of convenience - two incomplete people joining together to create one whole person, as the islanders say.

* Newspaper *"Empros"* (1896-1969), Issue: 1 August 1929, page 1 Abstract from article by Angelos Sgouros

"...The small church of Spinalonga welcomes several leper couples, who want to be legally married and receive the Church's blessing. And the priest who has accepted this post for a salary of 1,200 drachmas (...) and in the hope of saving his soul, blesses their union without formalities, wedding processions, sugared almonds or wedding veils..."

Morale

A few days after the wedding, Kostis arrives. He thanks the boatman and disembarks as one of the guards walks towards him.

'Hi there, Kostis!' the guard says warmly.

'Hi, yourself!'

'Have you come to see your wife?'

'Yes.'

'Ok, let's go,' he says, and the two of them start walking up the road that leads to the settlement.

'How long will you be?' the guard asks upon reaching Pipina's door.

'About half an hour...'

'Ok, I'll come pick you up.'

'All right.'

Kostis knocks on the door while calling Pipina's name.

Thrilled to hear her husband's voice, Pipina runs to welcome him. Kostis quickly steps inside, shuts the door behind him and takes her in his arms.

'My love!' he cries, holding her tightly and tenderly kissing her lips.

'Slow down!' Pipina giggles.

'How are you? Did you miss me?' he asks playfully.

'Of course I missed you!'

'I missed you too, my love, very much... I got your letter...'

'You did? Then why didn't you write back?'

'I prefer to speak face to face. Did you actually think I'd forgotten you?'

'I don't know...'

'Don't know? Have I ever neglected you? Aren't I your faithful and devoted husband?'

'You are...'

'Then what is it? Why the worried expression on your pretty face?'

Pipina looks deep into his eyes, as tears start blurring her vision.

'Let me see you...' Kostis says, as he holds her face in both his hands. 'Are you crying?'

At this, Pipina buries her face in Kostis' chest and cries silently. Kostis tightly wraps his arms around her and gently whispers in her ear:

'What is it, my love? What's wrong?'

Pipina doesn't reply, and Kostis lets her tears run their course.

'Do you love me?' Pipina asks after a few seconds.

'Of course I do, silly!'

'And you'll never leave me?'

'Are you serious? What would I do without you?'

'But I'm sick...'

'Nonsense! Who told you that? Were you tested?'

'No, but I've been here for so long...'

'Don't give up now, my love. We'll work something out, and I'll find a way to bring you back home. So, please don't cry.'

In an effort to cheer her up, Kostis starts to joke.

'Tell me now... Why are you asking me if I'll leave you? Have you set your sights on some rich guy here who's on his last legs?'

'Who, me?' Pipina asks, astonished.

'Yes, you! Come on now... Full confession.'

'Goodness gracious, now I've heard it all!' Pipina says laughing.

'What's so funny? Let me in on the joke.'

'Don't be silly, Kostis.'

'So you've been faithful all the time I've been away?'

'Of course I have!'

'All right... But don't think I'll just take your word for it. I'm going to ask around...' he says, with a playful grin.

'Ask anyone you want. I've nothing to hide.'

'So you've been a good girl?'

'I have, but the real question is... have *you* been faithful?'

'I have, too. But do you know why?'

'Why?'

'Because they don't allow women in the military.'

'Is that so? Ok, you asked for it!' she says, pretending to be mad and hitting him playfully.

'Ouch! Ouch! Stop it! I was lying! I was lying! I love you, and only have eyes for you! Ouch!'

'Only me?' Pipina asks, as she continues hitting him.

'You, only you!'

'Swear?'

'I swear!'

'Swear on what?'

'I swear on my life! I swear to God!'

'So you've never cheated on me?'

'Not once!'

'Swear!' she insists.

'I already told you; I swear!'

'All right then, I'll let you live...'

'Do you really think I could ever leave you? I didn't elope with you just to let them split us up now.'

Kostis holds Pipina tight, and, with their foreheads touching, whispers:

'Do you love me?'

'With all my heart...'

Kostis kisses her lips gently and, as one kiss leads to another, intimacy leads to passion and passion to love-making.

They only have fifteen minutes before the guard comes looking for them, but those few minutes are enough to prove to each other that their feelings are real. They are barely clothed when the guard knocks on Pipina's wooden door. A sweet kiss goodbye and the lovely memories they had just created will keep their passion alive until the next time.

26 July 1947 – The Eve of the Feast of Saint Panteleimonas

Tonight, the small church of Agios Panteleimonas is the centre of attention. It's the eve of the celebration in honour of the island's patron saint, and in a few minutes Spinalonga's priest will begin the Vesper service. All the islanders, young and old, have slowly been gathering at the church since early afternoon, but the nave is too small to accommodate the crowd. The oldest and weakest arrived early to find a seat inside, while the rest are standing outside in the courtyard or are seated beside the Venetian cisterns across from the church. Today's liturgy is just for the islanders, but tomorrow morning the island will open its gates to welcome people from across the Gulf, who come every year to celebrate along with the patients. The weather is fine, and the islanders are dressed in their most brightly-coloured clothing. Most of the patients have been on the island for so long that they have embraced their new lives, but Pipina and a handful of others continue to wear black - Pipina because she hasn't accepted her confinement yet. As for the others, she has never asked. They may be in mourning for a loved one on the islet or back home on the mainland - who knows? What is certain is that they wear black as a reminder of some loss: their family, a friend, their freedom... Pipina is in the courtyard with Yiannis and Sofia, with Argyro and Katina standing right behind them. In contrast with the separation of men and women inside the church, no such formalities are observed in the courtyard. Here, people are free to sit or stand next to whomever they please, so usually friends and relatives form small clusters, while the men stay close to wives and sisters.

Vespers are nearly over, and the islanders have already started to gossip. Their whispering grows more pronounced when Irene makes her appearance in a beautiful, long red dress, and although she isn't dressed all that provocatively, her complicated past and her current profession inspire the women to shift the tone of their gossip into a more mean-spirited vein. Sofia, who hasn't been participating in the others' conversation until now, suddenly breaks her silence.

'Well, well, well... Look who's here...' she says bitterly.

Although Yiannis knows what Sofia thinks of Irene, he reminds her that they are in church and asks her to show some respect and hold her peace.

Irene walks towards the entrance of the church, looking around for anyone she might know. Her eyes meet Pipina's, and she discreetly acknowledges her with a nod. Thinking that the greeting was meant for her husband, Sofia starts scolding Yiannis:

'Did she just nod at you?' she demands.

'No,' Yiannis replies calmly.

'But I saw her! Do you think I'm blind?'

'Stop it, Sofia. We're in church.'

'Haven't I told you I don't want you anywhere near her?'

'I've nothing to do with her, so please stop.'

'If that's true, then why the greeting?'

'She didn't nod at Yiannis, she nodded at me,' Pipina breaks in.

'You?' Sofia asks, surprised.

'Yes, me. Do you have a problem with that?'

'Are you two friends or something?'

'That's none of your business, now is it?'

'Yes, go on and befriend her. You'll end up just the same!'

'That's enough!' Yiannis snaps. 'I'm not going to say it again. One more word from you and I'm leaving!'

Fearing that Yiannis might make good on his threat, Sofia holds her tongue. Once Vespers are over, all the members of the congregation mingle in the courtyard, while Pipina turns to the others and proposes a glass of wine at her house.

'Sofia, you go along if you want,' Yiannis says to his wife. 'I have to stay.'

'What for?' Pipina asks.

'We've got to prepare the place for the feast tomorrow.'

'Can't you do that in the morning?'

'No.'

'Why not? What time does it start?'

'Right after communion, of course.'

'How about you, Sofia? Do you want to come?'

'No, I'd better get some sleep; I want to get an early start tomorrow.'

'Ok then, how about you two?' Pipina says, turning towards Argyro and Katina.

'We're also getting up early tomorrow, but we'll walk you home,' Argyro replies.

'All right, let's go.'

The four women leave the church together, and when they reach Pipina's door they arrange to meet the following morning, say their goodbyes and continue on to their own homes, while Yiannis stays behind at the church to help make ready for the feast. Like most of the other islanders, he would get very little sleep that night. The task of preparing for the feast and presenting their community to the outside world fills them with a mixture of pride and excitement, and sleep is of little concern.

27 July 1947 - The Celebration

The island's gates have been open since dawn, and the service boats have been busily ferrying people across from the mainland for the big celebration - the only day of the year one can see healthy and sick together, all dressed in their finest clothes and gathered in the same place for a common purpose. The islanders have done their best to make the island presentable and display a positive image to the mainlanders. They have planned everything down to the last detail and for days have been gathering and cooking all the necessities for the feast: bread, sweets, food, wine and *raki*.

The turnout is overwhelming, and the visitors have flooded both church and courtyard, while the islanders maintain a respectful distance from their guests and gather around the stone fountain, from where they can still see and hear the service. Some of the visitors have also brought their children along: young boys and girls dressed in their Sunday clothes, their faces smooth and angelic.

Among the visitors stands seven-year-old Kostakis Spithas, who is attending the service with his grandfather - the well-known contractor. As he scans the islanders' faces, a little girl around his age catches his attention. His heart races, and he finds himself unable to take his eyes off the young girl in the dark-green velvet dress. He marvels at her exquisite features, wondering if such a healthy-looking face could possibly be concealing the disease. On that day, little Kostakis falls madly in love. The girl's face will remain etched in his memory forever, and 60 years later he will still be telling people about the beautiful little girl of Spinalonga.

The service is over, and after the priest blesses the communion bread, he hands out little pieces of it to members of the congregation.

The first to receive the communion bread are the healthy people of the Gulf, while the islanders patiently await their turn. Year after year, their attitude never fails to impress the mainlanders. Although they are sick, isolated on this barren island and deprived of everything they cherish most, they never complain or show animosity or resentment to others. Instead of lashing out, they have come to terms with their situation and seem to truly care about the society which has condemned them to this exile, taking pains not to place others in danger or discomfort. Over time, their attitude makes the residents of the wider region value and respect them.

When the last islander has received his communion bread, everyone starts descending the cobbled street toward the village, where the feast will take place.

The celebration continues well into the night, and when the music finally stops the visitors board the service boats and head back to their homes across the narrow stretch of water separating the islet from the Cretan mainland.

Death

Yiannis died today, and Pipina is in shock. Her beloved brother, who did so much to help her adjust to life on the island, is no more. For hours, Pipina has been rocking back and forth in a kitchen chair, crying inconsolably and contemplating something Yiannis had said only months earlier: "One day, Sis, I'll get out of here and go back home to Sitia. I'm not going to be buried on Spinalonga." And yet, his body has already been consigned to the earth – in one of the islet's shallow graves. Yiannis will never taste the freedom he so craved or set eyes on his village again. Sunk in her own loss and despair, Sofia can't be there to console or share Pipina's grief.

The next morning, Pipina leaves the house to visit his grave. On the way, she walks past a low stone wall on which her brother had carved "Y.C. Solidakis, 1939" when he had finished building it. Yiannis was a prodigious craftsman, and one couldn't walk ten metres without stumbling on something he had made.

'Oh, my dear brother...' she whispers in tears, closing her eyes and running her fingers over the letters carved in the rough stone. She lingers for a few minutes, then continues on her way and soon arrives at her brother's freshly-covered grave. On the way, she has picked a small bouquet of wildflowers, which she now gently places on his headstone. Tears course down her cheeks, as she sits at the edge of the stone and starts talking to herself and to the departed:

'Oh, dear brother, you managed to escape this damn place, but what about me? What will I do here all alone with no one to care about me? Who will I turn to? Who will listen to my problems or protect and guide me now?' She recalls Yiannis' last words to her: "Pipina, I'll be gone before long, but you need to stay strong, just as you are now. Don't close yourself off again. I'm sick and have been suffering for a long time, but you will have to get tested before you find peace of mind. You know everything about the island; you're smart, and I know you can do it. Use your knowledge and experience as a weapon; don't give up, and never abandon hope that you'll someday go home. Take care of yourself..." Yiannis whispered, as he grew weaker and weaker in her arms.

Pipina stops crying and sternly says to herself, 'Enough is enough. I'm going to die here if I don't do something!' With that, she stands up and starts walking towards Agios Panteleimonas.

She walks into the church, kneels before the icon and crosses herself with her eyes closed.

'Help me, Saint Panteleimonas, help me...' she whispers over and over again. 'Please show me the way, and I vow to crawl to church on my hands and knees. Help me, please... What should I do? Show me; guide me. I have to get tested, but how? How do I leave the island? How can I go to Agios Nikolaos for the test when those people know I was sent here healthy? Oh, God, what should I do? Tell me... Tell me, because I'm losing my mind away from my children! I've suffered for eleven whole months! Isn't that enough?' Pipina presses her forehead against the cold stone floor of the church as tears stream down her face. After remaining motionless in this position for several minutes, she suddenly realises something.

'I don't have any spots or marks on me. I've got to tell Kostis, but how will I reach him?' She quickly stands up and crosses herself, then leaves the church and starts walking down the road that leads to her house. That night, instead of sleeping, Pipina struggles to come up with a plan to reach Kostis, but with the first pale light of dawn she still hasn't thought of anything.

Several days pass, yet Pipina is still without a solution, and Kostis has not visited in a while. One day, as she is sitting down by the pier staring at the sea, the boatman Alexandris is making his preparations to leave after having sold all of his merchandise. He is alone and seems to be in a good mood, so Pipina decides to talk to him. As one of his best customers, Pipina figures that Alexandris might agree to help her if it wouldn't land him in trouble. He is just what she needs, a man with access to the "outside world".

'Hello, Alexandris, how are you?' she calls out to him.

'Fine, Pipina, thank the Lord! How about you?'

'So and so... You heard about my brother, right?'

'I heard, Pipina. My condolences,' he says solemnly.

'Have you got a minute? I want to tell you something.'

Thinking that Pipina wants to place an order, Alexandris patiently waits for her to walk down to the boat.

'Good morning again,' she says a few moments later, now standing right in front of him.

'Hi, Pipina. How are you holding up? I was very sorry to hear about Yiannis. I would have come to the funeral, but by the time I found out it was too late. Yiannis was a fine man, and your family have all been good to me.'

'It's all right, Alexandris. That's over now. I wanted to talk to you about something else.'

'Anything, Pipina; as long as it's within my power.'

'Actually... I have quite a big favour to ask, Alexandris.'

'Go on...'

'Come; let's sit down for a minute and I'll tell you.'

After they are both seated, Pipina starts telling him her story. She starts with how she ended up on Spinalonga, then tells him about her two children who've been practically orphaned, her husband who is away on duty, her conviction that she's healthy and a number of other things she has seen and heard on the island.

Alexandris is deeply moved by her story.

'So what is it you're asking? To help you escape? If I do that, the entire Gendarmerie force will be looking for the both of us. What would we do then?'

'No, no, no, Alexandris! I don't want to escape!'

'What then?'

'I want you to go find Kostis in Sitia and tell him that I'm probably not sick, and ask him to come up with a plan for me to get tested. But it can't be in Agios Nikolaos, because the Medical Officer knows everyone there, and if he finds out, he'll make my life a living hell. Kostis will be going to the village on leave any day now. Can you please help me? I have no one else to turn to so you're my last hope...'

'To tell you the truth, Pipina, if it was anyone else I wouldn't even consider it... but for you, I'll do my best.'

'Thank you, Alexandris. May God repay you for your good deed and your kind heart. I will be forever obliged to you.'

After agreeing on the details, Alexandris boards his boat and slowly heads for the opposite shore.

Several days pass without a sign of the boatman. Pipina waits for him every day down by the pier, not for goods or groceries, but for news. Alexandris is a kind and compassionate man, so she is certain he will help her reach Kostis.

The plan

The sound of Alexandris' boat echoes across the islet, causing Pipina to drop what she is doing and hurry down to the pier along with all the other patients who depend on the merchant-boatman to supply their needs. Pipina stands off to one side as the others buy their goods, and only after he has sold all of his merchandise and the last customer has left does she walk over to him.

'Hello there, Alexandris.'

'Hi, Pipina!'

'Well?' she asks anxiously. 'What happened? Did you find him?'

'I did...'

'And what did he say? Was he at the village?'

'Yes, he's got three days off.'

'How about my children? Did you see them? Are they all right?'

'They're both fine. They were with their grandmother.'

'Ok then, tell me. What did Kostis say? Did you tell him what I said?'

'Yes, I told him everything. He said you need to ask for two or three days' leave for family reasons and go to Sitia.'

'What am I going to do in Sitia? I can't get tested there!'

'You won't actually be going to Sitia...'

'I won't?'

'Your husband has made arrangements for a driver and one of your fellow-villagers to take you to Dr. Markianos in Athens.'

'How?'

'Pipina, we shouldn't talk any more, or someone'll get suspicious. Everything's been taken care of; just make sure you get that leave.'

'Ok. When will this happen?'

'Tomorrow night. I'll come a bit later than usual tomorrow. You come find me at dusk, so we can get going. Go on now; you don't have much time.'

Pipina runs to the Medical Officer and follows Kostis' instructions: she says that she needs a leave for a family emergency, and, because she has been on her best behaviour, manages to get it. Trying to stay calm, but with a racing heart, she heads home to get ready, and, knowing that this may be her only chance to learn the truth, she only packs the bare necessities for such a visit - so that no one will suspect anything out of the ordinary.

* Note: With Rasidakis monitoring all letters arriving at or leaving Spinalonga, communicating with the outside world was difficult, and criticising him in this way was dangerous or impossible.

The great escape

Alexandris moors his boat at the pier and, after selling all of his merchandise, glances toward Pipina, who is patiently waiting to one side.

'Where are you off to, Pipina? Agios Nikolaos?' he asks casually.

'That's right, Alexandris.'

'Where's your leave paper? Let me see it.'

'Here you are,' she says, handing over the paper

'All right then, come aboard.'

The first part has gone according to plan, and no one has understood that anything unusual is afoot.

Alexandris and Pipina soon arrive at Agios Nikolaos, tie up and disembark. Then, Alexandris leads her by the hand to a car parked nearby.

'Go on; get in.'

'Where's Kostis?'

'You're going to meet him, but don't say too much now.'

Pipina bites her lip and gets into the car without further delay. Alexandris leans his head inside the window and says in a serious tone:

'Good luck, and may God be with you.'

'Thank you for everything,' she says sincerely, looking up into his eyes.

The driver starts the engine, and they are soon on their way. Pipina is lost in her own thoughts and avoids conversation. Worried that their plan will be uncovered and everyone involved arrested or punished, she silently prays over and over again, 'Please, God, help us. Please, God, help us....' The car comes to a stop just before Agios Nikolaos, and Pipina sees three men waiting for her: Kostis, Pervolaris - the driver who had taken them to Myrsini when they had eloped - and Michalis - a neighbour of theirs who is now a Gendarme in Piraeus. Although not on duty in Crete, Michalis is wearing his uniform.

'Kostis!' Pipina cries, and is so overcome with emotion that she bursts into tears.

Kostis takes her in his arms and strokes her hair, whispering, 'Hush now, my love. It will all be over soon'.

Pipina has so many things she wants to tell him, but the words refuse to come. Instead, she looks at him plaintively with tears running down her face.

'The children?' she finally asks.

'They're fine; they miss you... But we've got to go now; we don't have much time. My leave is about to end, and I should be reporting back for duty tomorrow.'

'So what are you going to do? We need at least three or four days to get to Athens and back! They'll shoot you, Kostis; we're at war!'

'I don't want a life without you! I'm not harming anyone - just trying to save my family, so if they want to try me as a deserter, then so be it. But we have to get going. There'll be plenty of time to talk on the way to Athens.'

'Oh, poor Michalis, we've dragged you into this mess too...' Pipina says, turning towards the Gendarme.

'You didn't drag me into anything, Pipina. I came willingly,' Michalis replies, as Pipina and Kostis get into back seat. The Gendarme climbs onto the running board on the passenger side and holds onto the mirror with one hand and the door with the other.

'Why doesn't he sit inside, Kostis?' Pipina asks.

'We're bound to run into roadblocks on the way, but if there's a Gendarme on board they won't think to stop us. He's got authority, understand?'

'I see,' Pipina says.

It's a long journey, but after several tiring hours they finally manage to reach their destination: the old airport at Heraklion, which only handles small aeroplanes carrying a few passengers each. The Gendarme leads Pipina and Kostis to the plane, which is getting ready to depart for Athens. To their dismay, the flight is full. Getting to Athens, however, is a matter of life and death for Pipina and Kostis, so the Gendarme improvises a solution.

'Come with me. You're getting on that plane!'

He finds the airport manager and tells him to remove two passengers so that Kostis and Pipina can take their seats, saying that it is imperative that they get to Athens without delay - but without providing any further explanation. The manager has no choice but to comply with the Gendarme's request, so within a couple of minutes two visibly unhappy passengers are escorted off the plane, and Pipina and Kostis are led on board.

They settle into their seats with a nervous sigh of relief and watch Crete disappear behind them.

Athens, 1947 - The examination

After a long and bumpy flight, the small aeroplane lands in Athens, where another neighbour of theirs is waiting. He now lives in the capital, knows his way around, and is therefore of great use to the young couple, who have never been to the big city before. Kostis had informed him about their arrival without knowing for certain whether they would make it. In either case, he would be waiting for them. The following morning, he would take them to Dr. Markianos, who was known throughout Greece as the leading leprosy specialist and whose medical opinion no one could question.

That night, Kostis and Pipina sleep in their fellow-villager's small house, and the next morning the three of them are up at dawn. It's the day of the examination which will determine the rest of the young couple's lives. They leave for the doctor's office at seven, and, when they arrive, sit in the waiting room and patiently wait for their turn.

'Don't be afraid now, my love. Everything will be ok,' Kostis says to Pipina, gently taking her hand in his.

'I know, Kostis dear.'

Although Pipina doesn't believe she is sick, she knows her life is about to change forever: After the examination, she will either return to her former life in the village or go back to Spinalonga forever.

After a short wait, a deep and imposing voice calls out:

'Next please.'

It's their turn, so Kostis helps Pipina up, and the two of them walk into the doctor's office.

'Stay calm now, Pipina. No crying,' whispers Kostis.

'Ok.'

'Have a seat,' Markianos says, gesturing to the empty chairs. 'So, tell me. Why are you here?'

Kostis starts telling their story:

'Well, Doctor, I won't bore you with too many details, so here's the short version: We came here today so you can test my wife, who's been confined on Spinalonga for the past eleven months. The local Medical Officer's men came and took her from our village, which is close to

Sitia, supposedly to take her to the Medical Centre in Agios Nikolaos to get tested for leprosy. They claimed she might have contracted the disease from her siblings, who were already on Spinalonga, although my wife hadn't been in contact with any them since they'd been sent to the islet years earlier – and didn't have a single mark or symptom. Anyway, although they supposedly took her away to get tested, that test never took place. When they reached Agios Nikolaos, they led Pipina and the others down to the port, put them right into a boat and ferried them straight to Spinalonga.'

'I'm sorry,' Markianos interrupts, surprised. 'Let me be sure I understand correctly: they sent her there without any tests?'

'That's right, Doctor! She's been imprisoned on that island for eleven whole months without tests! This business has destroyed my family. I'd understand it if she had any marks on her, but look at her: Her skin is radiant and there's not so much as a pimple on her! Please examine her, Doctor, and if she has the disease, I give you my word that I'll take her straight back to the island myself. But if she's been locked up without actually being sick... well that's unfair, isn't it? My children are growing up without their mother, and I can't support or protect them because I'm away on duty, so we've left the poor things with their grandmother. Please, Doctor, we need to know... Please examine her...'

Troubled by their story, Markianos agrees to examine Pipina, and, after the examination is over, he asks them to sit in the waiting room until the results are ready.

Time crawls by, every minute like a century. Finally, Markianos calls them back into his office and tells them to have a seat.

Kostis and Pipina hold their breath, nervously waiting for the Doctor to speak. They watch Markianos go over the test results again, and every time he flips a page, they grow more and more anxious.

'Well, Kyrios Kostis,' the Doctor finally says. 'I have good news.'

'Tell us, Doctor,' Kostis says, sitting on the edge of his chair in anticipation.

'Your wife is perfectly healthy and has never had Hansen's disease.'

'I knew it!' Pipina exclaims, as tears of joy and relief trickle down her face. 'Thank you, God! Thank you, my sweet Virgin Mary!' she cries, crossing herself over and over again.

Although Kostis is enormously relieved that his wife is healthy, he also finds himself overcome with anger at the Medical Officer and his men, who have done this to his family. Even so, he tries to control his anger so the doctor can walk them through the next steps.

'Doctor, when we get back to Crete, my wife is supposed to return to Spinalonga. What will we tell them? How do I get her out of there? I don't want her staying there another day!'

'Don't worry, Kyrios Kostis. I'll give you copies of the test results and my report. Show them to your Medical Officer; then take your wife and leave.'

'What if they claim I forged them just to get her out of there?'

'I don't think they'll go that far!'

'But, Doctor, these are the same people who wrongfully detained her there for eleven months! Why would they stop now? Please, for the sake of justice, can we go to the police station and have the copies certified? That way, they won't be able to doubt their authenticity.'

Kostis convinces Markianos to accompany him to the police station and have their copies stamped, and, with these precious documents in hand, Pipina and Kostis set off on their homeward journey.

"The big fight"

Alexandris has moored his boat at the port and is standing next to it on the pier when Pipina runs up to him in tears and throws her arms around him.

'Hey hey, Pipina, welcome back! What's wrong? Why are you crying?'

'Alexandris, I'm not sick, and according to Dr. Markianos, I never was! If Kostis hadn't taken me to get tested, I'd have died over there without ever learning the truth. So thank you!'

'For what?'

'For all your help. Thank you with all my heart.'

Kostis walks over to Alexandris and grabs his hand. 'Thank you, my friend. May God repay you tenfold for all you've done for us.'

The three of them sit down on some nearby crates while Kostis and Pipina tell him what had taken place in Athens. Then, Kostis stands up and says:

'All right, Alexandris, take us to the island so we can share our news with the Medical Officer. And may God keep me from cutting his throat like a lamb!'

'I can't blame you for feeling that way, Kostis, but it's not worth going to jail for that man...'

'You're right. God will deal with him.'

As the boat slowly approaches the islet, many patients walk down to the pier to meet it – and when it is close enough for them to make out Pipina's face in the bow, one of them raises a cry:

'It's Pipina! Pipina's back!'

Pipina had received a three-day leave, yet she's been away nearly a week. Naturally, everyone thought she had run away.

The boat docks, and Pipina gets out first, followed by Kostis, while Alexandris gets out last, distancing himself from the couple.

The crowd excitedly welcomes Pipina and bombards her with questions about her long absence.

Spinalonga, however, is a small island, and the news of her arrival doesn't take long to reach Rasidakis. He immediately rises from his desk, slams the door to the clinic behind him and marches to the port in a fury, scattering fearful patients left and right. Before he even reaches Pipina, he is already shouting at the top of his lungs:

'So you're back, eh? And you think you can just run away like that? Oh no, young lady, you've got it all wrong!'

Too terrified to move, Pipina simply watches him draw closer and closer.

The Medical Officer stops just a foot away and raises his hand to grab her, but Kostis leaps in between Pipina and Rasidakis and knocks the unwary Medical Director to the ground. But before he can get his hands around the man's neck, his henchmen intervene and try to drag him away.

'Step aside, or it's you who'll suffer!' Kostis yells angrily, and the men take a step back.

'Who the hell are you?' Rasidakis shouts, bruised by the fall and shocked by this turn of events. Kostis grabs him by his shirt and roughly shakes him back and forth:

'Don't you recognise me, you bastard? I'm the guy whose life you tried to destroy!'

'Me?'

'Yes, you, you son of a whore!'

'I don't understand; what are you talking about?' the Medical Officer replies, suddenly worried.

'Here, open your eyes and read this!' Kostis shouts, as he shoves the test results in his face.

'What's this?'

'Proof!'

Rasidakis reads the test results and Markianos' medical report.

'It can't be!'

'Oh yes it can, you cheap crook!'

The crowd is likewise in shock, never having seen the Medical Officer so shrunken and pale.

Kostis now turns to them and says:

'Pipina's not sick, and she never was! The Medical Officer and his goons have wrongfully sent her here - and other healthy people too - so those of you who haven't been tested, go get tested by yourselves and learn the truth! Don't just take their word for it! I'm taking my wife and leaving, so it's up to you now!'

Kostis then walks over to Rasidakis again:

'And as for you,' Kostis glares at Rasidakis with his fist raised, 'if you ever so much as come near my family again, I swear to God I'll kill you! You won't get away a second time; not you or that hotshot friend of yours. And may God punish you for all the evil you have done! You have my curse!' he yells and then spits on the fallen man before turning to leave. Rasidakis doesn't dare stand up, but simply lies on the ground staring at Kostis in shock.

'Let's go home, Pipina,' Kostis then says to his wife, taking her hand and helping her back into Alexandris' boat.

'Farewell!' Pipina cries to the others. 'Be strong, and go get tested!' she adds as the boat pulls away from the island.

After Pipina left Spinalonga, the patients revolted. Those who had never been tested did so, and the healthy ones returned to their homes. In fact, every single person admitted to the colony after the elections of 1946 left the islet. It turns out that none of them were sick. And those who were admitted without tests prior to the elections got the chance to learn whether they were actually sick or not. All uncertainty was now dispelled.

The cure for leprosy came to Greece in 1947, but it didn't reach Crete immediately. Lepers remained on Spinalonga until 1957, when the Greek Government decided to close the colony. If Pipina hadn't escaped when she did – and hadn't brought Rasidakis' tricks to light – all those who had been wrongfully confined would have had to endure another ten years of confinement. When the colony finally closed, the lepers were re-examined. Some were released and prescribed medication which they could take from the comfort of their own homes, while approximately twenty patients who had nowhere else to go to were transferred to "Limodon" - the specialised hospital for leprosy in Agia Varvara, Attica. They continued to receive their allowance, since the stigma that accompanied Hansen's disease prevented them from finding work. And if one visits the old "Limodon" today, you can still find healthy people who were born on Spinalonga but who now call the old hospital their home - home as well to an extensive archive on the lepers of Spinalonga.

* To this very day, witnesses still recall the events that took place that day at the port of Spinalonga. They still talk about "the big fight", about the Medical Officer lying there on the ground and the residents rising up and protesting their wrongful confinement.

For the record...

Pipina and Kostis went home, and life gradually returned to normal. In addition to Maria and Kostakis, they went on to have two more healthy children, making a happy family of six. Kostis was brought before a Military Tribunal on charges of desertion but was acquitted after the court reviewed the circumstances of the case. And when the Civil War ended, he returned to his family, which he never left again. He died at the age of 76, while Pipina lived to the ripe old age of 93. Over the course of their lives, they had many grandchildren and great-grandchildren; they loved their extended family and were deeply loved in return.

We forgot to mention that in 1952 Spinalonga was renamed "Kalydon", which had been the island's name throughout antiquity. Although modern maps now list the small islet by its official name, the locals have never ceased to think of it as "Spinalonga". After the leper colony closed in 1957, the Greek Government explored the possibility of using the islet for other purposes. Newspaper articles from that time report that the Government was considering establishing a public psychiatric hospital there, but these discussions were soon dropped.

After the leper colony closed, residents of the Gulf of Mirabello had to endure several difficult years. The construction of new roads, however, helped them adjust to the new reality. And over time, the unique beauty of the Gulf, in combination with the growth of tourism, established the area as one of the most attractive destinations in Greece. Its natural beauty caught the eye of major businessmen from Crete and elsewhere in Greece, and it wasn't long before luxury hotels started appearing along the coast, feeding a cycle of growth. Today, the Gulf of Mirabello, Elounda,

Plaka and Agios Nikolaos together welcome thousands of visitors each year from all over the world. As for Spinalonga, the former barren rock of exile rises from the waters of the Gulf like a precious stone. Every day, dozens of boats from the nearby villages ferry visitors to the small islet. A few years ago, the Ephorate of Byzantine Antiquities began work to restore the islet's buildings and soon hope to present a picture of how it looked during its years of operation as a leper colony. Although words alone can't hope to capture the island's special beauty, the incredible hospitality of the local people and an understanding of the area's story will ensure that visitors to the one-time leper colony of Spinalonga will never forget their experience.

* Newspaper "*Eleftheria*" (1944-1967), Issue: 26 March 1955, page 6

"GRADUAL SHUT-DOWN OF SPINALONGA BASED ON PLAN OF UNDER-SECRETARIAT OF MEDICAL ASSISTANCE

After a meeting held at the Ministry of Welfare, the said Ministry announced that the leper colony of Spinalonga is to be closed and the islet subsequently used for other public purposes.

The announcement also stated that the shut-down will take place gradually and according to a plan drafted by the Under-Secretary of Medical

Assistance. According to this plan, the first patients to be released from Spinalonga will be those who do not pose a threat to public health and are able to undergo treatment in their own homes. Other patients susceptible to treatment will be transferred to *Agia Varvara* – to a specialised hospital for leprosy, which will be reorganised as a model infirmary. Finally, the lepers who are not susceptible to treatment will be transferred to a specialised asylum. It was also announced that every patient who leaves the leper colony will continue to receive a special allowance."

It would be a grave oversight to close this story without mentioning another incident indirectly related to the case of Spinalonga. According to the testimony of various local residents of the region, in an effort to eradicate the disease, some of the patients' children were sterilised. According to these reports, these children were born healthy, and their only crime was to have leper parents. Not only were they heavily stigmatised as children of lepers, but their futures were also taken from them. The people behind this action had little knowledge of the disease, and this ignorance cost those children dearly.

Epilogue

The primary inspiration for undertaking the research which resulted in this book was Pipina herself. Our families were close, and I would often find myself a guest in her house. Pipina - a proud and upstanding Cretan woman who played a major role in forming my character - used to lull me to sleep by telling me stories from her life. To this day, if I close my eyes, I can still see her smiling face and hear her calming voice. Her dynamic character and disarming honesty would often shock people, while her wit, expressiveness and ability to laugh at herself would cause them to pay attention to what she was saying. This remarkable woman with a larger-than-life personality and strong maternal instinct remained mentally sharp and lucid till the very end of her long life. Although she lacked a formal education, her learning was ongoing and impressive. When talking to people, she would often make points at her own expense in order to get them thinking and to help prepare them for the difficulties that lay ahead. Pipina was talkative, but the simple language she used was easily understood, even by children. Moreover, her directness and deep kindness - evident in everything she said – kept us hanging on her every word.

One of her favourite subjects was Spinalonga, and I would listen to her in rapt silence for hours and hours with a mixture of love and fascination, even when too young to understand the importance of the events she was describing. I was around ten years old when Pipina first decided to share her story with me, and started, reticently to begin with, to recount the events of that time - events that clearly still pained her. I had the impression then that her stories were just her way of getting me to sleep, talking in the rhythms of a parent or grandparent reading a bedside story to a child. So many nights, I drifted off to sleep listening to her soothing voice telling the story of the lepers of Spinalonga. And during the day as well, she spent countless hours talking to me about the disease; about the hard times on the islet; about the poverty, hunger and sometimes even thirst they had to endure. This wise old woman used her own misfortunes as a way to strengthen and protect me: Regardless of the subject, she would always end her stories with a moral - like Aesop - using her own mistakes as examples to avoid. She also observed the evolution of modern society with a keen eye and interest, comparing each new advance or invention with the quaint and cumbersome old ways of doing things in the village when she was growing up.

I remember her sitting in a chair next to "my" bed at her house, peacefully knitting away and saying: "The way science is going, my child, soon everyone will live a hundred years! Up to now, we only lived this long by the grace of God, no help from medicine and sometimes not even the basics." And by "basics" she meant food. For most of her life, Pipina's diet consisted mainly of *dakos*, olives, wild plants and herbs, fruit and legumes. Only in the event of a feast, wedding or baptism would they slaughter one of their animals and eat meat. And in the absence of refrigeration, if they couldn't consume it all themselves, they would trade the rest for another product they needed or give the leftover meat to a neighbour who would give them the same quantity back again when they slaughtered one of *their* animals. The few high-protein foods regularly available to the average family were milk, cheese and eggs from the goats and chickens in their yard. Everyone in the family worked: parents, children and grandparents, and most people didn't attend school because the struggle to survive came before education.

In any case, going to school was often too expensive for the average family, since students had to buy books and a slate board and wear decent clothes. Even if they managed to buy a second-hand textbook, slate board and pencil from a former student, the majority of children still went to school barefoot, for shoes were a rare luxury. Older children would eventually pass down their books and school supplies to their younger siblings, somewhat lightening the family's financial burden. The younger children would also wear their older siblings' hand-me-down clothes or clothes reconfigured from older garments.

In those days, girls weren't treated the same as boys, and were usually married off at an early age in order to shift the cost of their upbringing to their husbands. Girls as young as twelve or thirteen were forced to move into a home of their own and suddenly shoulder all the responsibilities of an adult.

The harsh living conditions and the challenges of village life meant that girls had to grow up fast in order to cope with their new reality - with none of our modern-day conveniences or amenities.

As Pipina used to say: "I never dreamed there'd come a day when we'd be able to see at night without candles. You've got to love science!" Although I didn't realise it at the time, Pipina was trying to tell me something.

I was still in elementary school when she first used the miracle of electricity as a way to motivate me to study: "You, my child, are very fortunate, so you've got to knuckle down and study hard. Education is our greatest weapon, because when someone's educated it's hard to push them around. It was different when I was young... We couldn't read for long by candlelight because our eyes would hurt. Even the children who were fortunate enough to attend school had to help out in the family fields after class, so they would only go home after sundown. After washing up and eating something, they would have to do their homework by candlelight."

"Houses weren't like they are today," Pipina would continue. "They were made of stone and dirt, and had large wooden beams holding the sod roof in place. We'd often see mice running back and forth on the beams, and when it rained, water would drip down and form puddles on the floor. I'd gather my children in a dry corner and cover them with blankets so they wouldn't catch cold. We didn't have any medicine, so a simple cold could kill you - especially if it turned into pneumonia. Only the careful and strong survived..."

Pipina's stories were always lively and interesting and so full of colourful details that they made me feel as if I had entered a time machine and travelled to a strange world in the past. With repeated tellings, many of these stories changed in small ways over the years. The only stories that remained unaltered, however, no matter how many times she told them, were her tales of Spinalonga. She would describe the same people and events in exactly the same way, and her persistence in repeating these stories over and over again got me thinking. Although I eventually knew these stories, in every detail, by heart, I also knew how important the telling of them was to Pipina – and what a precious bond this was between us – so I gladly listened, over and over.

I learned a lot from Pipina. That uncomplicated, generous and immensely strong woman taught me many

important lessons, among the most important of which was never to passively accept what I was told - or told to do. I can remember her saying: "Don't simply take their word for anything, because things aren't always what they seem. What separates us from animals is our ability to reason, so always turn things over in your head. If they make sense, that's fine; if they don't, just ignore them. What's important is that you think for yourself and draw your own conclusions..."

These words so influenced me that when I was fourteen I even began questioning what Pipina herself told me. Was her story true? Why did she keep repeating it? Was she really trying to protect and guide me or did she just want to be admired? Was she telling the story as it happened, or was she distorting things for effect? I had many questions, but I was unable to cross-check any of the information. All I knew was her version of events and her scorching accusations. Uncovering the truth of her story became an obsession. In a storm of adolescent contrariness I wanted to make sure she wasn't lying to me, for if she was, she would come tumbling off the pedestal I had fashioned for her. So I started asking around - questioning anyone who would spare me some time and could tell me anything about Spinalonga or the lepers. But it seems my youth kept people from taking me seriously. They laughed or changed the subject and told me to find more "appropriate" interests for my age. These minor, though persistent, setbacks did nothing to dampen my determination. I finally received my first solid answers a few years later when my parents, Michalis and Maria, enrolled me in the Nursing School of Agios Nikolaos in the hopes of rendering me employable. I was still attending this school when I began my training in the General Prefectural Hospital of Agios Nikolaos. At first, without any meaningful nursing skills, we interns had to take the patients' temperature, check their blood pressure, tend to their general needs or simply keep them company – usually through conversation. And so my research began.

Pipina had told me that leprosy was a disease that was front and centre in people's consciousness back then. Armed with this and other things I had learned from her, I embarked upon my quest for the truth. This time, I had an advantage, since my nursing uniform lent me an air of authority and made the older patients seek out my company. It began as a kind of game: After completing my rounds, I would spend some time with a senior patient who was both mentally sound and in the mood for a chat. I'd start by asking them their age and where they grew up to see if they were from that area. After learning these initial details, I would slowly move on to the subject that really interested me: the story of Spinalonga. I would listen intently and then write down in a notebook everything I learned so I could go over it in peace later at home. To my immense surprise, narration by narration, answer by answer, Pipina's story was confirmed. As more and more information was cross-checked and verified, I found myself even more fascinated, yet still wondered... could it really be true?

In order to obtain and cross-check new information, I followed a particular process using facts I already knew to be true. By talking to my patients about certain people or incidents of the time, I would check their reactions: If what I was saying was untrue, they would object

and give me their version of events; if it was true, they'd agree and we'd move on to a new topic. This book only contains events which were described in the same way by most of the people interviewed.

These conversations continued for several years, during which time I graduated from high school with honours and worked as a nurse. I learned three other languages, studied graphics and web design, and learned sound processing and film editing, all of which helped me improve my writing skills and taught me how to structure a story. I started writing this book two years after I began gathering and cross-checking the first information about Spinalonga, and although the main story remains essentially the same, its pages were enriched and expanded over time, like a coral reef.

Pipina isn't with us today to see the completed book she inspired, but she did see its beginning. When she was 91 years old, I started reading her own story to her. Throughout these readings, I remember her crying from both sorrow and happiness; sorrow for the painful years she was reliving in her mind and happiness because the truth was finally going to be revealed. "Are you really going to publish it, my child?" she would ask in tears. "Yes," I would answer, though unsure back then if I would ever manage to complete it. "I wish you all the best! But before you publish anything, make sure you've got proof because certain people will come after you. Truth hurts, you know."

Pipina died two years later, and after her death my determination to publish her story grew even stronger. I spent five more years writing the book - a slow and painful process without the help and guidance of my beloved Pipina. Every time I sat down to add or change something, the memory of her loss forced me set the book aside, often for days or weeks at a time. I don't know how many times I thought I'd never finish, but when I recalled the love she'd given me and her desire to see the truth revealed, I regained my courage and continued.

Bibliography - Sources

1. Books

*Αρακαδάκη Μ., Το λιμάνι της Σπιναλόγκας. Κατάλογος σχεδίων, χαρτών και απεικονίσεων (XVII - XIX αι.), Κρητικά χρονικά Λ'(1990), pp. 127 -151

*Σαββάκης Μάνος, Οι Λεπροί της Σπιναλόγκας - Ιατρική, Εγκλεισμός, Βιωμένες Εμπειρίες (1903 - 1957), Πλέθρον 2008, pp. 70 - 111, 128 - 131, 137 - 143, 148 - 156, 167 - 171, 190.

*Μοσχόβη Γεωργία, 2005, Σπιναλόγκα, Ministry of Culture, Archaeological Receipts Fund, pp. 27 - 33

*J. Grivel, 2002, Η νόσος του Χάνσεν στην Ελλάδα και στην Κρήτη κατά τον 20ο αιώνα, Ψυχοκοινωνιολογικές Επιπτώσεις, Agios Nikolaos, Κ. ΕΠ. ΑΝ.ΕΛ. (Κοινοτική Επιχείρηση, Ανάπτυξη Ελούντας)

*Δετοράκης Ε.,1981, Η λέπρα στην Κρήτη. Μια σύντομη αναδρομή στο παρελθόν, Αμάλθεια, pp. 275 - 292

*Δετοράκης Ε.,1984, Φροντίδες της Κρητικής Πολιτείας για τη δημόσια υγεία, Λύκτος, pp. 167 - 182

*Δετοράκης Ε.,1986, Φροντίδες της Κρητικής Πολιτείας για τη

δημόσια υγεία, (Β' περίοδος 1905 - 1913), Λύκτος, pp. 165 - 225

*Δετοράκης Ε., 2003, Τα υγειονομία στην Κρήτη επί Τουρκοκρατίας, Κρητολογικά Γράμματα, pp. 159 - 179

*Ζερβογιάννης Ν., 1992, Η ιστορία της Σπιναλόγκας, Αμάλθεια, pp. 90 - 93

*Ζερβογιάννης Ν., 1993, Η ιστορία της Σπιναλόγκας, Αμάλθεια, pp. 94 - 97

*Ζερβογιάννης Ν., 1994α, Η ιστορία της Σπιναλόγκας, Αμάλθεια, pp. 98 - 99

*Ζερβογιάννης Ν., 1994β, Η ιστορία της Σπιναλόγκας, Αμάλθεια, pp. 103 - 120

*Ζερβογιάννης Ν., 1995α, Η ιστορία της Σπιναλόγκας, Αμάλθεια, pp. 3 - 15

*Ζερβογιάννης Ν., 1995β, Η ιστορία της Σπιναλόγκας, Αμάλθεια, pp. 83 - 93

*Καταπότης Μ., 1933α, Η Σπιναλόγκα, Μύσων, Β', pp. 1 - 36

*Καταπότης Μ., 1933β, Η λέπρα εν Κρήτη, Μύσων, Β', pp. 37 -194

*Καταπότης Μ., 1937, Δια την ιστορίαν της λέπρας εν Κρήτη, Μύσων, ΣΤ', pp. 127 - 128

*Ρεμουντάκης Ε., 1973, Αϊτός χωρίς φτερά, Self-published, Athens

*Ρεμουντάκης Ε., 1976, Το νησί του πόνου και των δακρύων, Ο κόσμος της Ελληνίδος, 2/ 1976, pp. 24 - 26

*Ρεμουντάκης Ε., 1976, Το ψέμα και η αλήθεια, Ο κόσμος της Ελληνίδος, 11/ 1976, pp. 287 - 288

*Ρεμουντάκης Ε., 1977, Σπιναλόγκα και η μεγάλη θυσία, Ο κόσμος της Ελληνίδος, 2/ 1977, pp. 63 - 64

*Giuseppe Gerola, I monumenti Veneti nell' isola di Creta, Instituto Veneto di Scienze, Lettere ed Arti, vol. I 1, 1905, vol. 12, 1906, vol. I I , 1917, vol. I V,1932 – 1940

* Thesis titled "Public health in Crete during the first half of the 20th Century", Kaparounaki Ekaterini, Perantoni Aristea, Frouzaki Eleni, Supervising Professor: Konstandinidis Theoharis, T.E.I. of Heraklion, Crete, 2007 – 2008.

* Vies et morts d'un Crétois lépreux, Maurice Born, ANACHARSIS Publications, Paris 2015

*Στέφανος Ξανθουδίδης, ¨Χάνδαξ, ιστορικά σημειώματα¨, 1929

* *L'Illustration*, Paris, n° 4473, 24 Novembre 1928, p. 599

2. Records and archives consulted

a) Vikelaia Municipal Library of Heraklion

b) Koundoureios Municipal Library of Agios Nikolaos

c) *Demogerondia* of Lasithi (Community Council of Elders)

d) General State Records (Neapoli branch)

e) Metropolis of Petra

f) Ministry of Health, Athens

g) Ministry of Culture, Athens

h) National Library (Digital newspapers)

i) J.P. Destelle

j) Kostis Spithas

k) Anna Giakoumaki

l) Maurice Born

m) General Kallaris

n) blogs.editions-anacharsis.com

o) Kostis Mavrakakis

p) Newspaper "*Anatoli*", Agios Nikolaos, Crete

q) JD Pollet, "*L'Ordre*"

Acknowledgements

My long-standing dream of completing and publishing this book has finally come true. This would never have happened without the valuable contribution of certain people who now deserve my thanks.

First and foremost, I would like to thank my family: father Michalis, mother Maria and brother Kostis, for their moral support and discreet presence throughout my life. A big thank-you to "Panagiotidis G.P." and "Heraklion Diving Center Panagiotidis" for their contribution to the printing of the first edition of the book. Thank you to Mr. Kostis Spithas from Neapoli, Crete, for his invaluable assistance in my research. Thank you also to Manolis Metaxakis and "SITIA FM 95.5" for processing all the image and sound files, as well as for his active, personal support. A special thank-you to Nikolaos Kounalis and his family, who eagerly ferried me from Plaka to Spinalonga in their boat "Archangelos" more times than I can remember.

My sincere appreciation to Mr. Manolis Koumbanakis and his wife Kile for their help in tracing documents, as well as to the family of Stavros and Sofia Rosoudakis from Armeni, Sitia, for their warm hospitality and for helping me locate witnesses in the area. A big thank-you to the following individuals for their testimonies: Mrs. Maria, Pipina's daughter; Mrs. Eleni Aeraki from Armeni; Mrs. Marika, the Medical Officer's wife; Mr. Georgios Sfyrakis, former police officer from Elounda; Mrs. Eleftheria Mattheaki, former nurse on Spinalonga; Father Nikodimos and his wife from Dories, Lasithi; Mrs. Maria, tavernkeeper from Plaka, Elounda, as well as her children - the Vrahasotakis family. A special thanks to her son Aristides for the many times he ferried me to the islet in his small boat. I am extremely grateful to Mr. Manolis Foundoulakis for his testimony, the documents he provided and for welcoming me with open arms; to Mr. Tsatsaronis from the newspaper "*Isotimia*" and current president of the Pan-Thessalian Association of Attica, for taking the time to talk to me and for his belief in my endeavour; and to Evangelia Androulidaki from Siva, Pyrgiotissa, president of the cultural association "Siva - Themos Kornaros". I would also like to thank the boatmen of the Vrahasotakis family: Dimitrios Mavrikakis, Nikos

Venetos and Manolis Tsangarakis for being so kind, patient and helpful every time they ferried me to Spinalonga to take photographs or examine the area. Thank you to Mr. Yiannis Tsihlis for the documents and books he provided for my research; to the Municipality of Agios Nikolaos, the
Koundoureios Municipal Library and its staff for helping me trace and gather documents; to the Vikelaia Municipal Library and its staff for the photographic material and documents they so kindly provided; to the Municipality of Neapoli, the Folklore Museum and its staff for the books and records they let me borrow; to Mrs. Maria Sergaki and the staff at the General State Archives of the Prefecture of Lasithi for the documents and assistance they so willingly provided. I would also like to thank all the many people who devoted time and energy to this project and provided constructive feedback along the way, as well as all those who provided assistance but prefer to remain anonymous. I couldn't end without a warm thank-you to all those people who pushed me to continue and encouraged me to keep fighting to dispel the various myths about the lepers of Spinalonga. My final thank-you goes to you, the reader. Thank you for doing me the honour of reading this book.

Anna Giakoumaki

Archival material on Spinalonga, with comments by Anna Giakoumaki.

Section A

Photographs of Spinalonga, old and new.

Pipina, Kostis and their two children, Maria and Giorgis. Archives of Anna Giakoumaki.

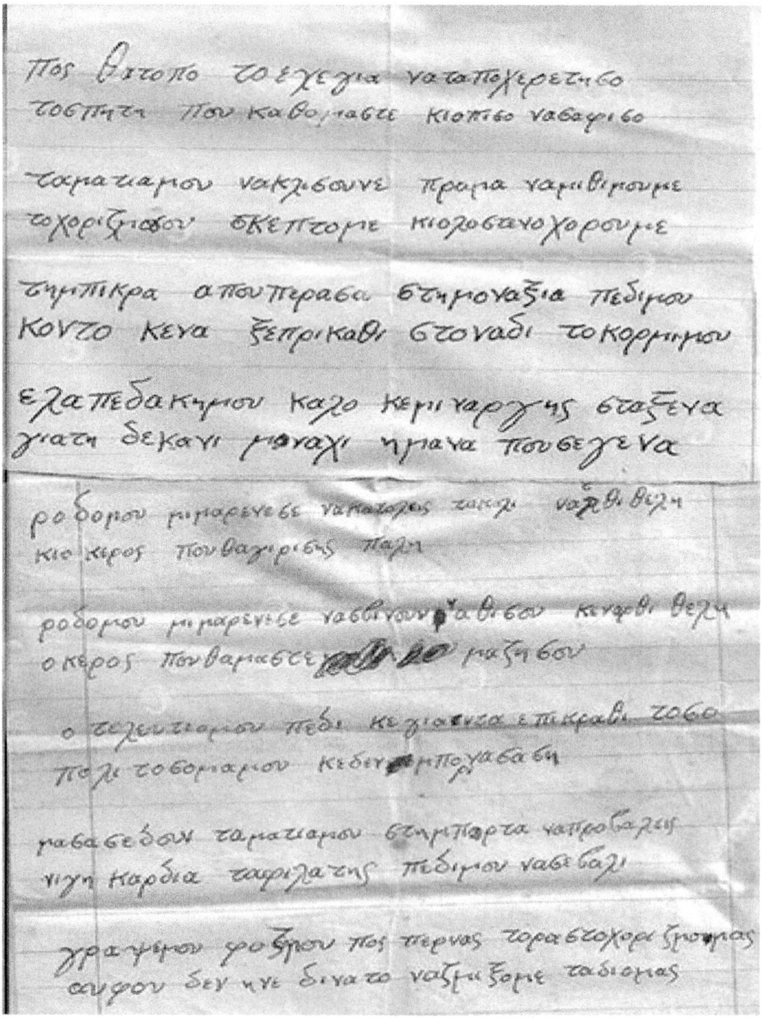

πος θατοπο τοεχεγια νατα ποχερετησο
τοσπητη που καθομασε κιοπισο νασαφισο

ταματιαμου νακλισουνε πραμα ναμηθιμουμε
τοχοριζιοσου σκεπτομε κιολοσανοχορουμε

στημπικρα απουπερασα στημοναξια πεδιμου
κοντο κενα ξεπρικαθι στοναδι τοκορμιμου

ελαπεδακιμου καλο κεμιναργης σταξενα
γιατη δεκανι μοναχι ημανα πουσεγενα

ροδομου μημαρενεσε [illegible] ναθι θελη
κιο κερος πουθαμαρισης παλη

ροδομου μημαρενισε [illegible] κεν [illegible] θελη
ο κερος πουθαμασετ [illegible] μαζη σου

ο τελευτιαμου πεδι [illegible] επικραθι τοσο
πολι τοσομαμου [illegible] ναβαση

ναβασεσου ταματιαμου στημπορτα [illegible]
νιγη καρδια ταφιλατης πεδιμου [illegible]

γραψεμου [illegible] πος περνας τορα στοχορι [illegible]
αυφου δεν ηνε δινατο [illegible] ταδιομας

Somarou's mandinadas. Archives of Anna Giakoumaki.

Pipina's brother, Yiannis. Archives of Anna Giakoumaki.

Spinalonga in 1903. Photograph by Giuseppe Gerola, Vikelaia Municipal Library, Heraklion, Crete.

Crete's first Members of Parliament with Eleftherios Venizelos, 1915. Vikelaia Municipal Library. The handwritten caption reads:

"ELECTIONS OF 31 MAY 1915 - CRETE'S FIRST MEMBERS OF PARLIAMENT IN THE HELLENIC PARLIAMENT

Bottom row (seated) from left: Michail Manasakis, Michail Saklambanis, Dimitrios Anagnostakis, Eleftherios Venizelos, Michail Makrakis.

Second row, from left: Michail Papamichelakis, Emmanouel Tsouderos, Kyriakos Mitsotakis, Vasileios Skoulas, Georgios Kokkinakis, Har. Ploumidakis, Michail Katapotis.

Third row (back): Georgios Maris, Nikolaos Papadakis, G. Markandonakis, G. Mylogiannakis, Manousos Voloudak is, Ioannis Lekanidis"

The caption also states that "Mich. Kothris is absent", when in fact three other MPs were also absent that day: Athanasios Zitakis, who was elected in Heraklion, Michail Sfakianakis from the prefecture of Lasithi and Andreadakis from Rethymnon. Kothris' name appears in the 1946 election results, so he must have stood against the Medical Officer's friend - the Doctor, MP and Senator of Lasithi - who is among the people in the photograph. The Doctor-Senator of Lasithi seemed to have an excellent relationship with Venizelos, at least up to 1915, when he became one the Members of Parliament elected from the latter's party. The Medical Officer also seemed to enjoy a very good relationship with Venizelos. At the end of 1924, he received training and went on to temporarily fill the post of Medical Officer of Spinalonga, (with salary and expenses paid by Venizelos himself), and was appointed to the permanent post approximately two years later. The Medical Officer and the MP were both very powerful men, like-minded doctors and, a few years later, they also became son- and father-in-law. Further down in Section B, "Excerpts from various documents", we will see that they also had shared business interests involving public works on Spinalonga. Did they have a reason to support each other? Readers can draw their own conclusions.

Various photographs of Spinalonga from 1905 to 1932. Giuseppe Gerola, Monumenti Veneti & Archives of the Vikelaia Municipal Library of Heraklion.

Image of the sanatorium's interior, where most patients spent their final, painful days. In an effort to somewhat brighten their surroundings, they gathered what strength remained and hand-painted decorative motifs on the walls of the sanatorium wards. For even greater emphasis, they painted the wall above the motifs one colour and the wall below them another. These motifs were not simply an aesthetic luxury; they represented the islanders' need to improve their harsh environment and make it more like the "outside world". The motifs were usually painted in a dark shade of turquoise, the upper part of the wall in beige and the lower part in a lighter shade of turquoise.

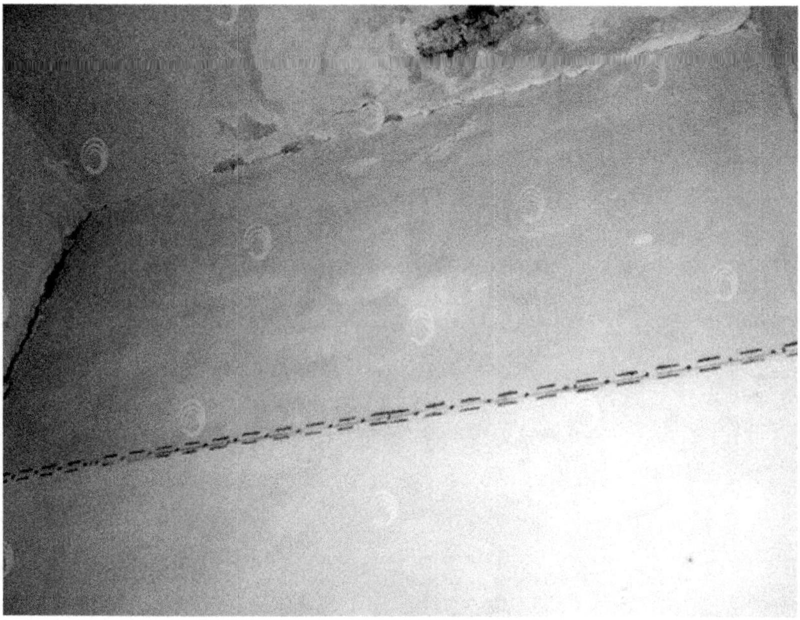

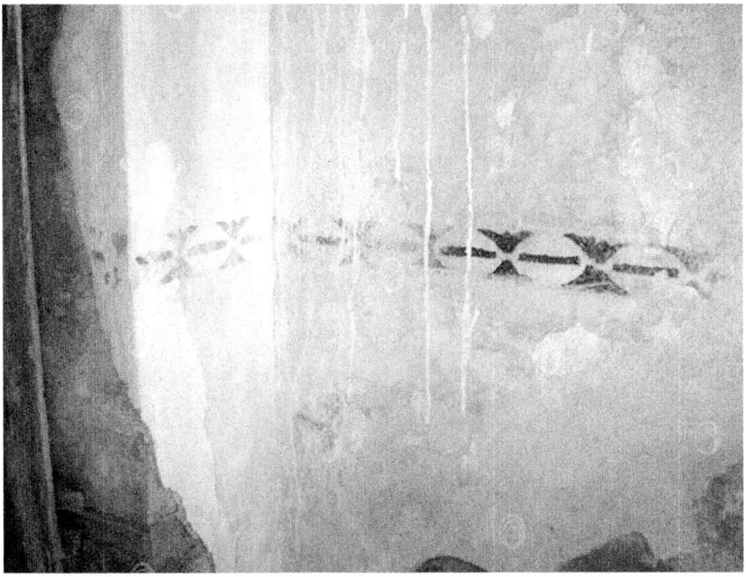

Then, in June 2012, under unknown circumstances, permission was given for a large and "violent" project to take place on much-afflicted Spinalonga. The following photographs speak for themselves. As evident from the dates in the drawings and writing on the wall, this is how that same ward looked just one month later. The motifs are no longer visible, but we can see drawings of genitals. For obvious reasons, the artist's name is not printed here.
Considering, however: that Spinalonga and Knossos are candidates for inclusion in UNESCO's World Heritage List; the islet's long history, which stretches back into antiquity; and the hundreds of people who died horrible deaths on the islet, often in excruciating physical and psychological pain, one wonders why such a project was ever given the green light.
Personal archives of Anna Giakoumaki.

Η πρώτη υπογραφή εδώ.
Ίδιο δωμάτιο.
RELENTLESS
MARIA

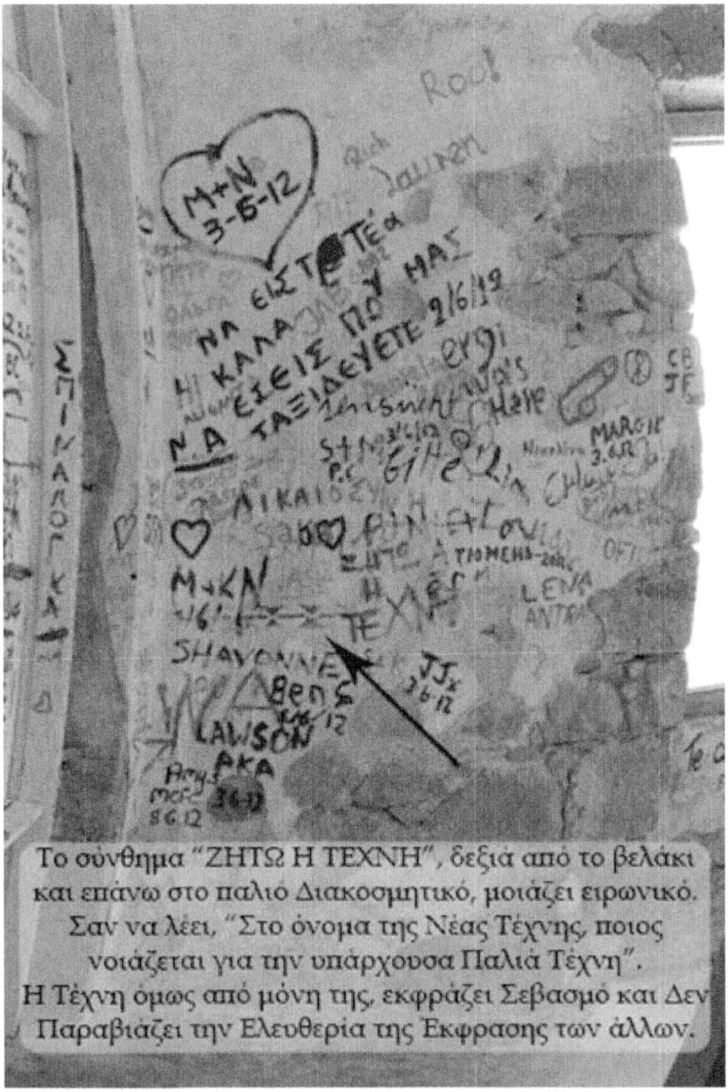

Το σύνθημα "ΖΗΤΩ Η ΤΕΧΝΗ", δεξιά από το βελάκι
και επάνω στο παλιό Διακοσμητικό, μοιάζει ειρωνικό.
Σαν να λέει, "Στο όνομα της Νέας Τέχνης, ποιος
νοιάζεται για την υπάρχουσα Παλιά Τέχνη".
Η Τέχνη όμως από μόνη της, εκφράζει Σεβασμό και Δεν
Παραβιάζει την Ελευθερία της Έκφρασης των άλλων.

One hopes that, over time, the real art of Spinalonga, which is scattered all over the small islet, will be recorded, preserved and showcased. The following images depict some of the peculiar "art" of Spinalonga.

Rock art. Images carved in the soft limestone all over the islet depict various games, boats, aeroplanes or whatever else the islanders saw or felt while spending time at those sites. According to Kostis Spithas, one of the images may portray the eruption of the volcano on Santorini. A flower carved in the stone steps of a house reveals that an islander devoted some of his or her time to aesthetic concerns. These images, the decorative motifs in the sanatorium and the elaborate wood and stone constructions found all across the islet, together comprise a vast and valuable historical-artistic "installation". One can still trace games of tic-tac-toe and other games carved in the limestone next to the Mezzaluna Bastion, unchanged from the day one of the islanders sat there and patiently carved them, an islander with a thirst for life, physical and mental health, joy, love, peace and freedom. Personal archives of Anna Giakoumaki.

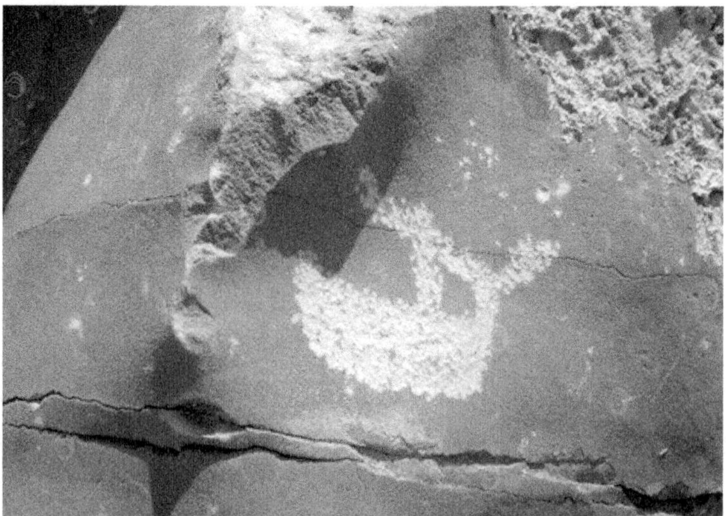

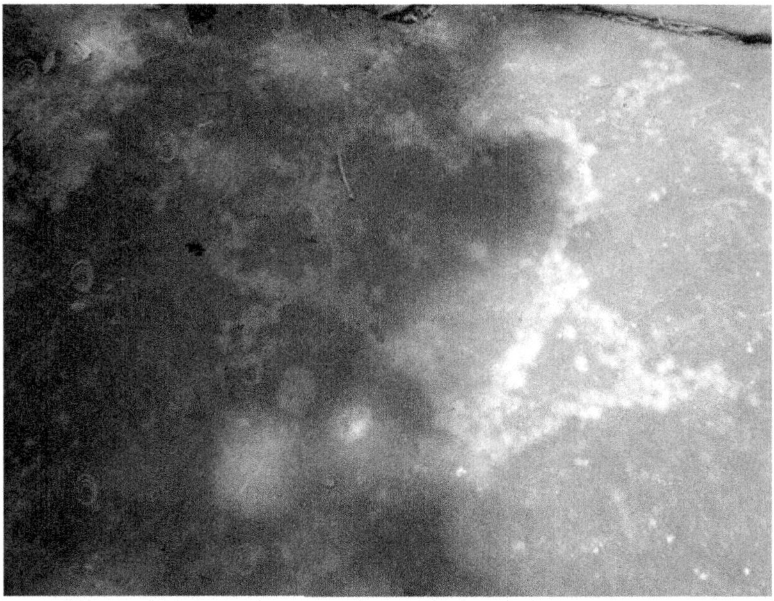

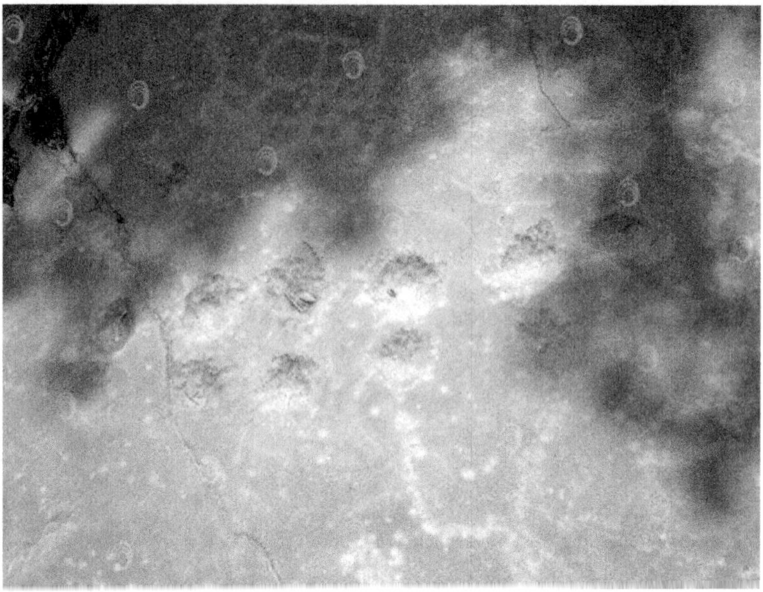

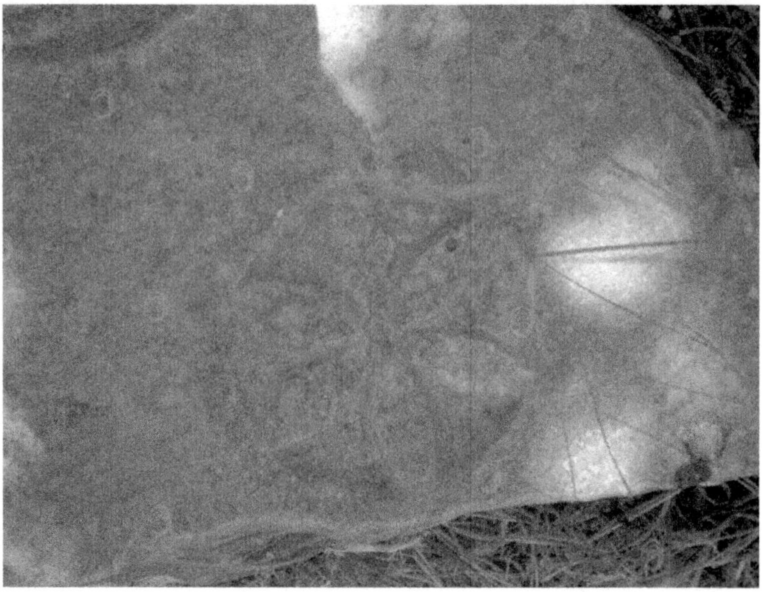

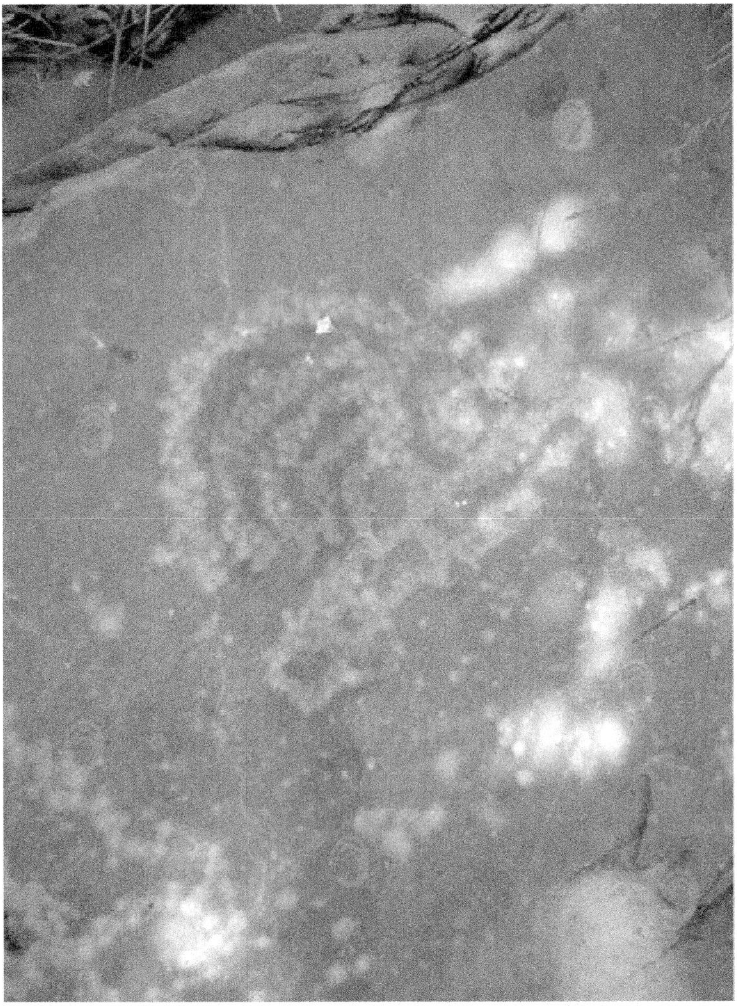

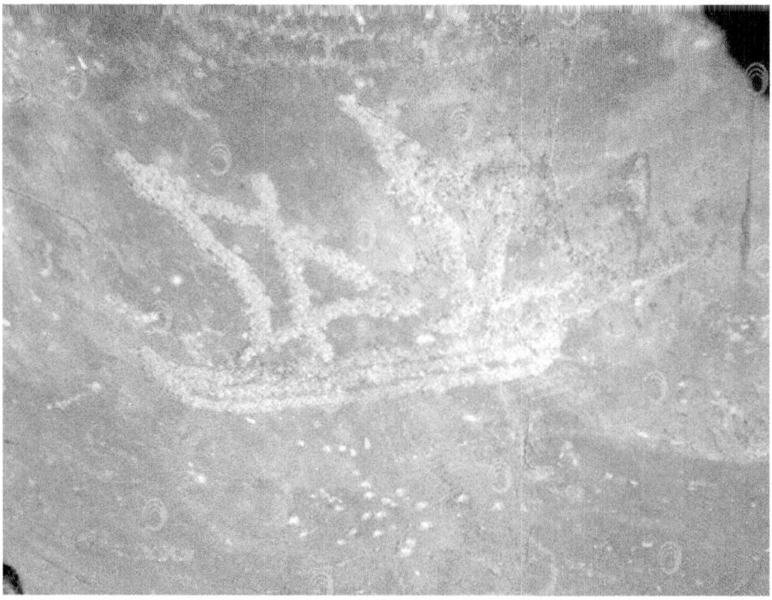

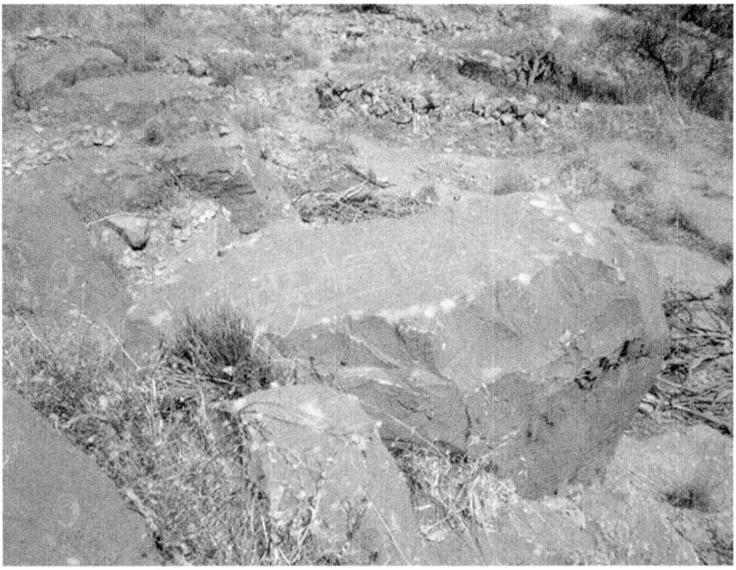

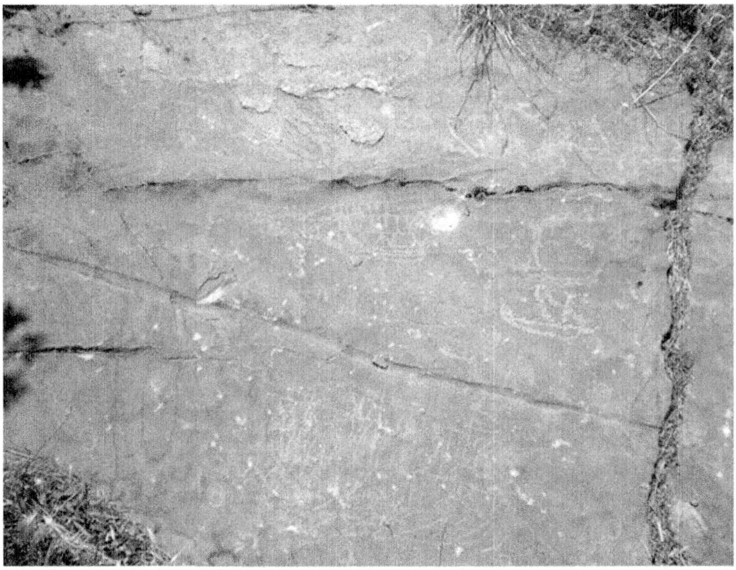

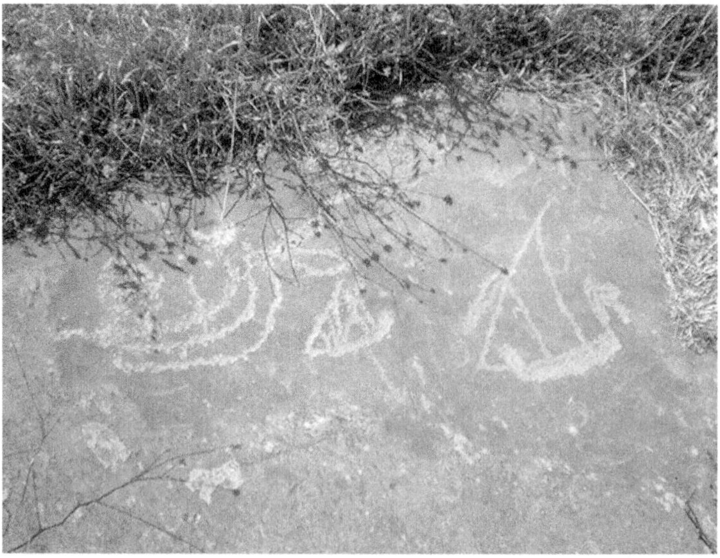

A photograph taken by Anna Giakoumaki, in 2007 shows the phrase "This is the 20th century's Golgotha" painted in white on the sanatorium wall. Personal archives of Anna Giakoumaki.

Section B

Excerpts from various documents from the archives of Anna Giakoumaki.

ΔΙΑΤΑΓΜΑ

Περὶ διακανονισμοῦ τῶν τῆς ἐσωτερικῆς ὑπηρεσίας τοῦ Λεπροκομείου.

ΗΜΕΙΣ ΠΡΙΓΚΗΨ ΓΕΩΡΓΙΟΣ ΤΗΣ ΕΛΛΑΔΟΣ

Ὕπατος Ἁρμοστὴς ἐν Κρήτῃ

Ἔχοντες ὑπ' ὄψει τὸ ἄρθρον 7 τοῦ ὑπ' ἀριθ. 375 Νόμου καὶ τὸν ὑπ' ἀριθ. 463 Νόμον, προτάσει τοῦ Ἡμετέρου ἐπὶ τῶν Ἐσωτερικῶν Συμβούλου,

Ἀποφασίζομεν καὶ διατάσσομεν:

Ἄρθρον 1. Ἀπὸ τῆς ἐγκαταστάσεως τῶν λεπρῶν ἐν Σπίνᾳ Λόγγᾳ πᾶσα ἐπικοινωνία αὐτῶν μετὰ τῆς Νήσου ἢ τοῦ ἐξωτερικοῦ ἐκτελεῖται ὡς ὁρίζει τὸ 5 ἄρθρον τοῦ ὑπ' ἀριθ. 375 Νόμου.

Ἐπιτρέπεται νὰ ἐπικοινωνῇ μετὰ τῆς Νήσου τὸ προσωπικὸν τῆς ὑπηρεσίας τοῦ λεπροκομείου· συγγενεῖς τῶν λεπρῶν δύνανται νὰ ἐπισκέπτωνται αὐτοὺς ἐν τῷ Λεπροκομείῳ προηγου-

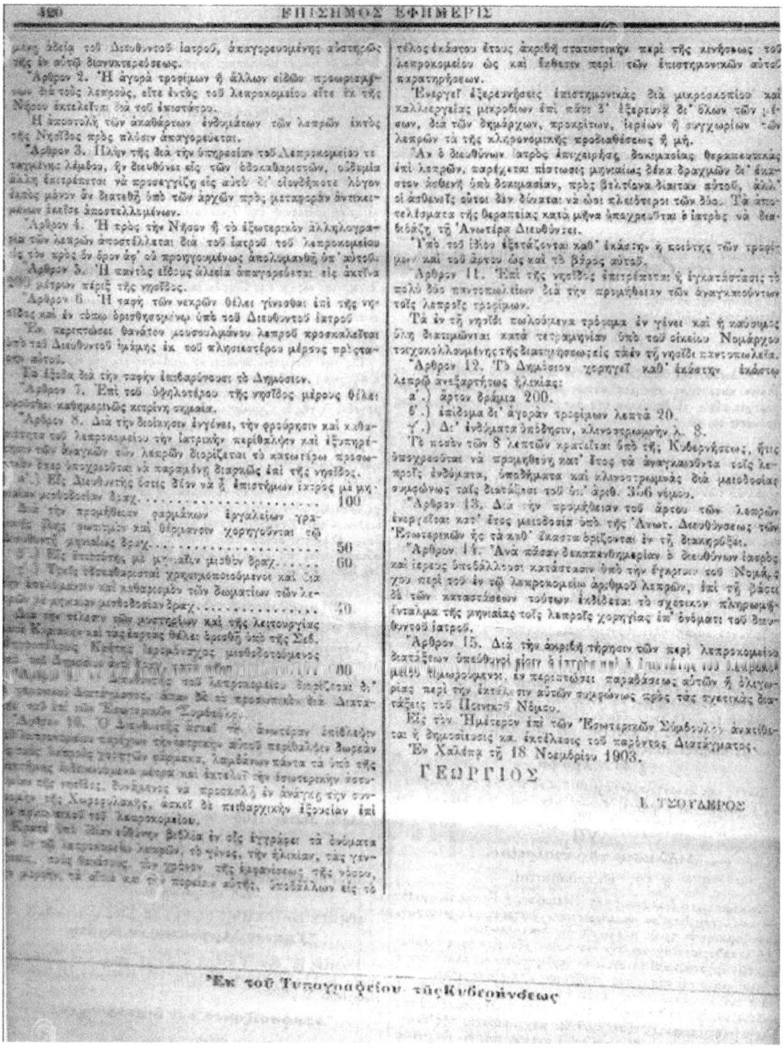

420 ΕΠΙΣΗΜΟΣ ΕΦΗΜΕΡΙΣ

τέλος εκάστου έτους ακριβή στατιστικήν περί της κινήσεως του λεπροκομείου ως και έκθεσιν περί των επιστημονικών αυτού παρατηρήσεων.

Ἐνεργεῖ ἐξερευνήσεις ἐπιστημονικάς διὰ μικροσκοπίου καὶ καλλιεργείας μικροβίων ἐπὶ πάντ[illegible] ἐξερευνᾷ δι' ὅλων τῶν μέσων, διὰ τῶν δημάρχων, προκρίτων, ἱερέων ἢ συγχωρίων τῶν λεπρῶν τὰ τῆς κληρονομικῆς προδιαθέσεως ἢ μή.

Ἂν ὁ διευθύνων ἰατρὸς ἐπιχειρήσῃ δοκιμασίας θεραπευτικὰς ἐπὶ λεπρῶν, παρέχεται πίστωσις μηνιαίως δέκα δραχμῶν δι' ἕκαστον ἀσθενῆ ὑπὸ δοκιμασίαν, πρὸς βελτίωσιν δίαιταν αὐτοῦ, ἀλλ' οἱ ἀσθενεῖς οὗτοι δὲν δύνανται νὰ ὦσι πλειότεροι τῶν δύο. Τὰ ἀποτελέσματα τῆς θεραπείας κατὰ μῆνα ὑποχρεοῦται ὁ ἰατρὸς νὰ διαβιβάζῃ τῇ Ἀνωτέρᾳ Διευθύνσει.

Ὑπὸ τοῦ ἰδίου ἐξετάζονται καθ' ἑκάστην ἡ ποιότης τῶν τροφίμων καὶ τοῦ ἄρτου ὡς καὶ τὸ βάρος αὐτοῦ.

Ἄρθρον 11. Ἐπὶ τῆς νησῖδος ἐπιτρέπεται ἡ ἐγκατάστασις τὸ πολὺ δύο παντοπωλείων διὰ τὴν προμήθειαν τῶν ἀναγκαιούντων τοῖς λεπροῖς τροφίμων.

Τὰ ἐν τῇ νησῖδι πωλούμενα τρόφιμα ἐν γένει καὶ ἡ καύσιμος ὕλη διατιμῶνται κατὰ τετραμηνίαν ὑπὸ τοῦ οἰκείου Νομάρχου τοιχοκολλουμένης τῆς διατιμήσεως εἰς τὰ ἐν τῇ νησῖδι παντοπωλεῖα.

Ἄρθρον 12. Τὸ Δημόσιον χορηγεῖ καθ' ἑκάστην ἑκάστῳ λεπρῷ ἀνεξαρτήτως ἡλικίας:

α'.) ἄρτον δράμια 200.

β'.) ἐπίδομα δι' ἀγορὰν τροφίμων λεπτὰ 20.

γ'.) Δι' ἐνδύματα ὑπόδησιν, κλινοστρωμνὴν λ. 8.

Τὸ ποσὸν τῶν 8 λεπτῶν κρατεῖται ὑπὸ τῆς Κυβερνήσεως, ἥτις ὑποχρεοῦται νὰ προμηθεύῃ κατ' ἔτος τὰ ἀναγκαιοῦντα τοῖς λεπροῖς ἐνδύματα, ὑποδήματα καὶ κλινοστρωμνὰς διὰ μειοδοσίας συμφώνως ταῖς διατάξεσι τοῦ ὑπ' ἀριθ. 356 νόμου.

Ἄρθρον 13. Διὰ τὴν προμήθειαν τοῦ ἄρτου τῶν λεπρῶν ἐνεργεῖται κατ' ἔτος μειοδοσία ὑπὸ τῆς Ἀνωτ. Διευθύνσεως τῶν Ἐσωτερικῶν ἧς τὰ καθ' ἕκαστα ὁρίζονται ἐν τῇ διακηρύξει.

Ἄρθρον 14. Ἀνὰ πᾶσαν δεκαπενθημερίαν ὁ διευθύνων ἰατρὸς καὶ ἱερεὺς ὑποβάλλουσι κατάστασιν ὑπὸ τὴν ἔγκρισιν τοῦ Νομάρχου περὶ τοῦ ἐν τῷ λεπροκομείῳ ἀριθμοῦ λεπρῶν, ἐπὶ τῇ βάσει δὲ τῶν καταστάσεων τούτων ἐκδίδεται τὸ σχετικὸν πληρωμῆς ἔνταλμα τῆς μηνιαίας τοῖς λεπροῖς χορηγίας ἐπ' ὀνόματι τοῦ διευθυντοῦ ἰατροῦ.

Ἄρθρον 15. Διὰ τὴν ἀκριβῆ τήρησιν τῶν περὶ λεπροκομείου διατάξεων ὑπεύθυνοι εἰσὶν ὁ ἰατρὸς καὶ ὁ [illegible] τοῦ λεπροκομείου [illegible], ἐν περιπτώσει παραβάσεως αὐτῶν ἢ ὀλιγωρίας περὶ τὴν ἐκτέλεσιν αὐτῶν συμφώνως πρὸς τὰς σχετικὰς διατάξεις τοῦ Ποινικοῦ Νόμου.

Εἰς τὸν Ἡμέτερον ἐπὶ τῶν Ἐσωτερικῶν Σύμβουλον ἀνατίθεται ἡ δημοσίευσις και ἐκτέλεσις τοῦ παρόντος Διατάγματος.

Ἐν Χαλέπᾳ τῇ 18 Νοεμβρίου 1903.

ΓΕΩΡΓΙΟΣ

Ι. ΤΣΟΥΓΑΡΟΣ

Ἐκ τοῦ Τυπογραφείου τῆς Κυβερνήσεως

O.G.G.C.S., Year E', 1903, pp. 419 & 420, Decree on the internal operation of the leper colony. In 1901, the Cretan State passed Law 375 "Law on the Isolation of Lepers" (O.G.G.C.S., Year B', p.44, 12 July 1901), declaring that lepers should be isolated somewhere, without proposing a specific location. The leper colony of Spinalonga was established in 1903, following a decree of the newly established Cretan State (1900-1913) signed by Eleftherios Venizelos. Law 463 "Law on the Settlement of the Lepers of Crete" (O.G.G.C.S., Year C', p. 25, 7 June 1903) identified Spinalonga as the place where the lepers of Crete were to be settled. Laws and Decrees passed prior to the "Decree on the internal operation of the leper colony" were as follows:

a) Law 375/1901, which stated that the lepers had to be isolated somewhere.
b) Decree of 1903 & Law 463/1903, which identified Spinalonga as the place where the lepers of Crete were to be settled.
c) Decree on the internal operation of the leper colony, 1903, which defined how the leper colony of Spinalonga was to operate.
On 13 October 1904, the first 251 lepers (148 men and 103 women) settled on the islet of Spinalonga. According to Michail Katapotis, by 22 December 1926, a total of 730 people had been admitted to the leper colony. 465 of them died; 28 were found to be healthy and were released, while 16 escaped, never to return or be captured by the authorities. During this same period of time, as a result of marriages which took place on the islet, 39 children were born, 16 of whom died. The high mortality rate observed from 1904 to 1930 was

mainly due to the lack of medical supplies and equipment; the absence of a hospital and specialised units for the sick; the lack of medical, nursing and support staff; malnutrition and unsanitary living conditions. Spinalonga had not been built as an infirmary but as a fortress, and there was no need for a hospital on the islet before the lepers were sent there. The previous inhabitants of the islet, the Turk ish squires, were healthy and able to travel to the mainland to see a doctor if the need arose.

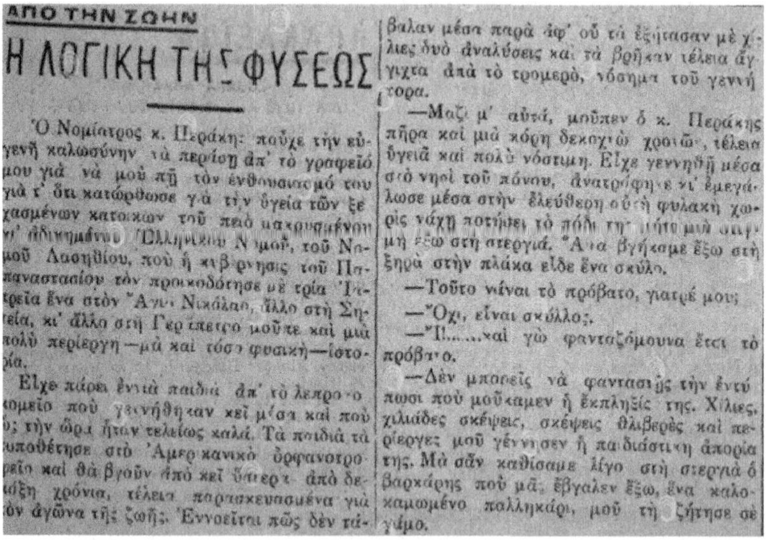

ΑΠΟ ΤΗΝ ΖΩΗΝ

Η ΛΟΓΙΚΗ ΤΗΣ ΦΥΣΕΩΣ

Ὁ Νομίατρος κ. Περάκης πούχε τὴν εὐγενῆ καλωσύνην νὰ περάσῃ ἀπ' τὸ γραφεῖό μου γιὰ νὰ μοῦ πῇ τὸν ἐνθουσιασμό του γιὰ τ' ὅτι κατώρθωσε γιὰ τὴν ὑγεία τῶν ξεχασμένων κατοίκων τοῦ πειὸ [illegible] Ἑλληνικοῦ Νησιοῦ, τοῦ Νησιοῦ Λασηθίου, ποὺ ἡ κυβέρνησις τοῦ Πανασταναστικοῦ τὸν προικοδότησε μὲ τρία Ἰατρεῖα ἕνα στὸν Ἅγιο Νικόλαο, ἄλλο στὴ Σητεία, κι' ἄλλο στὴ Γεράπετρο μοῦπε καὶ μιὰ πολὺ περίεργη—μὰ καὶ τόσο φυσική—ἱστορία.

Εἶχε πάρει ἐννιὰ παιδιὰ ἀπ' τὸ λεπροκομεῖο ποὺ γεννήθηκαν κεῖ μέσα καὶ ποὺ τὴν ὥρα ἦταν τελείως καλά. Τὰ παιδιὰ τὰ ὑποθέτησε στὸ Ἀμερικανικὸ ὀρφανοτροφεῖο καὶ θὰ βγοῦν ἀπὸ κεῖ ὕστερα ἀπὸ δεκάξη χρόνια, τέλεια παρασκευασμένα γιὰ τὸν ἀγῶνα τῆς ζωῆς. Ἐννοεῖται πῶς δὲν τάβαλαν μέσα παρὰ ἀφ' οὗ τὰ ἐξήτασαν μὲ χίλιες δυὸ ἀναλύσεις καὶ τὰ βρῆκαν τέλεια ἄγγιχτα ἀπὰ τὸ τρομερό, νόσημα τοῦ γεννήτορα.

—Μαζὶ μ' αὐτά, μοῦπεν ὁ κ. Περάκης πῆρα καὶ μιὰ κόρη δεκοχτὼ χρονῶν, τέλεια ὑγειᾶ καὶ πολὺ νόστιμη. Εἶχε γεννηθῇ μέσα στὸ νησὶ τοῦ πόνου, ἀνατράφηκε κι' ἐμεγάλωσε μέσα στὴν ἐλεύθερη αὐτὴ φυλακὴ χωρὶς νάχῃ ποτέ [illegible] μη ἔξω στὴ στεργιά. Ἅμα βγήκαμε ἔξω στὴ ξηρὰ στὴν πλάκα εἶδε ἕνα σκύλο.

—Τοῦτο νεἶναι τὸ πρόβατο, γιατρέ μου;

—Ὄχι, εἶναι σκύλος.

—Π......καὶ γὼ φανταζόμουνα ἔτσι τὸ πρόβατο.

—Δὲν μπορεῖς νὰ φαντασθῇς τὴν ἐντύπωσι ποὺ μοὖκαμεν ἡ ἔκπληξίς της. Χίλιες, χιλιάδες σκέψεις, σκέψεις θλιβερὲς καὶ περίεργες μοῦ γέννησεν ἡ παιδιάστικη ἀπορία της. Μὰ σὰν καθίσαμε λίγο στὴ στεργιὰ ὁ βαρκάρης ποὺ μᾶς ἔβγαλεν ἔξω, ἕνα καλοκαμωμένο παλληκάρι, μοῦ τὴ ζήτησε σὲ γάμο.

When an 18-year-old girl, who was born and lived her entire life in the "open prison" of Spinalonga, first stepped out into the "real world", she saw a dog and mistook it for a sheep. Article published in "Nea Efimeris", 2 February 1924.

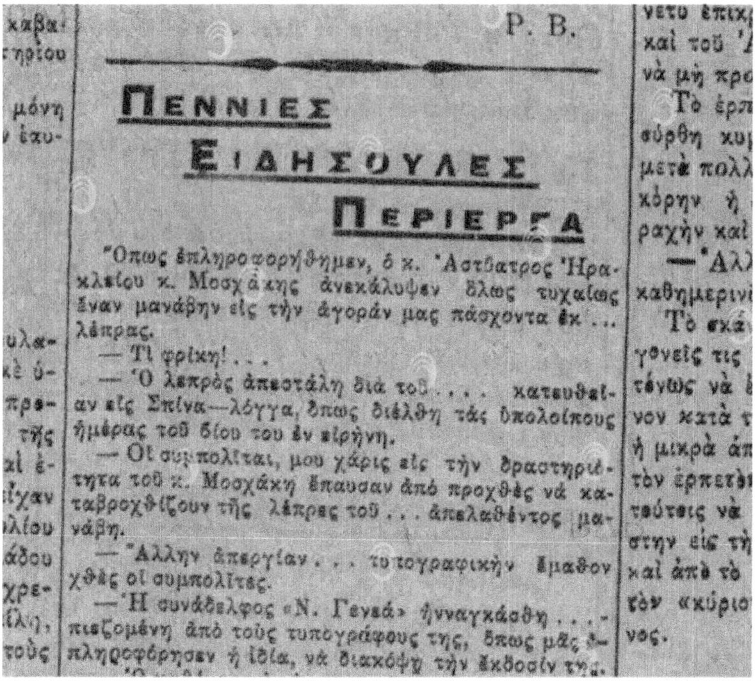

P. B.

ΠΕΝΝΙΕΣ
ΕΙΔΗΣΟΥΛΕΣ
ΠΕΡΙΕΡΓΑ

Ὅπως ἐπληροφορήθημεν, ὁ κ. Ἀστίατρος Ἡρακλείου κ. Μοσχάκης ἀνεκάλυψεν ὅλως τυχαίως ἕναν μανάβην εἰς τὴν ἀγορὰν μας πάσχοντα ἐκ ... λέπρας.

— Τί φρίκη!...

— Ὁ λεπρὸς ἀπεστάλη διὰ τοῦ .... κατευθεῖαν εἰς Σπίνα—λόγγα, ὅπως διέλθῃ τὰς ὑπολοίπους ἡμέρας τοῦ βίου του ἐν εἰρήνῃ.

— Οἱ συμπολῖται, μου χάρις εἰς τὴν δραστηριότητα τοῦ κ. Μοσχάκη ἔπαυσαν ἀπὸ προχθὲς νὰ καταβροχθίζουν τῆς λέπρας τοῦ ... ἀπελαθέντος μανάβη.

— Ἄλλην ἀπεργίαν ... τυπογραφικὴν ἔμαθον χθὲς οἱ συμπολῖτες.

— Ἡ συνάδελφος «Ν. Γενεά» ἠναγκάσθη ... πιεζομένη ἀπὸ τοὺς τυπογράφους της, ὅπως μᾶς ἐπληροφόρησαν ἡ ἰδία, νὰ διακόψῃ τὴν ἔκδοσίν της.

The social exclusion and discrimination lepers had to endure is clearly evident in the journalist's words: "We were informed that Dr. Moshakis, Heraklion's Municipal Doctor, accidentally came across a greengrocer in our market who suffers from... leprosy. How horrendous! The leper was sent by... straight to Spinalonga, where he will live out the remainder of his days in peace.
Thanks to Dr. Moshakis' actions two days ago, our fellow-citizens will no longer consume the now-deported greengrocer's filth." Article in "Esperini", 19 February 1925.

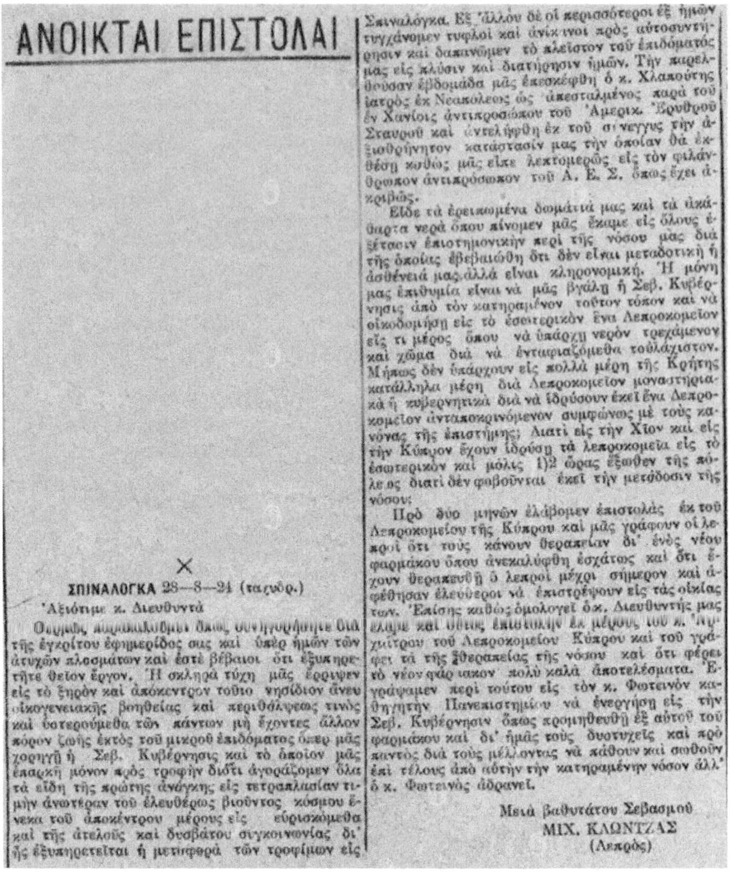

ΑΝΟΙΚΤΑΙ ΕΠΙΣΤΟΛΑΙ

×

ΣΠΙΝΑΛΟΓΚΑ 28—8—24 (ταχυδρ.)

Ἀξιότιμε κ. Διευθυντά

Θερμῶς παρακαλοῦμεν ὅπως συνηγορήσητε διὰ τῆς ἐγκρίτου ἐφημερίδος σας καὶ ὑπὲρ ἡμῶν τῶν ἀτυχῶν πλασμάτων καὶ ἔστε βέβαιοι ὅτι ἐξυπηρετῆτε θεῖον ἔργον. Ἡ σκληρὰ τύχη μᾶς ἔρριψεν εἰς τὸ ξηρὸν καὶ ἀπόκεντρον τοῦτο νησίδιον ἄνευ οἰκογενειακῆς βοηθείας καὶ περιθάλψεως τινὸς καὶ ὑστερούμεθα τῶν πάντων μὴ ἔχοντες ἄλλον πόρον ζωῆς ἐκτὸς τοῦ μικροῦ ἐπιδόματος ὅπερ μᾶς χορηγῇ ἡ Σεβ. Κυβέρνησις καὶ τὸ ὁποῖον μᾶς ἐπαρκῆ μόνον πρὸς τροφὴν διότι ἀγοράζομεν ὅλα τὰ εἴδη τῆς πρώτης ἀνάγκης εἰς τετραπλασίαν τιμὴν ἀνωτέραν τοῦ ἐλευθέρως βιοῦντος κόσμου ἕνεκα τοῦ ἀποκέντρου μέρους εἰς ὃ εὑρισκόμεθα καὶ τῆς ἀτελοῦς καὶ δυσβάτου συγκοινωνίας δι' ἧς ἐξυπηρετεῖται ἡ μεταφορὰ τῶν τροφίμων εἰς Σπιναλόγκα. Ἐξ ἄλλου δὲ οἱ περισσότεροι ἐξ ἡμῶν τυγχάνομεν τυφλοὶ καὶ ἀνίκανοι πρὸς αὐτοσυντήρησιν καὶ δαπανῶμεν τὸ πλεῖστον τοῦ ἐπιδόματός μας εἰς πλύσιν καὶ διατήρησιν ἡμῶν. Τὴν παρελθοῦσαν ἑβδομάδα μᾶς ἐπεσκέφθη ὁ κ. Χλαπούτης ἰατρὸς ἐκ Νεαπόλεως ὡς ἀπεσταλμένος παρὰ τοῦ ἐν Χανίοις ἀντιπροσώπου τοῦ Ἀμερικ. Ἐρυθροῦ Σταυροῦ καὶ ἀντελήφθη ἐκ τοῦ σύνεγγυς τὴν ἀξιοθρήνητον κατάστασίν μας τὴν ὁποίαν θὰ ἐκθέσῃ καθὼς μᾶς εἶπε λεπτομερῶς εἰς τὸν φιλάνθρωπον ἀντιπρόσωπον τοῦ Α. Ε. Σ. ὅπως ἔχει ἀκριβῶς.

Εἶδε τὰ ἐρειπωμένα δωμάτιά μας καὶ τὰ ἀκάθαρτα νερὰ ὅπου πίνομεν μᾶς ἔκαμε εἰς ὅλους ἐξέτασιν ἐπιστημονικὴν περὶ τῆς νόσου μας διὰ τῆς ὁποίας ἐβεβαιώθη ὅτι δὲν εἶναι μεταδοτικὴ ἡ ἀσθένειά μας ἀλλὰ εἶναι κληρονομική. Ἡ μόνη μας ἐπιθυμία εἶναι νὰ μᾶς βγάλῃ ἡ Σεβ. Κυβέρνησις ἀπὸ τὸν κατηραμένον τοῦτον τόπον καὶ νὰ οἰκοδομήσῃ εἰς τὸ ἐσωτερικὸν ἕνα Λεπροκομεῖον εἴς τι μέρος ὅπου νὰ ὑπάρχῃ νερὸν τρεχάμενον καὶ χῶμα διὰ νὰ ἐνταφιαζόμεθα τοὐλάχιστον. Μήπως δὲν ὑπάρχουν εἰς πολλὰ μέρη τῆς Κρήτης κατάλληλα μέρη διὰ Λεπροκομεῖον μοναστηριακὰ ἢ κυβερνητικὰ διὰ νὰ ἱδρύσουν ἐκεῖ ἕνα Λεπροκομεῖον ἀνταποκρινόμενον συμφώνως μὲ τοὺς κανόνας τῆς ἐπιστήμης; Διατί εἰς τὴν Χίον καὶ εἰς τὴν Κύπρον ἔχουν ἱδρύσῃ τὰ λεπροκομεῖα εἰς τὸ ἐσωτερικὸν καὶ μόλις 1)2 ὥρας ἔξωθεν τῆς πόλεως διατί δὲν φοβοῦνται ἐκεῖ τὴν μετάδοσιν τῆς νόσου;

Πρὸ δύο μηνῶν ἐλάβομεν ἐπιστολὰς ἐκ τοῦ Λεπροκομείου τῆς Κύπρου καὶ μᾶς γράφουν οἱ λεπροὶ ὅτι τοὺς κάνουν θεραπείαν δι' ἑνὸς νέου φαρμάκου ὅπου ἀνεκαλύφθη ἐσχάτως καὶ ὅτι ἔχουν θεραπευθῇ 5 λεπροὶ μέχρι σήμερον καὶ ἀφέθησαν ἐλεύθεροι νὰ ἐπιστρέψουν εἰς τὰς οἰκίας των. Ἐπίσης καθὼς ὁμολογεῖ ὁ κ. Διευθυντής μας ἔλαβε καὶ οὗτος ἐπιστολὴν ἐκ μέρους τοῦ κ. Ἀρχιάτρου τοῦ Λεπροκομείου Κύπρου καὶ τοῦ γράφει τὰ τῆς θεραπείας τῆς νόσου καὶ ὅτι φέρει τὸ νέον φάρμακον πολὺ καλὰ ἀποτελέσματα. Ἐγράψαμεν περὶ τούτου εἰς τὸν κ. Φωτεινὸν καθηγητὴν Πανεπιστημίου νὰ ἐνεργήσῃ εἰς τὴν Σεβ. Κυβέρνησιν ὅπως προμηθευθῇ ἐξ αὐτοῦ τοῦ φαρμάκου καὶ δι' ἡμᾶς τοὺς δυστυχεῖς καὶ πρὸ παντὸς διὰ τοὺς μέλλοντας νὰ πάθουν καὶ σωθοῦν ἐπὶ τέλους ἀπὸ αὐτὴν τὴν κατηραμένην νόσον ἀλλ' ὁ κ. Φωτεινὸς ἀδρανεῖ.

Μετὰ βαθυτάτου Σεβασμοῦ

ΜΙΧ. ΚΛΩΝΤΖΑΣ

(Λεπρός)

A leper's letter of complaint regarding the patients' isolation on Spinalonga. He decries the miserable living conditions and mentions that there is no running water or arable land on the islet - and that they are forced to buy goods at four times the regular cost. They request to be transferred to another location in Crete. Letter in "Nea Efimeris", 7 September 1924.

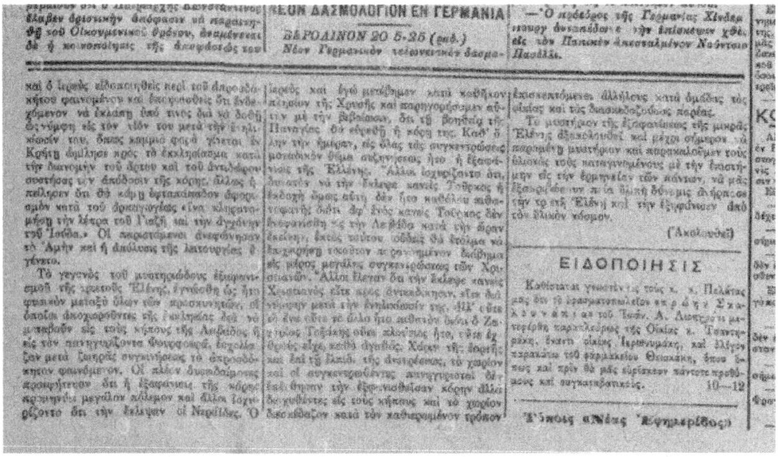
ΝΕΟΝ ΔΑΣΜΟΛΟΓΙΟΝ ΕΝ ΓΕΡΜΑΝΙΑ

ΒΕΡΟΛΙΝΟΝ 20 5-25 (ειδ.)

ΕΙΔΟΠΟΙΗΣΙΣ

(Ἀκολουθεῖ)

Τύποις «Νέας Ἐφημερίδος»

A three-year-old girl had gone missing and was thought to have been abducted. During church service, a priest addressed the congregation and threatened to "put a curse on him (the abductor) to catch leprosy." Curses and imprecations related to leprosy were considered especially severe. Article in "Nea Efimeris", 21 May 1925.

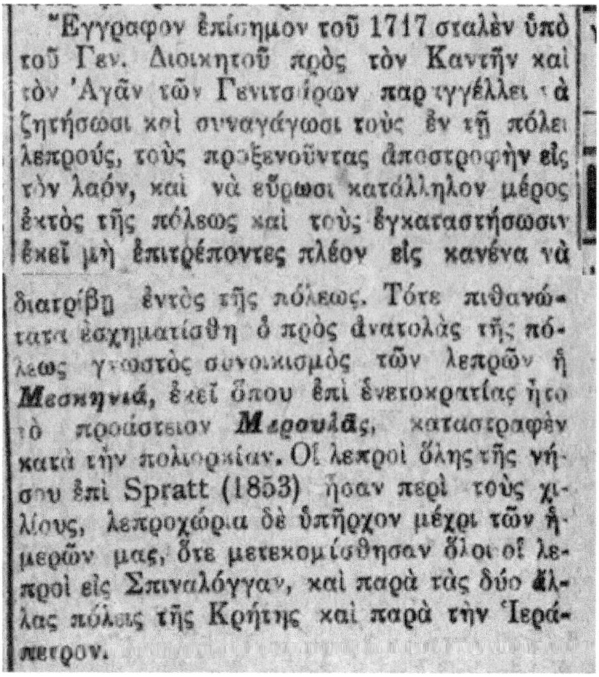

Ἔγγραφον ἐπίσημον τοῦ 1717 σταλὲν ὑπὸ τοῦ Γεν. Διοικητοῦ πρὸς τὸν Καντῆν καὶ τὸν Ἀγᾶν τῶν Γενιτσάρων παραγγέλλει τὰ ζητήσωσι καὶ συναγάγωσι τοὺς ἐν τῇ πόλει λεπρούς, τοὺς προξενοῦντας ἀποστροφὴν εἰς τὸν λαόν, καὶ νὰ εὕρωσι κατάλληλον μέρος ἐκτὸς τῆς πόλεως καὶ τοὺς ἐγκαταστήσωσιν ἐκεῖ μὴ ἐπιτρέποντες πλέον εἰς κανένα νὰ διατρίβῃ ἐντὸς τῆς πόλεως. Τότε πιθανώτατα ἐσχηματίσθη ὁ πρὸς ἀνατολὰς τῆς πόλεως γνωστὸς συνοικισμὸς τῶν λεπρῶν ἡ **Μεσκηνιά**, ἐκεῖ ὅπου ἐπὶ ἐνετοκρατίας ἦτο τὸ προάστειον **Μερουλᾶς**, καταστραφὲν κατὰ τὴν πολιορκίαν. Οἱ λεπροὶ ὅλης τῆς νήσου ἐπὶ Spratt (1853) ἦσαν περὶ τοὺς χιλίους, λεπροχώρια δὲ ὑπῆρχον μέχρι τῶν ἡμερῶν μας, ὅτε μετεκομίσθησαν ὅλοι οἱ λεπροὶ εἰς Σπιναλόγγαν, καὶ παρὰ τὰς δύο ἄλλας πόλεις τῆς Κρήτης καὶ παρὰ τὴν Ἱεράπετρον.

Article on "Meskinia" and how the first lepers were thought to have been settled there. It says: "...An official document from 1717 which was sent by the General Commander to Kantis and the Agha of the Janissaries, instructs them to locate and gather all of the city's lepers, who are an object of disgust and aversion to the people, find a suitable location outside the city for them to settle and not let any of them freely wander within city limits. That is probably when the leper settlement of "Meskinia" was established to the east of the city - where the "Meroulas" suburb was located during the Venetian Occupation, and which was subsequently destroyed during the [Turk ish] siege. Article in "Nea Efimeris", 15 April 1925.

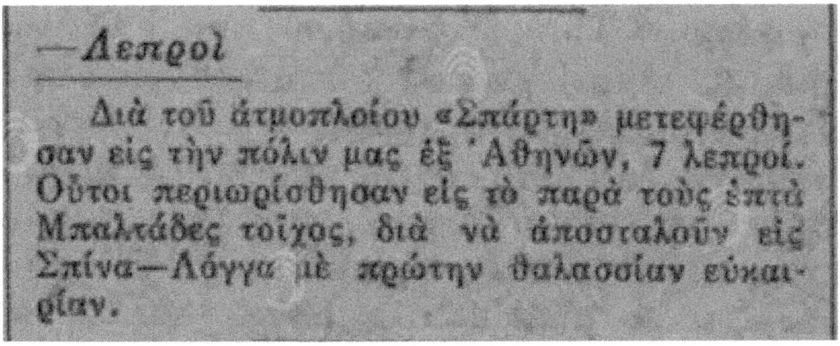

—Λεπροὶ

Διὰ τοῦ ἀτμοπλοίου «Σπάρτη» μετεφέρθησαν εἰς τὴν πόλιν μας ἐξ Ἀθηνῶν, 7 λεπροί. Οὗτοι περιωρίσθησαν εἰς τὸ παρὰ τοὺς ἑπτὰ Μπαλτάδες τοῖχος, διὰ νὰ ἀποσταλοῦν εἰς Σπίνα—Λόγγα μὲ πρώτην θαλασσίαν εὐκαιρίαν.

Lepers from Greece transferred to Spinalonga. "Nea Efimeris", 11 September 1926.

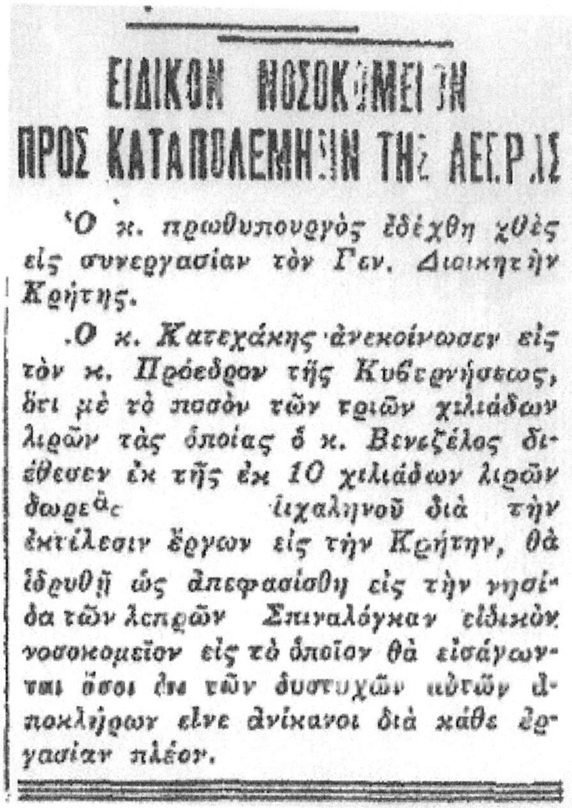

ΕΙΔΙΚΟΝ ΝΟΣΟΚ·ΜΕΙ·ΟΝ
ΠΡΟΣ ΚΑΤΑΠΟΛΕΜΗΣΙΝ ΤΗΣ ΛΕΠΡΑΣ

Ὁ κ. πρωθυπουργὸς ἐδέχθη χθὲς εἰς συνεργασίαν τὸν Γεν. Διοικητὴν Κρήτης.

Ὁ κ. Κατεχάκης ἀνεκοίνωσεν εἰς τὸν κ. Πρόεδρον τῆς Κυβερνήσεως, ὅτι μὲ τὸ ποσὸν τῶν τριῶν χιλιάδων λιρῶν τὰς ὁποίας ὁ κ. Βενιζέλος διέθεσεν ἐκ τῆς ἐκ 10 χιλιάδων λιρῶν δωρεᾶς [illegible]ιχαλινοῦ διὰ τὴν ἐκτέλεσιν ἔργων εἰς τὴν Κρήτην, θὰ ἱδρυθῇ ὡς ἀπεφασίσθη εἰς τὴν νησίδα τῶν λεπρῶν Σπιναλόγκαν εἰδικὸν νοσοκομεῖον εἰς τὸ ὁποῖον θὰ εἰσάγωνται ὅσοι ἐκ τῶν δυστυχῶν αὐτῶν ἀποκλήρων εἶνε ἀνίκανοι διὰ κάθε ἐργασίαν πλέον.

The article reports that a hospital will finally be built on Spinalonga. The first patients were transferred to the islet in 1904. This article, published in "Empros" on 24 November 1928, confirms that there still was no hospital on Spinalonga but that there were plans to build one. It says: "...SPECIALISED HOSPITAL FOR COMBATING LEPROSY. Yesterday, the Prime Minister received the Governor-General of Crete in his office. Mr. Katehakis announced to the Head of the Government that they will use the sum of 3,000 [Turk ish] liras which Mr. Venizelos has set aside from the 10,000 liras which Mr. Mihailinos has donated for the execution of construction works in Crete to establish a specialised hospital on the leper island of Spinalonga to house the unfortunate outcasts who are no longer able to perform physical work or care for themselves..." This marks the beginning of the project to build a hospital or a "sanatorium" as it was called then.

Handwritten receipts of the contractor Konstantinos Tsihlis or Spithas for work executed on Spinalonga. The receipts are dated 1929 & 1930. Personal archives of Anna Giakoumaki.

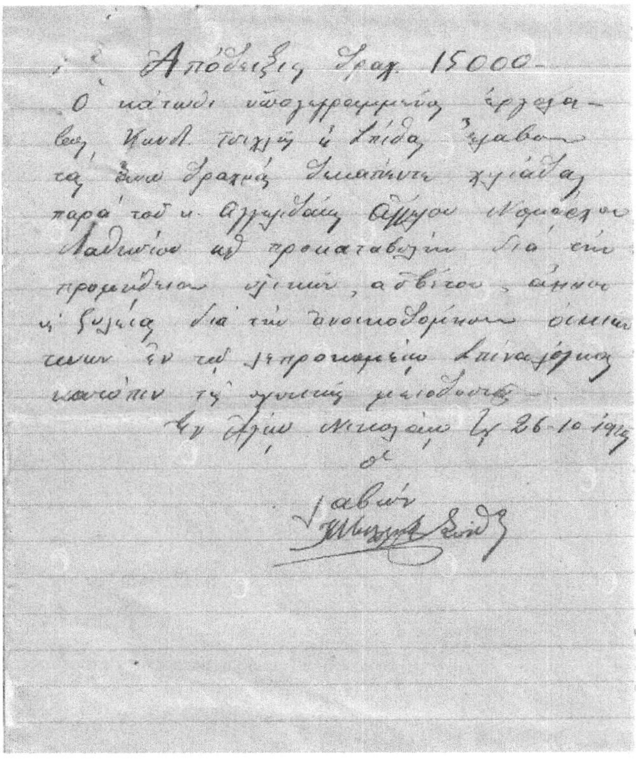

Απόδειξις δραχ. 15000

Ο κάτωθι υπογεγραμμένος εργολάβος Κωνστ. Τσιχλής ή Σπίθας έλαβον τας άνω δραχμάς δεκαπέντε χιλιάδας παρά του κ. [illegible] [illegible] [illegible] Λασιθίου ως προκαταβολήν δια την προμήθειαν [illegible], ασβέστου, άμμου και ξυλείας δια την ανοικοδόμησιν οικημάτων εν τω λεπροκομείω Σπιναλόγκας κατόπιν της [illegible] [illegible]

Εν Αγίω Νικολάω τη 26-10-1929

Ο λαβών

[illegible]

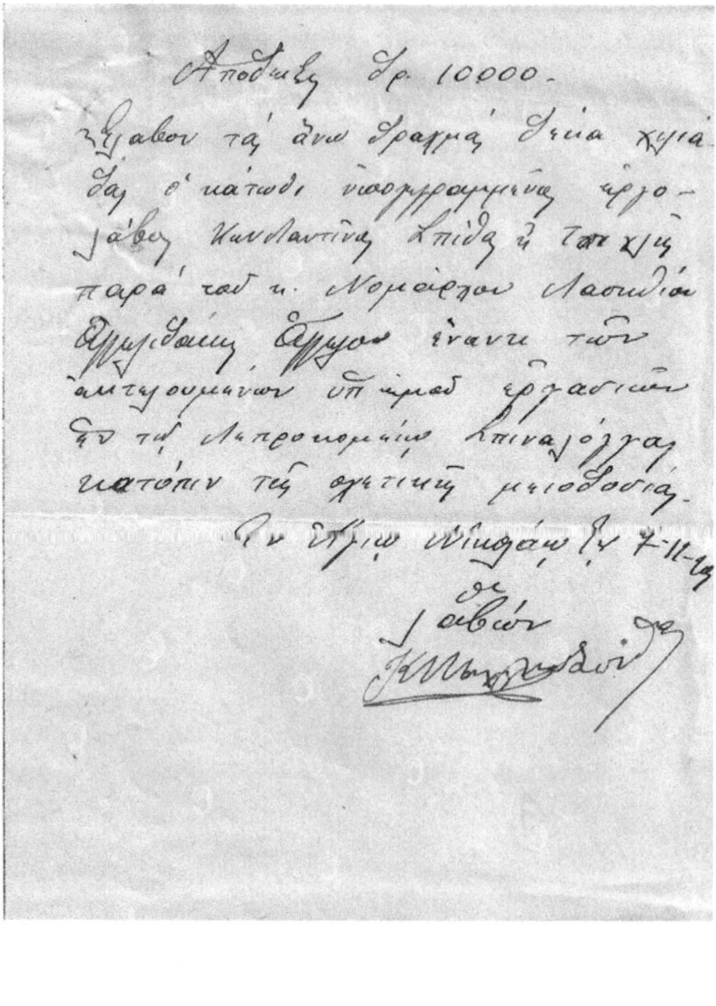

Απόδειξις δρ. 10.000.

Έλαβον τας άνω δραχμάς δέκα χιλιάδας ο κάτωθι υπογεγραμμένος εργολάβος Κωνσταντίνος Σπιθάς ή Τσαχλής παρά του κ. Νομάρχου Λασιθίου [illegible] [illegible] έναντι των εκτελουμένων υπ' εμού εργασιών εν τω Λεπροκομείω Σπιναλόγγας κατόπιν της σχετικής μισθοδοσίας.

Εν Αγίω Νικολάω τη 7-11-19[illegible]

Ο λαβών

[illegible]

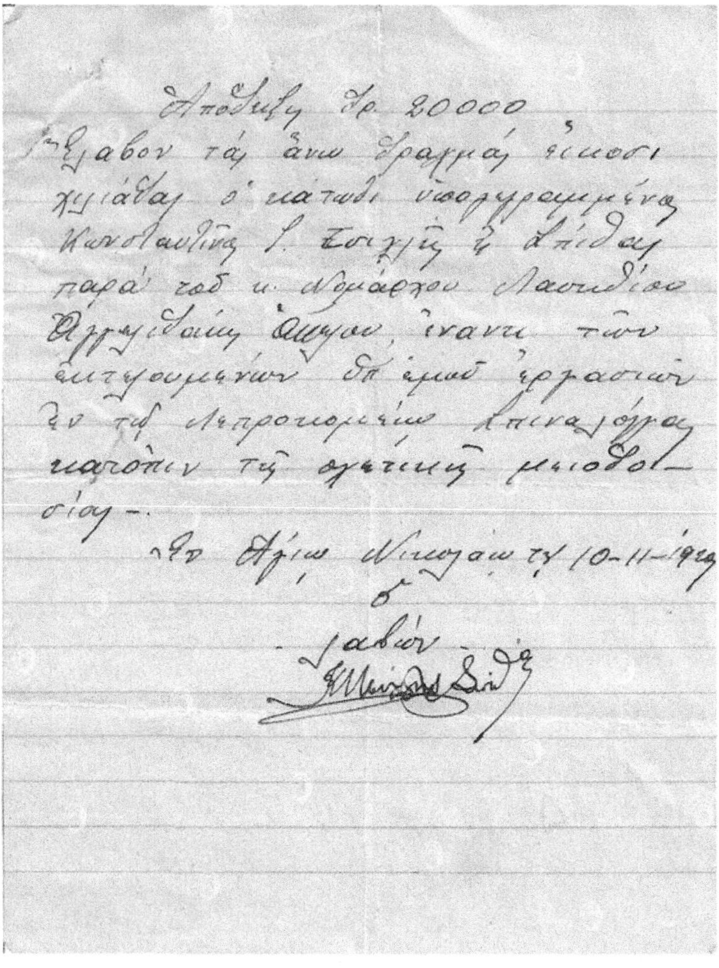

Απόδειξις Δρ. 20000
Έλαβον τάς άνω δραχμάς είκοσι
χιλιάδας ο κάτωθι υπογεγραμμένος
Κωνσταντίνος Ι. Στειχής ή Σπίθας
παρά του κ. Δημάρχου Λασυθίου
Αγγελιδάκη Ομήρου, έναντι των
εκτελουμένων υπ' εμού εργασιών
εν τω Λεπροκομείω Σπιναλόγγας
κατόπιν της σχετικής μισθοδοσίας.
Εν Αγίω Νικολάω τη 10-11-1929
ο
λαβών
[illegible]

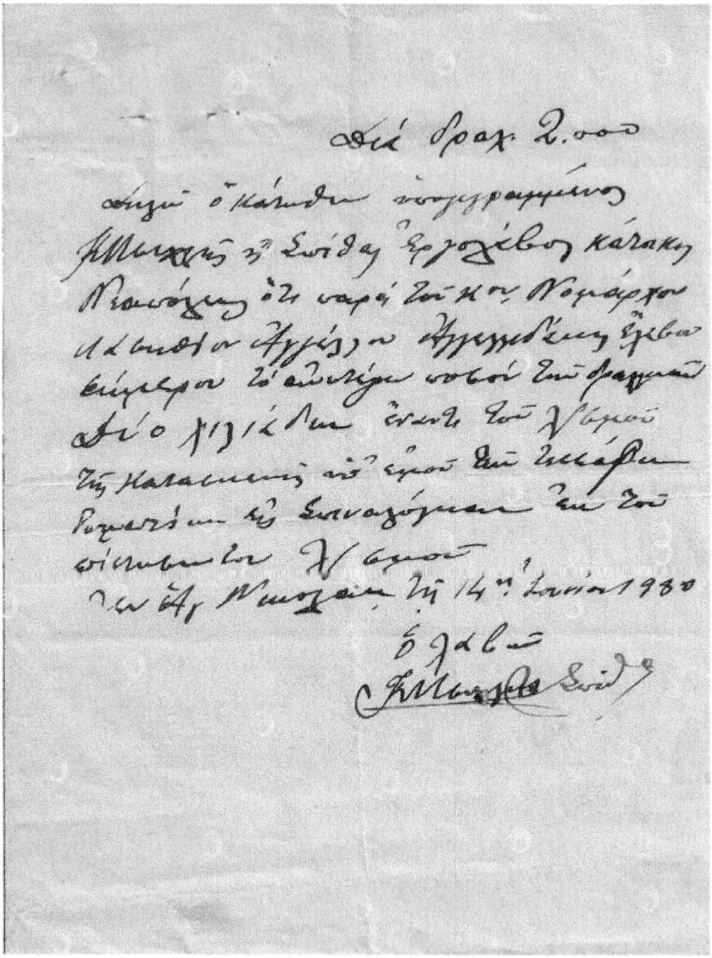
Διά δραχ. 2.000

Δηλώ ὁ κάτωθι ὑπογεγραμμένος
Μιχαήλ Ι. Σωίδας ἐργολάβος κάτοικος
Νεαπόλεως ὅτι παρά τοῦ κ. Νομάρχου
Λασηθίου [illegible] [illegible] ἔλαβον
ἐπί μέρους τό ποσόν [illegible] δραχμῶν
δύο χιλιάδων ἔναντι τοῦ [illegible]
τῆς κατασκευῆς [illegible] [illegible]
[illegible] [illegible] [illegible] τοῦ
[illegible] [illegible]
ἐν Ἁγ. Νικολάῳ τῇ 14ῃ Ἰουνίου 19[illegible]0

ὁ λαβών
Μιχαήλ Σωίδας

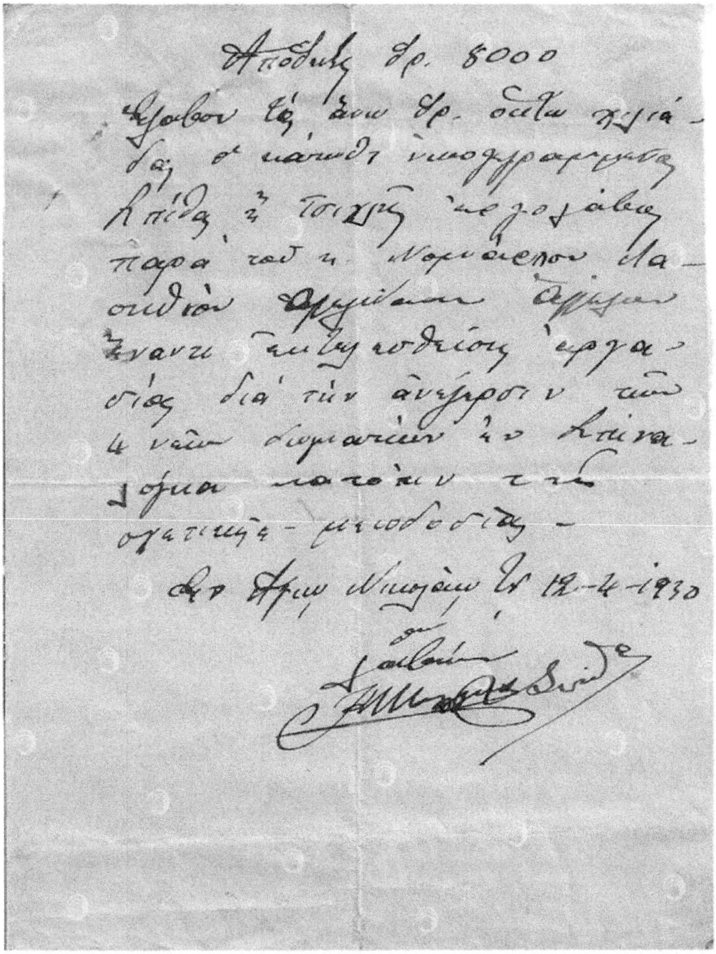

Απόδειξις δρ. 8000

Έλαβον εγώ άνω δρ. οκτώ χιλιάδας ο κάτωθι υπογεγραμμένος
[illegible] ως εργολάβος
παρά του κ. Νομάρχου Λα-
σιθίου [illegible] [illegible]
έναντι [illegible] εργα-
σίας διά την ανέγερσιν των
4 νέων δωματίων εν Σπινα-
λόγκα [illegible] [illegible]
στρατιωτικής μισθοδοσίας

Εν Αγίω Νικολάω τη 12-4-1930

Ο λαβών

[illegible]

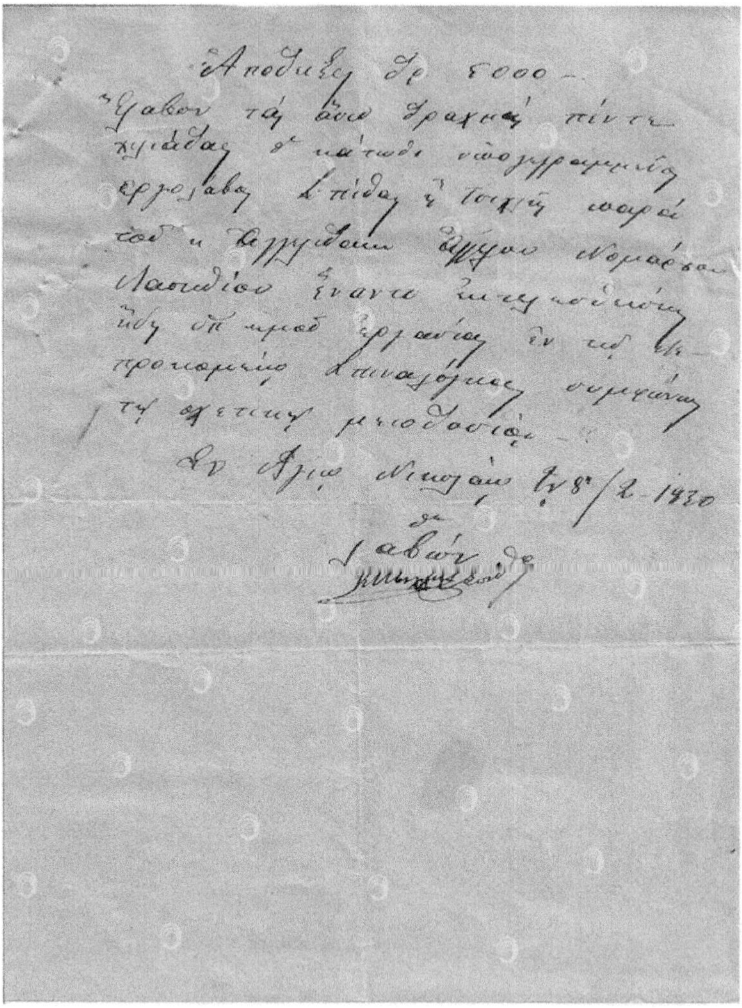

Απόδειξις δρ. 5000 –

Έλαβον τας άνω δραχμάς πέντε χιλιάδας ο κάτωθι υπογεγραμμένος εργολάβος [illegible] παρά του κ. [illegible] Νομάρχου Λασιθίου έναντι [illegible] εργασίας εν τω λεπροκομείω Σπιναλόγγας συμφώνως τη σχετική μισθοδοσία. –

Εν Αγίω Νικολάω τη 8/2-1930

ο λαβών

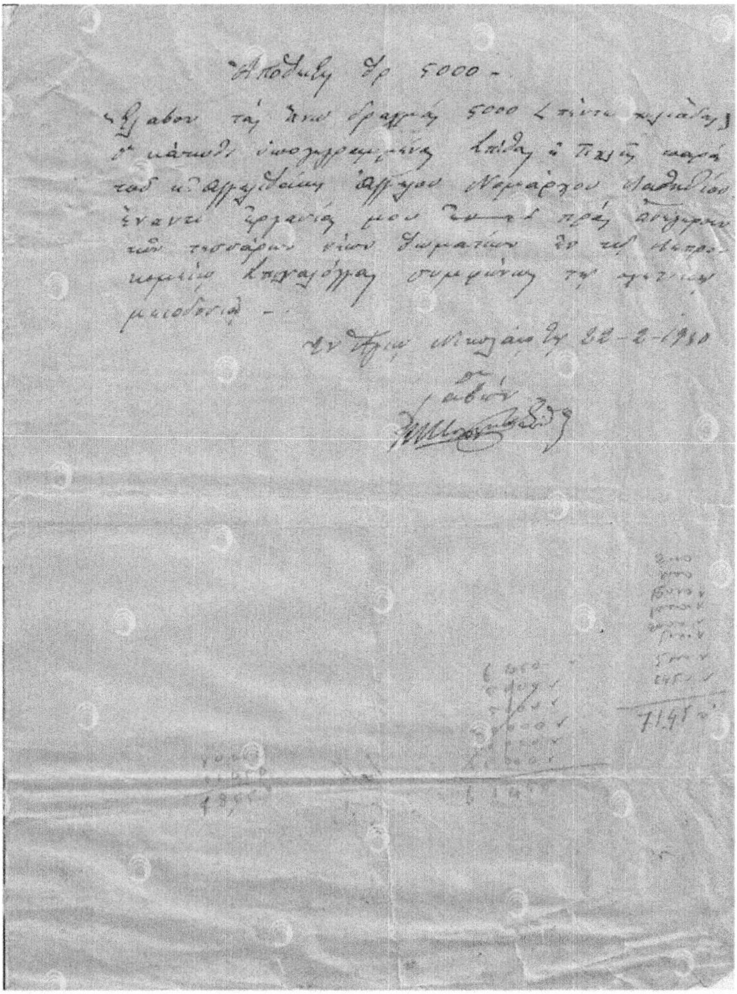

Απόδειξις δρ. 5000-

Έλαβον τας άνω δραχμάς 5000 (πέντε χιλιάδας) ο κάτωθι υπογεγραμμένος [illegible] παρά του κ. [illegible] Νομάρχου Λασηθίου έναντι εργασίας μου [illegible] προς ανέγερσιν των τεσσάρων νέων δωματίων εν τω λεπροκομείω Σπιναλόγγας συμφώνως τη [illegible] μισθοδοσία -

εν [illegible] Μιραμπέλλου 22-2-1930

ο λαβών

[illegible]

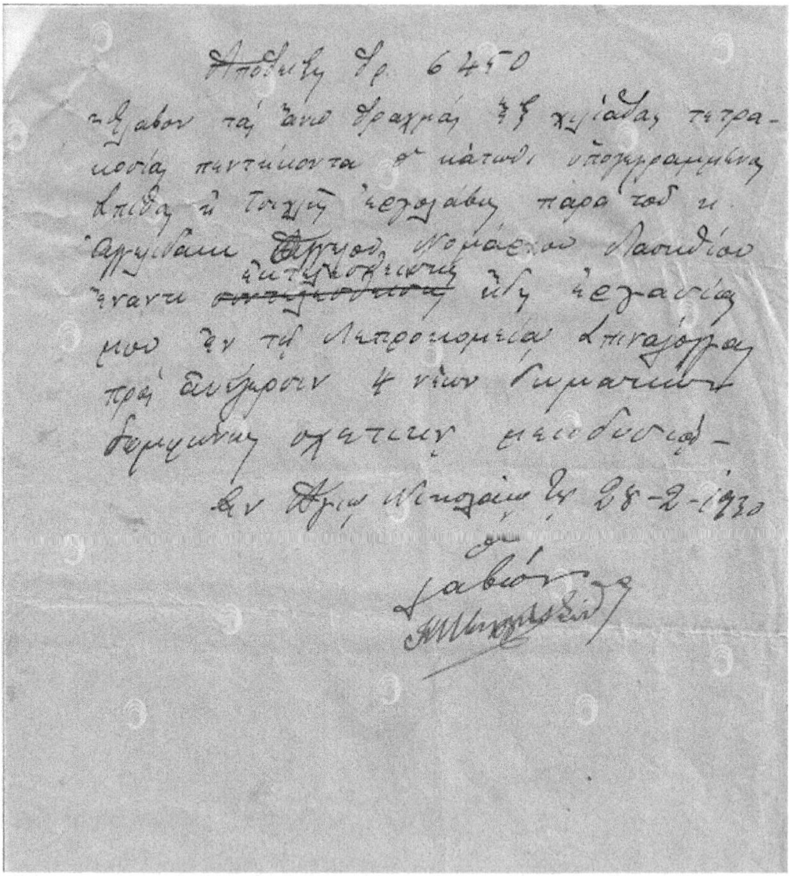

Απόδειξις δρ. 6450

Έλαβον τάς άνω δραχμάς έξ χιλιάδας τετρα-
κοσίας πεντήκοντα ο κάτωθι υπογεγραμμένος
επειδή ή τοιαύτη ελήφθη παρά του κ.
Αργυράκη Αρχηγού Νομάρχου Λασιθίου
έναντι ~~[illegible]~~ επιχορηγήσεως της εργασίας
μου εν τη Λεπροκομεία Σπιναλόγγας
προς διόρθωσιν 4 νέων δωματίων
[illegible] σχετικής [illegible]

εν Αγίω Νικολάω τη 28-2-1930

ο λαβών

[illegible]

The contractor in charge of the works on Spinalonga tells Eleftherios Venizelos that the delay in their execution is due to the fact that the staff of the Engineering Department of the Prefecture of Lasithi is busy with other projects, so he cannot find an available engineer to estimate the cost of the work and determine the amount of money to be paid to the contractor and labourers, who are under his supervision. Therefore, on 3 February 1933, Eleftherios Venizelos sends a letter to Konstantinos Drandakis, Inspector of Public Work s of Crete, saying the following: "Athens, 3 February 1933. To the Directorate of Public Work s of Crete. Mr. Director, The contractor in charge of the works on Spinalonga has informed me that the delay in their execution is due to the fact that the staff of the Engineering Department of the Prefecture of Lasithi is busy with other projects. He cannot find an engineer for his public works and thus cannot expedite the process of submitting invoices for the work carried out. Because of this delay, he lacks the funds needed to continue the project. Because, as you know, the works were commenced 4 years ago and must be completed as soon as possible in order to improve the fate of the poor lepers of Spinalonga, I would be obliged if you would kindly provide the appropriate instructions to the Engineering Department of the Prefecture of Lasithi, whose jurisdiction includes the district where the work is being executed, and assist us in our charitable work by submitting any invoices to us as soon as possible so we can settle them immediately. I also kindly request that you convey to the said Department that I have asked Mr. Katapotis, doctor and Senator of Lasithi, to submit a reconstruction plan for a leprosy Sanatorium with approximately thirty (30) wards not costing more than one-million drachmas. (Venizelos had trusted the doctor-Senator of Lasithi with preparing the reconstruction plan for Spinalonga's Sanatorium, with everything that this implied about the relationship between Venizelos, the Senator and the Medical Officer of Spinalonga). Since Mr. Katapotis will need an engineer for the selection of the plot of land and the drafting of relevant plans, I kindly request that you make the engineer of the Prefecture of Lasithi available to him, keeping in mind that the said engineer will be paid by me for his additional work. Eleftherios Venizelos." On 17 February 1933, the Inspector of Public Work s of Crete makes a certified copy of Venizelos' letter, attaches a letter of his own and on 22 February 1933 sends both of them to the Engineer of the Prefecture of Lasithi, making these documents also known to Mr. Katapotis, doctor-Senator of Lasithi. (The official four-page document, states that the copy was made on 17 October 1933, but this is a typing error. The correct chronological order of the letters is the following: a) On 3 February 1933, Eleftherios Venizelos sent a letter to the Inspector of Public Work s of Crete; b) on 17 February 1933, the Inspector made a certified copy of that letter. Since Venizelos had instructed the Inspector to promptly inform the other people involved, the latter couldn't possibly have done that in October - 8 whole months later; and finally c) on 22 February 1933, the Inspector sent both his own and Venizelos' letters to the Engineer). The letter of the Inspector of Public Work s of Crete says: "Chania, 22 February 1933. To the Engineer of the Prefecture of Lasithi in Agios Nikolaos. We hereby communicate to you the order of the Head of the Government, Mr. Eleftherios Venizelos, dated 3 February 1933, and we request that you immediately call upon the contractor in charge of the construction of the buildings in the leper colony of Spinalonga to complete the approved work of the aforementioned project within a timeframe set by yourselves, adopting the measures provided for in article 27 of Decree dated 12 July 1932 in pursuance of Law 5367 "Law on execution of Public Work s". To date, the failure observed in the execution of the work can be partly justified by the shortage of staff in your office, but this is no longer the case since public works have stalled due to lack of financial resources. (Here, Drandakis is saying that there is a problem with payments, leading to the suspension of public works). We therefore request that, in consultation with Mr. Katapotis, doctor- Senator of Lasithi, you proceed with preparing the said reconstruction plan for a leprosy Sanatorium and submit it to us for approval as soon as possible. Please confirm the receipt and execution of the present [Letter - Order]. The Inspector of Public Work s of Crete, Konstantinos Drandakis. Copy sent to Mr. Katapotis in Athens." Personal archives of Anna Giakoumaki.

'Αθῆναι τῇ 3ῃ Φεβρουαρίου 1933

ΠΡΟΣ

ΤΗΝ ΔΙΕΥΘΥΝΣΙΝ ΤΩΝ ΔΗΜΟΣΙΩΝ ΕΡΓΩΝ ΚΡΗΤΗΣ

ΧΑΝΙΑ

Κύριε Διευθυντά,

'Ο ἐργολάβος τῶν ἔργων Σπιναλόγκας δικαιολογῶν τήν βραδύτητα, ἥτις παρατηρεῖται κατά τήν ἐκτέλεσιν αὐτῶν μοί ἀνέφερεν ὅτι, λόγῳ ἀπασχολήσεως τοῦ προσωπικοῦ τῆς μηχανικῆς ὑπηρεσίας τοῦ Νομοῦ Λασηθίου, διά τά δημόσια ἔργα αὐτοῦ δέν εὑρίσκει διαθέσιμον μηχανικόν πρός ταχυτέραν ὑποβολήν τῶν λ/σμῶν τῶν ἑκάστοτε ἐκτελουμένων ἔργων, καί ὅτι ἐκ τῆς οὕτω ἐξελισσομένης ἀναβολῆς στερεῖται τῶν ἀναγκαίων χρημάτων καί δέν δύναται νά προχωρήσῃ ὡς ἐπιθυμεῖ, εἰς τήν ἐκτέλεσιν τῶν ἐργασιῶν.

'Επειδή ὡς γνωρίζετε τά ἔργα ἤρξαντο πρό 4/ετίας καί ἐπιβάλλεται νά τερματισθοῦν διά νά χρησιμοποιηθοῦν τό ταχύτερον πρός βελτίωσιν τῆς τύχης τῶν δυστυχῶν λεπρῶν τῆς Σπιναλόγκας, θά σᾶς ἤμην λίαν ὑπόχρεως, ἐάν εἴχετε τήν καλωσύνην νά διά [illegible] τάς δε- [illegible] περιφέρειαν τῆς ὁποίας ἐκτελοῦνται τά ἔργα, ἵνα μᾶς βοηθήσῃ εἰς τό ἀναληφθέν φιλανθρωπικόν ἔργον, ὑποβάλλουσα ἡμῖν τό ταχύτερον τούς ἑκάστοτε λ/σμούς πρός ταχεῖαν ἐξόφλησιν αὐτῶν.

'Επί τῇ εὐκαιρίᾳ ταύτῃ παρακαλῶ νά γνωρίσητε ἐπίσης εἰς τήν αὐτήν ὑπηρεσίαν, ὅτι παρεκάλεσα τόν κ. Κατακόπην ἰατρόν Γερουσιαστήν Λασηθίου νά μοί ὑποβάλῃ μελέτην ἀνοικοδομήσεως Σανατορίου λεπρῶν μέ τριάκοντα (30) περίπου αἰθούσας ἐπί τῇ βάσει δαπάνης ἑνός ἑκατομμυρίου περίπου δραχμῶν.

'Επειδή δέ διά τήν ἐργασίαν ταύτην θά χρειασθῇ ὁ κ. Κατακόπης μηχανικόν διά τήν ἐκλογήν τοῦ γηπέδου καί σύνταξιν τοῦ σχετικοῦ σχεδίου, παρακαλῶ ὅπως θέσητε εἰς τήν διάθεσιν αὐτοῦ τόν

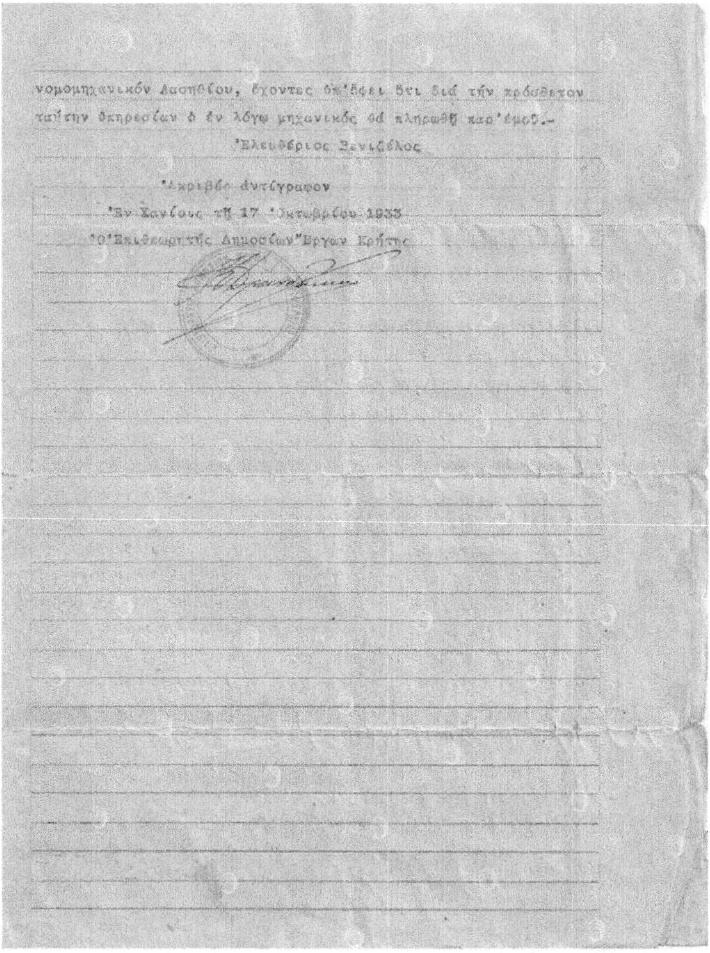

νομομηχανικόν Λασηθίου, ἔχοντες ὑπ'ὄψει ὅτι διά τήν πρόσθετον ταύτην ὑπηρεσίαν ὁ ἐν λόγῳ μηχανικός θά πληρωθῇ παρ'ἐμοῦ.-

'Ελευθέριος Βενιζέλος

'Ακριβές ἀντίγραφον

'Εν Χανίοις τῇ 17 'Οκτωβρίου 1933

'Ο'Επιθεωρητής Δημοσίων "Εργων Κρήτης

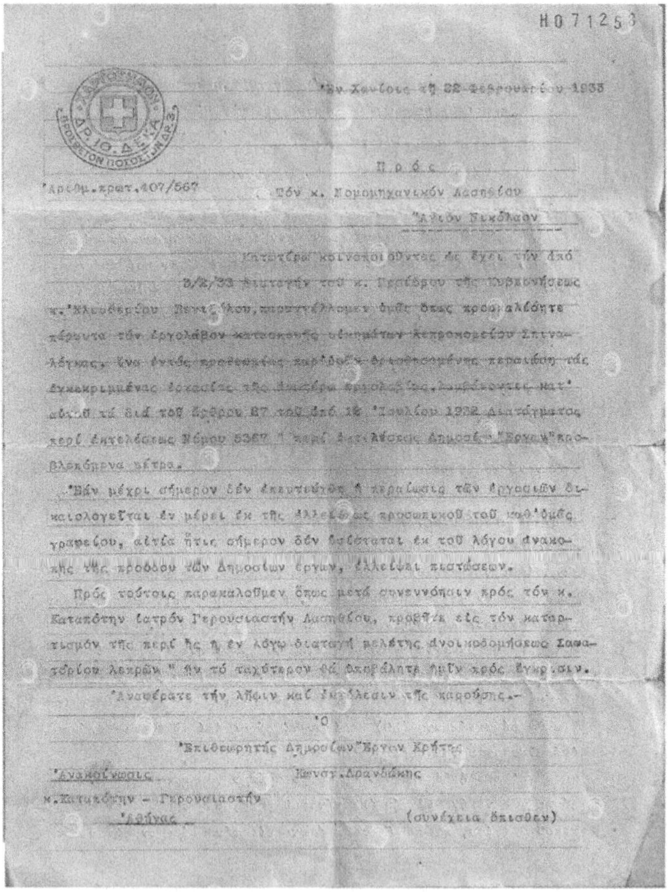

H 0 7 1 2 5 3

Ἐν Χανίοις τῇ 22 Φεβρουαρίου 1933

Ἀριθμ. πρωτ. 407/567

Πρός

Τόν κ. Νομομηχανικόν Λασηθίου

Ἅγιον Νικόλαον

Κατωτέρω κοινοποιοῦντες σᾶς ἔχει τήν ἀπό 3/2/33 διαταγήν τοῦ κ. Προέδρου τῆς Κυβερνήσεως κ. Ἐλευθερίου Βενιζέλου, παραγγέλλομεν ὑμᾶς ὅπως προσκαλέσητε πέρυντα τόν ἐργολάβον κατασκευῆς οἰκημάτων λεπροκομείου Σπιναλόγκας, ἵνα ἐντός προθεσμίας [illegible] περαιώση τάς ἐγκεκριμένας ἐργασίας [illegible], λαμβάνοντες κατ' αὐτοῦ τά διά τοῦ ἄρθρου 87 τοῦ ἀπό 1? Ἰουλίου 1932 Διατάγματος περί ἐκτελέσεως Νόμου 5367 "περί Ἐκτελέσεως Δημοσίων Ἔργων" προβλεπόμενα μέτρα.

Ἐάν μέχρι σήμερον δέν ἐπετεύχθη ἡ περαίωσις τῶν ἐργασιῶν δικαιολογεῖται ἐν μέρει ἐκ τῆς ἐλλείψεως προσωπικοῦ τοῦ καθ' ὑμᾶς γραφείου, αἰτία ἥτις σήμερον δέν ὑφίσταται ἐκ τοῦ λόγου ἀνακοπῆς τῆς προόδου τῶν Δημοσίων ἔργων, ἐλλείψει πιστώσεων.

Πρός τούτοις παρακαλοῦμεν ὅπως μετά συνεννόησιν πρός τόν κ. Καταπότην ἰατρόν Γερουσιαστήν Λασηθίου, προβῆτε εἰς τόν καταρτισμόν τῆς περί ἧς ἡ ἐν λόγῳ διαταγή μελέτης ἀνοικοδομήσεως Σανατορίου λεπρῶν" ἥν τό ταχύτερον θά ὑποβάλητε ἡμῖν πρός ἔγκρισιν.

Ἀναφέρατε τήν λῆψιν καί ἐκτέλεσιν τῆς παρούσης.-

Ὁ

Ἐπιθεωρητής Δημοσίων Ἔργων Κρήτης

Κωνστ. Δρανδάκης

Ἀνακοίνωσις

κ. Καταπότην - Γερουσιαστήν

Ἀθήνας

(συνέχεια ὄπισθεν)

Handwritten letter of contractor Kostis Tsihlis or Spithas, which he apparently intended to send to the doctor-Senator of Lasithi and to another individual called Vasileios Skoulas, (V. Skoulas was also among Venizelos' elected MPs pictured in the photograph of 1915 - Image 9, Section A) who seem to be connected to payments for work done on Spinalonga. The letter is dated 8 November 1933, so we can reasonably assume that after Venizelos' letter in February 1933, certain payments were made and some progress was made on Spinalonga. The problem of finding an engineer seems to have been solved, since the contractor doesn't mention the subject in his letter, but he does bring up the issue of payments again. The handwritten letter reads: "Two recipients: Katapotis - Senator, Hotel Megas Alexandros, Athens & Vasileios Skoulas, Venizelos' residence, Athens. I kindly request that you communicate to me the results of your actions with Venizelos regarding the payment of the leper colony account, attaching the relevant document of the Inspectorate of Public Work s of Crete, and give both to Vasileios Skoulas to deliver to me when he comes here [to Crete]. If not, I shall halt all work on the project in protest against the [economic] damage and losses we have sustained. Contractor Spithas, 8 November 1933." Personal archives of Anna Giakoumaki.

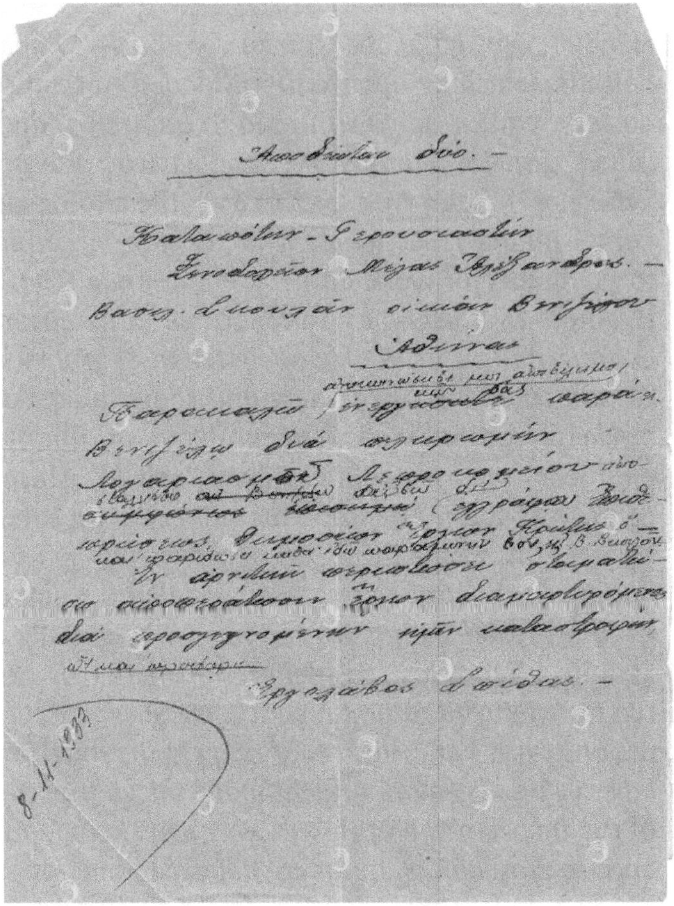

Στρατάρχου ... Αλεξάνδρου.-

Αθήνας

8-11-1933

The works on Spinalonga progressed, and the contractor continued to undertake projects on the islet. This is a certificate issued to Spithas in 1936 by the Municipality of Neapoli, Lasithi, Crete - of which he was a resident - so he could participate in a new tender concerning works on Spinalonga. His grandson, a friend of mine also named Konstantinos Tsihlis or Spithas, says that his grandfather was always awarded the contracts for Spinalonga, but that the day after he received payment for each such contract, he would follow a specific routine: He would go to the kafenion and play cards with the person in charge of awarding the contracts - and would always "lose" a large, and previously agreed-upon, sum of money. My 75-year-old friend Kostis is the perfect example of the clear-sighted people encountered during my research, people whose simplicity and honesty compel them to tell things as they happened, without embellishment. Personal archives of Anna Giakoumaki.

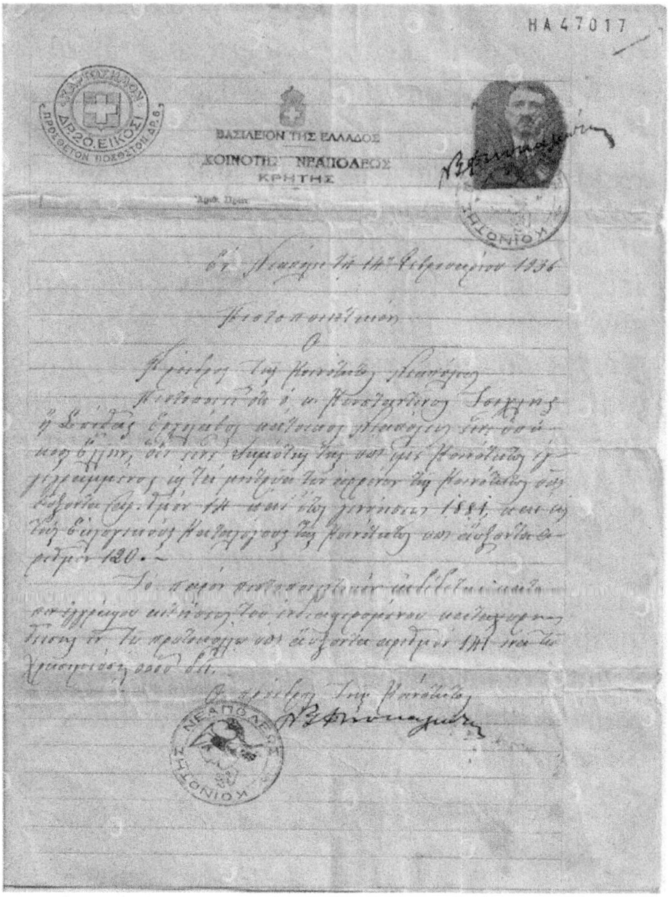
HA 47017

ΒΑΣΙΛΕΙΟΝ ΤΗΣ ΕΛΛΑΔΟΣ

ΚΟΙΝΟΤΗΣ ΝΕΑΠΟΛΕΩΣ

ΚΡΗΤΗΣ

Εν Νεαπόλει τη 14η Φεβρουαρίου 1936

Πιστοποιητικόν

Σελὶς 3η «ΚΡΗΤΙΚ

ΑΠΟ ΤΟ ΝΗΣΙ ΤΟΥ ΠΟΝΟΥ

Η ΖΩΗ ΤΩΝ ΑΣΘΕΝΩΝ ΤΗΣ ΣΠΙΝΑ-ΛΟΓΚΑΣ

ΠΩΣ ΔΙΑΙΤΩΝΤΑΙ - ΕΙΣ ΤΙ ΚΑΤΑΓΙΝΟΝΤΑΙ

Ἀξιότιμε κ. Διευθυντά,

Σᾶς ἀποστέλλομεν τὴν ἐσώκλειστον αὐτὴν Ἔκκλησιν ὅπως τὴν καταχωρίσετε εἰς τὰς στήλας τῆς ἐγκρίτου ὑμῶν Ἐφημερίδος συνηγοροῦντες ἅμα, ὅπως σᾶς Ἐπιβάλλουν τὰ Φιλανθρωπικά καὶ ἀλτρουϊστικά σας αἰσθήματα διὰ τὴν κατάπαυσιν τοῦ ἐγκλήματος τῆς ἀπομονώσεώς μας. Ἐκόντες—ἄκοντες εὑρισκόμεθα ἐπάνω σ' [illegible] νῆσι. Ἀξίζει τι αὐτὴ ἡ τόσον φρικτὴ καταδίκη μας. Τὸν ἴδιον τὸν ἑαυτόν μου διαλελημένον μέσα σὲ βραχὴν νερό. Ἐν ὀνόματι τοῦ πολιτισμοῦ, ἐν ὀνόματι τοῦ ἀνθρωπισμοῦ, ἐν ὀνόματι τῆς ἀνθρωπίνης ἀλληλεγγύης, ὑψώσατε φωνὴν διαμαρτυρίας διὰ τὴν μὴ διαιώνισιν τοῦ αἴσχους καὶ μαρτυρικοῦ μας αὐτοῦ Γολγοθᾶ Σπιναλόγκας.

Μετὰ ἐξαιρετικῆς ἐκτιμήσεως
Θαμένοι ζωντανοὶ οἱ Λεπροὶ
Σπιναλόγκας

Ἐνῷ κόσμος ὁλόκληρος ὁ πιὸ σκληρὰ δεινοπαθὴς καὶ κανονιστικῶς δοκιμαζόμενος κόσμος τοῦ ἀπομάχου, οἱ πιὸ τραγικοὶ ναυαγοὶ τῆς σήμερον.

Οἱ λεπροὶ Σπιναλόγκας, ἀποκαμωμένοι, κατατσακισμένοι, ὄχι τόσον ἀπὸ τὰ δεινὰ ποὺ μᾶς ἐκληροδότησεν ἡ ἐπάρατος νόσος ὅσον ἀπὸ τὰ πολλαπλασίως φρικτότερα, ἀβάστακτα βασανιστήρια, εἰς τὰ ὁποῖα μᾶς ὑποβάλλει ἀδιαλείπτως ἡ ἀπομόνωσίς μας μέσα σ' αὐτὴ τὴ φρικτὴ—λίαζώντανη—κόλασι τῆς Σπιναλόγκας, ἀπευθύναμεν ἀπεγνωσμένας ἐκκλήσεις εἰς ὅλας τὰς Διευθύνσεις, πρὸς τοὺς κ. κ. ἁρμοδίους πρὸς τὸν ἐπιστημονικόν μας κόσμον, πρὸς ὅλας τὰς χριστιανικάς, φιλανθρωπικάς, ἀνθρωπιστικάς, ἐπαγγελματικάς, ἐργατικὰς κλπ. ὀργανώσεις. Πρὸς τὴν Ἐκκλησίαν μας, πρὸς τὸν τύπον, μὲ τὴν θερμοτάτην παράκλησιν ὅπως κάμουν ὅτι τοὺς ἐπιβάλλει ἡ φιλανθρωπία καὶ πολιτισμένη των συνείδησις διὰ νὰ ἐπισπεύσθῇ ἐπὶ τέλους ἡ ἀπαλλαγή μας ἀπὸ τὰ ἀφόρητα αὐτὰ πρόσθετα Σπιναλόγκεια δεινοπαθήματά μας καὶ ἀνθρωπίνη μας ἀπομάκρυνσις εἰς ἕνα ἄλλο μέρος ποὺ νὰ ἔχῃ ΧΩΜΑ καὶ ΝΕΡΟ ἀπὸ ἐδῶ λοιπόν, ἀπὸ τὴν ξεκουρασιὰν διὰ τὴν ποίησιν τῆς Σπιναλόγκας, τὸ νεκροταφεῖον μας αὐτὸ ἐπάνω στὸ ὁποῖον διερχόμεθα ἀγωνιώδεις στιγμές, μόλις καὶ μετὰ βίας κατορθώσαντες νὰ συγκεντρώσωμεν τὰς ὑπολειφθείσας ἀσθενεῖς μας δυνάμεις, σᾶς, ἐκλιπαροῦμεν διὰ τοῦ ἡμερησίου τύπου. Σπεύσατε νὰ δώσητε χεῖρα βοηθείας εἰς ἡμᾶς τοὺς πνιγομένους ἀπὸ τὴν δυστυχίαν συναδελφούς σας. Μὴ λησμονεῖτε ὅτι ἄνθρωποι καὶ ἡμεῖς ἦσμεν καὶ ἀνάρρωστήσαμεν ἀπὸ αὐτὴν τὴν ἀρρώστια δὲν εἶναι [illegible] δικό μας, ὥστε νὰ δικαιολογεῖται ἔστω καὶ πόρρωθεν ἀπόμη, μιὰ τόσον φοβερὰ ἀνθρωπίνη καταδίκη.

Οἱ ἐκκαλοῦντες ἀθῷοι κατάδικοι Λεπροὶ Σπιναλόγκας.

Ἰ. Παυλάκη, Βιρ. Τσαλόσμα Ε. Τσαλόσμας, Θεόδ. Νικολάου Α. Γατάκης, Α. Κούτρας, Β. Κούτρας, Μ. Ἀζαρδάκης, Α. Διαδάκης, Γ. Μανιδάκης, Στ. Στ. Σταματιάδης, Θ. Τουτουτζῆς Στ. Κουτσουρῆς, Στ. Μεγαλέζόγλου, Ἐμ. Κοκκινάκις, Α. Χ'' Μιχάλης, Σ. Σκορνοβάς Κ. Καρασωτηρίου, Α. Μαρκάκης, Ν. Νειφιδάκη, Ἐμμαν. Σαριδάκης, Φίλιππος Μακρῆς, Μ. Μακρῆς, Φ. Βοριζάνης, Ι. Γιαλδάσης, Γ. Μαρκετάκης, Χ. Μανιαδάκης, Α. Καβαδᾶς, Α. Καλλάκος, Κ. Καββαδᾶ, Ν. Μπαρούνης, Α. Κλάδης, Μ. Μπαρούνη, Ν. Μανουσάκης, Α. Μάστορας, Ι. Πάγκαλος, Ελ. Κρίτσα, Ν. Παπαδημητρίου, Κ. Πατσῆς, Κ. Τάσσου, Μ. Φραγκιαδάκη, Μ. Φραγκιαδάκης Μ. Παναγιωτάκης, Α. Παναγιωτάκις, Ι. Παπαδόγελος, Μ. Κλώντσας, Ἀργ. Ζαγοράκης, Δ. Ἰωαννίδης, Μ. Θεοδωράκης, Ἐμ. Λιαράκις, Κ. Λιοσαράκις, Ν. Ζῶμος, Δ. Παπαχαραλάμπου Μ. Σκαρβελῆς, Α. Παυλάκις, Ν. Κοκάκις, Ι. Χρόνης, Μ. Μηκράκις, Α. Ἀγγέλου, Ν. Κοσυκλᾶς Ελ. Ἀρβανίτου Δ. Μιλάκης, Ε. Πετράκης, Α. Συμεωνίδης, Α. Βαρδαλίνης, Κ. Κουκουβάκης Μ. Τσιλιάτου Ε. Πρατσινάκης, Γ. Κριτσίλας, Γ. Παπαγέλου, Ν. Ἀναστασόπουλος, Ι. Νιάρχου, Ἀρ. Δρακουλάκης Ν. Θεοδωράκης, Δ. Πετράκης, Ε. Κρίτσα, Ν. Καπελώνη, Ι. Φραγκιαδάκης, Ν. Μοσχολιδάκης, Γ. Μελᾶς, Ν. Β[illegible]άκης, Γ. Βάκος, Δ. Ἀναστασόπουλος, Μ. Κωνσταντοπούλου, Κ. Φραγκιαδάκης, Ε. Φραγκιαδάκης, Γ. Χριστοδουλάκης, Ν. Κυριατζῆς, Α. Κυριατζῆς, Μ. Βοριζανάκης, Ε. Κουτσουρῆς, Π. Παρασκευάκη, Δ. Κλαμπανάκη, Σ. Πλακαντωνάκης, Α. Στρατῆς, Κ. Βογιατζῆς, Ζ. Μανέτας, Γ. Κονταάκης, Ν. Τσιμπίδας Ν. Τρίφωνα, Α. Μαρινίκα, Ε. Μαρανίκα, Ε. Κλιματιανὸς, Α. Τζημινάκη, Ι. Κλάδης, Ι. Τσατσαρῆς, Α. Μανιωάτου, Σ. Βαλμᾶς, Α. Δημητρόπουλος, Μ. Παπαϊωάννου, Ε. Φουρνούνης, Μ. Χρυσάκης, Π. Κουλῆ, Κ. Χρυσάκης, Α. Μασσαάκης, Ν. Βλάχος Γ. Βόλακας, Δ. Δαφνῆς, Μ. Δαφνῆ, Χ. Τσαρουχάν, Ε. Μπαρούτη, Ν. Τρεντάκη Μ. Παγώνης, Ἀρ. Ντουράκη, Α. Μουντουράκης, Ἐμ. Καψάκης, Ε. Σταυρετάκης, Β. Ἔξαρχος, Α. Καρμαρᾶς, Α. Κονδυλόπουλος Γ. Χρονάκης, Μ. Τσίκουρας, Μ. Φιστικάκη Π. Προϊμάκη, Κ. Κουτσουράκη Μ. Σταυρακάκη, Χ. Σταυρουλάκη, Α. Σκαρβελάκη, Γ. Μητροφάνη Π. Τσουρῆς Ι. Περιφεράκης, Ἠλ. Ἀνδρουλάκης, Ἠλ. Γιολδάσης Φ. Ἀνδρονικοπούλου, Μ. Ἀνδρονικοπούλου Μ. Σιμιώτου Γ. Χαρδαβέλας Π. Παπαδόπουλος, Σ. Γιολδάσης, Μ. Παπουτσῆς, Μ. Βλαχογιάννη, Δ. Μουζάκη, Ε. Σταμπλάκη Δ. Ξαγοράρης Κ. Ροδόπουλος Ε. Χριστοδουλάκη, Αἰκ. Παπαδάκη, Ι. Καραϊσκάκης Μ. Διαλυνᾶς Κ. Μακράκης, Α. Μοσχολιδάκης, Α. Τζινῆς, Ε. Χαραλάμπης Ε. Τουλουπάκης Ζ. Ρ[illegible]άκη, Ζ. Νιτσάκη, Ι. Καραντζῆς, Κ. Τ[illegible], Κ. Μάστορα, Γ. Πεζεβεγκόπουλος, Η. Καλαμπάκη, Π. Ἀγγέλου, Ν. Κληρονόμος, Ε. Κουκουρίτη Ε. Κλάδης, Ε. Κλάδη, Π. Κλάδη, Β. Πετράκης, Μ. Πετράκη, Γ. Πετράκη, Γ. Μπρανίκα, Α. Παγώνη Α. Μιχελάκη, Μ. Καλογιάκη, Π. Καραμανώλης, Σ. Βαλμᾶ, Μ. Βαλμᾶ, Γ. Γιατρᾶς, Π. Γιατρᾶ, Σ. Καρκίδης, Μ. Αὐγουλᾶς Ζ. Καρκίδης Α. Κατσαρός, Σ. Κατσαροῦ, Ε. Παπάζογλου Γεωργ. Βαϊνάκης Μ. Τσακίρη, Ε. Λεϊζάκη, Ν. Μαΐστης, Μ. Τσιγγρῆ, Ι. Σταματάκης, Ε. Κανάκης, Σ. Κλάδης, Α. Δρετάκης, Α. Σκαραμανώλης, Δ. Τζανῆς, Δ. Καραβελάκη, Μ. Καμπουριανοῦ, Ι. Καμπουριανός, Ε. Καλομοιράκης, Α. Βαγιανάκης, Ε. Κουκουρίτης, Δ. Τσάκας, Μ. Ἀρτσουλᾶ, Π. Μαραλῆς, Ι. Ἀλιφιέρης, Α. Ἀλιφιέρη, Μ. Μαρκετάκης, Κ. Ἀποστολάκης, Μ. Φακέλα, Ι. Δρίβας, Ι. Κολυβᾶς, Μ. Μαϊνας, Κ. Ἀδαμοπούλου, Ν. Τσαπλάνης, Γασιμάκοβον, Ψυχογιός.

Ἀκριβὲς ἀντίγραφον

Ἐν Σπίνα Λόγκα τῇ 27η Ἰουλίου 1935. Ἡ ἐξουσιοδοτηθεῖσα ἐπιτροπή.

Γ. Βοριζανός, Γ. Μανιδάκης Ν. Μπαρούτης.

Rare letter sent by the lepers of Spinalonga to the editor of "Kritika Nea", published on 13 August 1935. In the letter, the residents of Spinalonga describe their lives on the islet and request to be transferred to another location with arable land and running water. The rarity of the letter lies in the fact that the patients have signed their full names, knowing that by doing so they would be stigmatised even further. This action reflects their frustration and can be interpreted as a desperate cry for help. The article reads: "From the island of pain. The life of the patients of Spina-Longa. How they live - What they do. Honourable Director [of the newspaper], we are sending you this letter so you can publish it among the articles of your reputable newspaper, in the hope that it will appeal to your philanthropy and altruism, and motivate you to help us put an end to the criminal isolation we endure. Whether we like it or not, we are isolated on this inaccessible and barren island. Oh, why is our confinement so terrible? Broken bodies surrounded by nothing but water. In the name of civilisation; in the name of humanity and solidarity, raise your voices in protest against the prolongation of the torturous and disgraceful Golgotha we have to endure on Spinalonga. Yours faithfully." And it continues: "The living-dead lepers of Spinalonga. An entire community; a community which has to endure the heaviest of fates; people who are tested again and again in every way possible; the most tragic castaways of our times. We, the lepers of Spinalonga, who are haggard and worn-out, not so much by the misfortunes thrust upon us by this damnable disease, but by the manifold horrendous and unbearable tortures caused by our confinement in this dreadful hell, launch a desperate appeal to the authorities; to the scientific community; to all Christian, charitable, humanitarian and labour organisations; to the Church and the Press and beseech you to do everything your charitable and civilised conscience guides you to do, and help to liberate us from the unbearable suffering we endure isolated on Spinalonga by transferring us to another location with LAND and WATER. Living agonising lives on notoriously horrific Spinalonga, we barely managed to summon the strength to launch this appeal through the press to beg you to lend a helping hand to your fellow-men who are drowning in misery. Don't forget that we are people too and we didn't choose to get sick; we didn't choose such a dreadful fate. The innocent supplicants of Spinalonga (followed by the names of the 229 patients who signed the Letter- Complaint), Certified Copy. On Spina Longa, 27 July 1935. The authorised committee. G. Vorizinos, G. Manidakis, N. Baroutis".

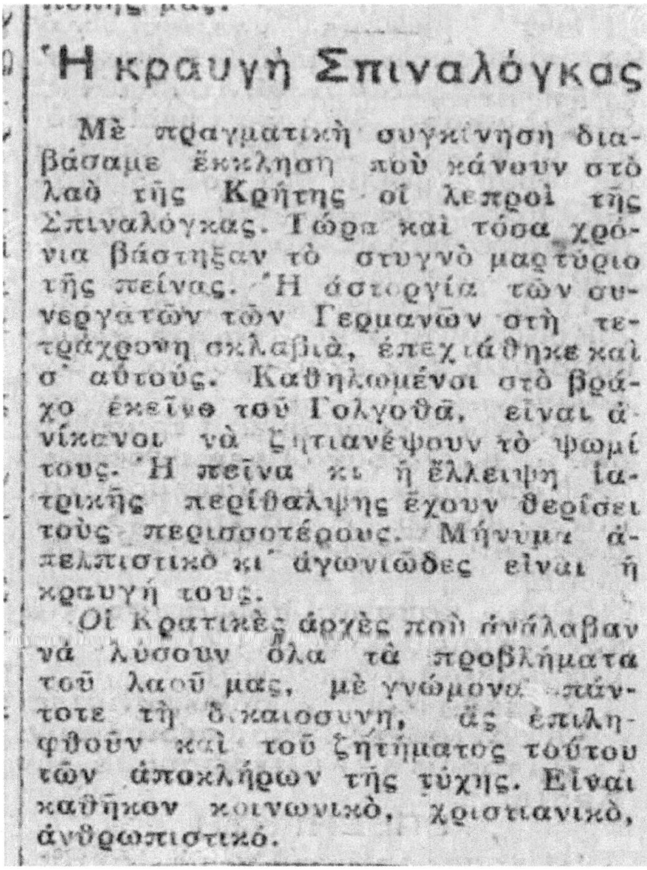

Ἡ κραυγὴ Σπιναλόγκας

Μὲ πραγματικὴ συγκίνηση διαβάσαμε ἔκκληση ποὺ κάνουν στὸ λαὸ τῆς Κρήτης οἱ λεπροὶ τῆς Σπιναλόγκας. Τώρα καὶ τόσα χρόνια βάστηξαν τὸ στυγνὸ μαρτύριο τῆς πείνας. Ἡ ἀστοργία τῶν συνεργατῶν τῶν Γερμανῶν στὴ τετράχρονη σκλαβιά, ἐπεκτάθηκε καὶ σ' αὐτούς. Καθηλωμένοι στὸ βράχο ἐκεῖνο τοῦ Γολγοθᾶ, εἶναι ἀνίκανοι νὰ ζητιανέψουν τὸ ψωμί τους. Ἡ πεῖνα κι ἡ ἔλλειψη ἰατρικῆς περίθαλψης ἔχουν θερίσει τοὺς περισσοτέρους. Μήνυμα ἀπελπιστικὸ κι' ἀγωνιῶδες εἶναι ἡ κραυγή τους.

Οἱ Κρατικὲς ἀρχὲς ποὺ ἀνάλαβαν νὰ λύσουν ὅλα τὰ προβλήματα τοῦ λαοῦ μας, μὲ γνώμονα πάντοτε τὴ δικαιοσύνη, ἂς ἐπιληφθοῦν καὶ τοῦ ζητήματος τούτου τῶν ἀποκλήρων τῆς τύχης. Εἶναι καθῆκον κοινωνικό, χριστιανικό, ἀνθρωπιστικό.

On 20 November 1944, an article in "Eleftheri Kriti" reads: "The outcry of Spinalonga. We were truly moved when we read the appeal by the lepers of Spinalonga addressed to the people of Crete. Today, and for so many years, they have endured the brutal torture of hunger. The heartlessness of the Germans' accomplices throughout the four years of slavery has taken its toll on them. Isolated on the rock of Golgotha, they cannot even beg for a loaf of bread. Hunger and the lack of medical care have decimated them.

(At this point, we'd like to remind you that more than a hundred people died on Spinalonga during the Occupation because the State didn't pay salaries to the leper colony's staff; didn't send the patients their allowances - with all the consequences this would have on their diet and medical care - and at the same time, it didn't even set them free to scavenge for food on the Cretan mainland. The massive number of deaths led to a debate on closing the leper colony). Their outcry is full of desperation and agony. The Cretan authorities in charge of solving people's problems without prejudice should also see to the matter of these outcasts of fortune. It's our duty as citizens; as Christians; as human beings."

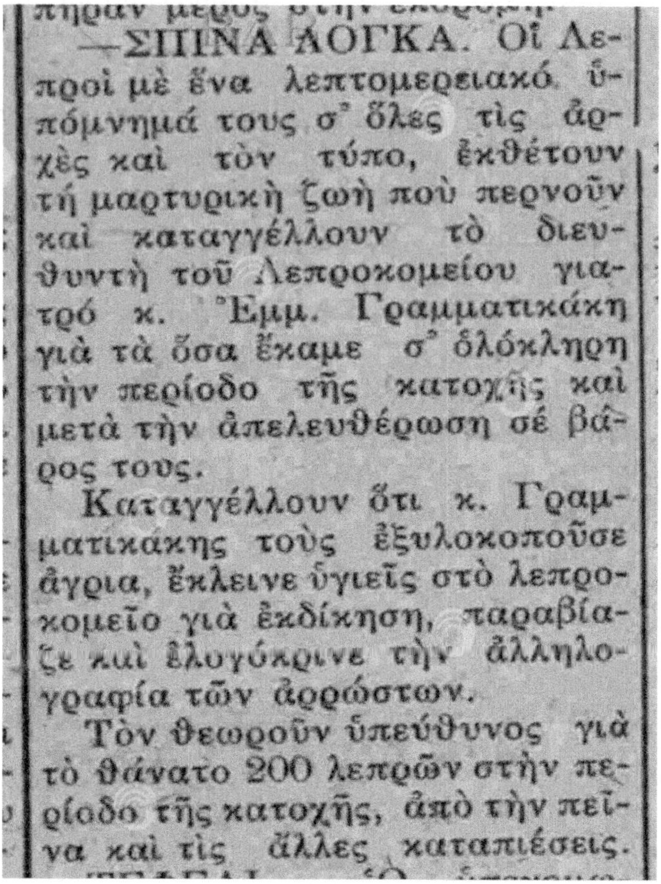

—ΣΠΙΝΑ ΛΟΓΚΑ. Οἱ Λεπροὶ μὲ ἕνα λεπτομερειακό ὑπόμνημά τους σ' ὅλες τὶς ἀρχὲς καὶ τὸν τύπο, ἐκθέτουν τή μαρτυρικὴ ζωὴ ποὺ περνοῦν καὶ καταγγέλλουν τὸ διευθυντὴ τοῦ Λεπροκομείου γιατρό κ. Ἐμμ. Γραμματικάκη γιὰ τὰ ὅσα ἔκαμε σ' ὁλόκληρη τὴν περίοδο τῆς κατοχῆς καὶ μετὰ τὴν ἀπελευθέρωση σέ βάρος τους.

Καταγγέλλουν ὅτι κ. Γραμματικάκης τοὺς ἐξυλοκοποῦσε ἄγρια, ἔκλεινε ὑγιεῖς στὸ λεπροκομεῖο γιὰ ἐκδίκηση, παραβίαζε καὶ ἐλογόκρινε τὴν ἀλληλογραφία τῶν ἀρρώστων.

Τὸν θεωροῦν ὑπεύθυνος γιὰ τὸ θάνατο 200 λεπρῶν στὴν περίοδο τῆς κατοχῆς, ἀπὸ τὴν πεῖνα καὶ τὶς ἄλλες καταπιέσεις.

An article in "Eleftheri Kriti" on 1 June 1945, reads: "SPINA LONGA. In an extensive letter to the authorities and the press, the lepers reveal details of their torturous lives and denounce the Leper colony's Director - Dr. E. Grammatikakis - for abusing them during and after the Occupation. They accuse Mr. Grammatikakis of beating them; of confining healthy people in the leper colony for revenge and of opening and censoring the patients' letters. They hold him responsible for the death of 200 lepers during the Occupation, from starvation and other hardships."

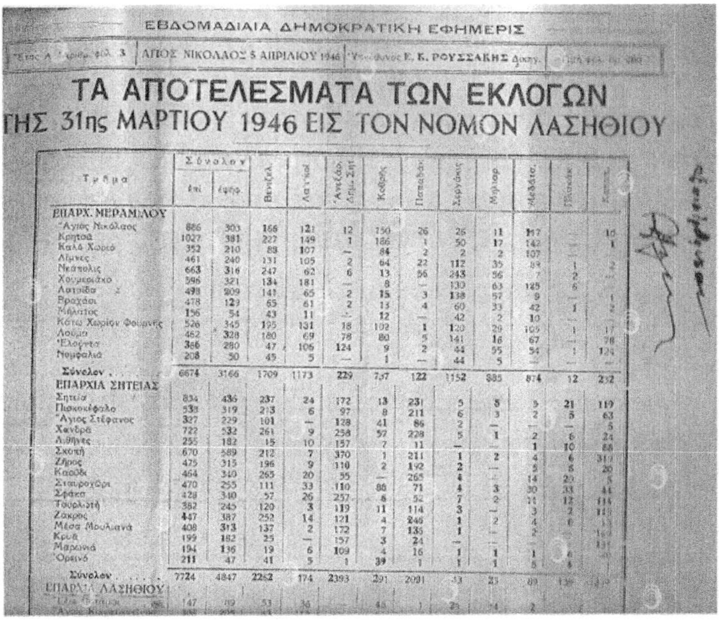

ΕΒΔΟΜΑΔΙΑΙΑ ΔΗΜΟΚΡΑΤΙΚΗ ΕΦΗΜΕΡΙΣ

Έτος Α' Αριθμ. φύλ. 3 | ΑΓΙΟΣ ΝΙΚΟΛΑΟΣ 5 ΑΠΡΙΛΙΟΥ 1946 | Υπεύθυνος Ε. Κ. ΡΟΥΣΣΑΚΗΣ Δικηγ. | [illegible]

ΤΑ ΑΠΟΤΕΛΕΣΜΑΤΑ ΤΩΝ ΕΚΛΟΓΩΝ ΤΗΣ 31ης ΜΑΡΤΙΟΥ 1946 ΕΙΣ ΤΟΝ ΝΟΜΟΝ ΛΑΣΗΘΙΟΥ

Τμήμα	Σύνολον		Βενιζελ.	[illegible]	Ανεξάρ. Δημ. Σητ.	Κοθρής	Παπαδάκ.	[illegible]	Μηλιαρ.	Μοδάτσ.	[illegible]	[illegible]
	επί	εψηφ.										
ΕΠΑΡΧ. ΜΕΡΑΜΠΕΛΛΟΥ												
Άγιος Νικόλαος	886	303	166	121	12	150	26	26	11	117		16
Κριτσά	1027	381	227	149	1	186	1	50	17	142	—	1
Καλό Χωριό	352	210	88	107	—	84	2	2	2	107	—	
Λίμνες	461	240	131	105	2	64	22	112	35	89	1	2
Νεάπολις	663	316	247	62	6	13	56	243	56	7	2	[illegible]
Χουμεριάκο	596	321	134	181	—	8	—	130	63	125	6	
Λατσίδα	498	209	141	65	2	15	3	138	57	9	—	1
Βραχάσι	478	129	65	61	2	13	4	60	33	42	1	2
Μίλατος	156	54	43	11	—	12	—	42	2	10	—	
Κάτω Χωριό Φουρνής	526	345	195	131	18	102	1	120	20	105	1	17
Λούμα	462	328	180	69	78	80	5	141	16	67	—	78
Ελούντα	366	280	47	106	124	9	2	44	55	54	1	124
Νοφαλιά	208	50	45	5	—	1	—	44	5	—	—	—
Σύνολον	6674	3166	1709	1173	229	757	122	1152	385	874	12	232
ΕΠΑΡΧΙΑ ΣΗΤΕΙΑΣ												
Σητεία	834	436	237	24	172	13	231	5	8	5	21	119
Πισκοκέφαλο	538	319	213	6	97	8	211	6	3	2	5	63
Άγιος Στέφανος	327	229	101	—	128	41	86	2	—	—	—	5
Χανδρά	722	532	261	9	258	57	228	5	1	2	6	24
Λιθίνες	255	182	15	10	157	7	11	—	—	1	10	88
Σκοπή	670	589	212	7	370	1	211	1	2	4	6	319
Ζήρος	475	315	196	9	110	2	192	2	—	5	5	20
Καρύδι	464	340	265	20	55	—	265	4	—	14	23	5
Σταυροχώρι	470	255	111	33	110	88	71	4	3	30	33	44
Σφάκα	428	340	57	26	257	8	52	7	2	11	12	114
Τουρλωτή	382	245	120	3	119	11	114	3	—	3	2	111
Ζάκρος	447	387	252	14	121	4	246	1	2	4	6	[illegible]
Μέσα Μουλιανά	408	313	137	2	172	7	135	1	—	2		[illegible]
Κρυά	199	182	25	—	157	3	24	—	—			[illegible]
Μαρωνιά	194	136	19	6	109	4	16	1	1	1	6	[illegible]
Ορεινό	211	47	41	5	1	39	1	1	1	5	4	[illegible]
Σύνολον	7724	4847	2262	174	2393	291	2091	33	23	89	139	[illegible]
ΕΠΑΡΧΙΑ ΛΑΣΗΘΙΟΥ												
[illegible]	147	89	53	36	[illegible]	48	1	23	[illegible]	2		

The results of the elections of 1946 published in "Democratikos", on 5 April 1946, issue 3, Koundoureios Municipal Library, Agios Nikolaos, Crete. Modatsos and Kothris were powerful politicians of the time and front-runners in the region of Mirabello, yet the preference of the residents of Elounda is clear. Victims of the Medical Officer's propaganda, they voted for his good friend and fellow-doctor, thus helping to keep the leper colony open. Even though they weren't aware of the two men's devious intentions, over the following months dozens of people from all over the Prefecture were sent to Spinalonga without testing so that the Medical Officer and his friend could keep their pre-election promises. The victims of their scheme were the elderly, women and children because - with the Civil War raging - all the young and able-bodied men were away fighting. It should be remembered that, in the absence of a road network and mass media, politicians were unable to reach a wide audience with their campaigns, so it was extremely unlikely for the locals to vote for a candidate from another region. Although these two men sent so many innocent people into exile, stigmatised them as lepers and destroyed entire families, they were never brought to justice.

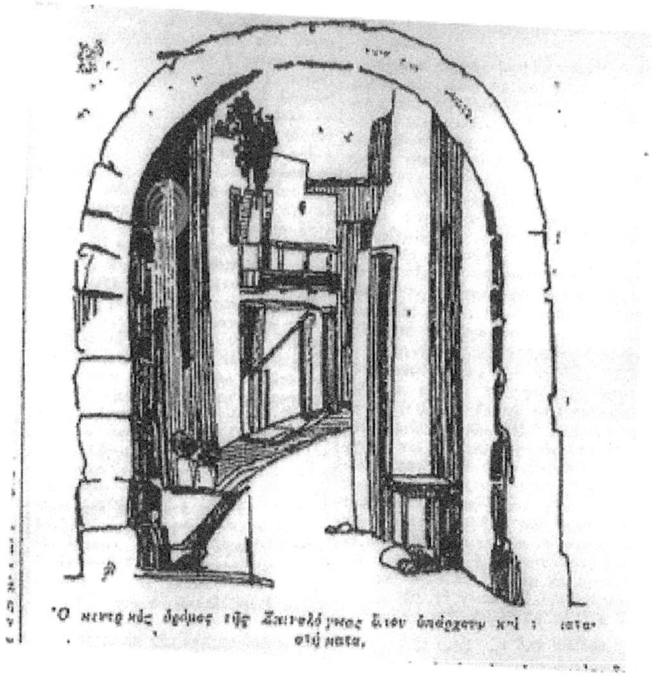

The central road, Spinalonga. Sketch by Angelos Sgouros, published in "Empros", 31 July 1929.

Ὁ λεπρὸς καταστηματάρχης Χριστοδουλάκης.

Sketches of patients of Spinalonga by Angelos Sgouros, "Empros", 1 August 1929.

Dear Reader,

This concludes my book on Spinalonga. I hope it sets you thinking, even just a little, and causes you to reflect on the times you may have stood by, a passive spectator to injustice. The pleasant and unpleasant situations we come across in our lives only occur because the generations before us nurtured them and helped them occur. However, the work of those generations ends there. If something continues to occur in the present it means that we are the ones who have nurtured and preserved it. So let us consciously decide what we want in our lives. It's never too late to get rid of unhealthy situations and determine - as free human beings - which of our ancestors' examples are worth preserving so that they become part of our future and our children's futures, and which we need to jettison. Dear Reader, you are a free human being. Trust your judgment and your heart and, as they say in Crete, "Never infringe on your fellow-men's freedom or be unjust to them, but also never let others infringe on your freedom or be unjust to you". For myself, I have only two wishes: May God protect us from malicious or ignorant people in positions of authority, and may we truly love and value our fellow men, despite - or because of - their problems.

Thank you from the bottom of myheart.
Yours very truly.
Anna Giakoumaki

Contents

Printed in Great Britain
by Amazon

43209722R00260